THIS
WHEEL'S
ON FIRE

Books by Stephen Davis

Reggae Bloodlines
Reggae International
Bob Marley
Hammer of the Gods
Say Kids! What Time Is It?
Moonwalk (with Michael Jackson)
Fleetwood (with Mick Fleetwood)
Jajouka Rolling Stone
This Wheel's on Fire (with Levon Helm)

THIS WHEEL'S ON FIRE

LEVON HELM
AND THE STORY OF THE BAND

LEVON HELM WITH STEPHEN DAVIS

William Morrow and Company, Inc.
New York

It is the policy of William Morrow and Company, Inc., and its imprints and affiliates, recognizing the importance of preserving what has been written, to print the books we publish on acid-free paper, and we exert our best efforts to that end.

Library of Congress Cataloging-in-Publication Data

Helm, Levon.
    This wheel's on fire : Levon Helm and the story of The Band /
Levon Helm with Stephen Davis. — 1st ed.
      p.   cm.
    Includes index.
    ISBN 0-688-10906-3
    1. Helm, Levon. 2. Rock musicians—United States—Biography.
3. Band (Musical group). I. Davis, Stephen. II. Title.
ML419.H42A3   1993
782.42166'092'2—dc20
[B]   93-4413
                                          CIP
                                        MN

Printed in the United States of America

First Edition

1 2 3 4 5 6 7 8 9 10

BOOK DESIGN BY BRIAN MALLOY, CIRCA 86, INC.

Isn't everybody dreaming!
Then the voice I hear is real
Out of all the idle scheming
Can't we have something to feel.

"IN A STATION"
RICHARD MANUEL

CONTENTS

Prologue

TIME TO KILL

The Band had always had a pact that if one of us died on the road of a heart attack or an overdose or a jealous boyfriend, or whatever might kill a traveling musician, the others would put him on ice underneath the bus with the instruments and haul him back to Woodstock before the police started asking questions. This flashed through my mind as I ran half-dressed down the motel corridor at nine o'clock on the morning of March 4, 1986, in Winter Park, Florida.

Richard Manuel and I had been laughing for years at stuff that wasn't even funny anymore, when he went and took his own life. We were on what had been jokingly called the "Death Tour" because the gigs were in small places hundreds of miles apart. We tried to approach it with good humor, but I know Richard felt we weren't getting the kind of respect we were used to. This was ten years after *The Last Waltz*, fifteen years after we were playing the biggest shows in American history, twenty years after Bob Dylan had "discovered" us, and twenty-five years after Ronnie Hawkins had molded us into the wildest, fiercest, speed-driven bar band in America. It had been almost thirty years since I'd left my daddy's cotton farm in Phillips County, Arkansas, to seek my fortune on the rockabilly trail.

For sweet, ultrasensitive Richard Manuel, the trail ended on a spring morning in Florida.

Richard's wife, Arlie, was screaming hysterically, "He's *dead*! Oh my God, *he's dead*!" Rick Danko and his wife, Elizabeth, were already in Richard's room, and I heard Rick kind of gasp and say, "Oh, no, man . . ." I went inside: The room was in disarray, the bed unmade, the TV on, an empty bottle of Grand Marnier on the dresser. The light was on in the bathroom. Suddenly I got a terrible sense of pure dread and felt surrounded by the chill of death. I wanted to run the other way as fast as I could, but instead I walked to the bathroom door and looked in.

What I saw just broke my heart. That's for damn sure. It would've broken yours too.

Five days later Rick and I and Richard's brothers carried his metal casket into Knox Presbyterian Church in Stratford, Ontario. Richard had been raised a Baptist, but the bigger church was needed to accommodate his last sold-out show. The organist was Garth Hudson, who set the tone of the service with his old Anglican hymns. My mind was wandering through the prayers and the Scripture readings. Jane Manuel, Richard's ex-wife, and her children were there, dozens of Richard's relations, and many friends from our days in Toronto. It was hard to see so many beloved sad faces on such an occasion. I never did like funerals.

Robbie Robertson had been asked to deliver a eulogy, but he didn't show up. Friends of Richard's remembered his laughter, his jokes, his scary driving, his love for music. Then Garth played "I Shall Be Released," which Bob Dylan had written for Richard to sing. Through all three verses there wasn't a dry eye in the church.

I had a funny experience while Garth was playing. I was thinking about Richard and asking myself *why,* when I clearly heard Richard's voice in the middle of my head. It came in as clear as a good radio signal. And he said, *"Well, Levon, this was the one action I could take that was gonna really shake things up. It's gonna shake 'em up and change things round some more, because that's what needs to happen."*

Now, to understand this—and I think I have come to an understanding—you would have to know what Richard had been through, although that would be hard to convey. In fact, you'd have to know what we all had been through: the story of The Band, from 1958 until today. Because from then to now we went through the best of times as well as times that were full of pain and disappointment. But those bad times are important. They give you a chance to practice, listen, take stock, have a life, get your feet back on the ground, and maybe you'll live to tell the story.

That's what this book is all about. My story is recalled and written from my perspective on the drum stool, which I've always felt was the best seat in the house. From there you can see both the audience and the show. Along the way we'll check in with friends and family, and I thank them for their memories and the ability to share them. In the end, though, the story must be my own, with apologies in advance to those I neglect to mention or damn with faint praise. Memory Lane can be a pretty painful address at times, but in any inventory of five decades of American musical experience you've got to take the good with the bad. So draw up a chair to my Catskill bluestone fireplace while I roll one, and we'll crack open a couple of cold beers. The game's on the cable with the sound off, and I'm gonna take you back in time, specifically to cotton country: the Mississippi Delta just after World War II. We're gonna get this damn show on the road.

Chapter One

THE ROAD FROM TURKEY SCRATCH

Waterboy! Hey, *waterboy!*

That's my cue. It's harvesttime, 1947, and I'm the seven-year-old waterboy on my daddy Diamond Helm's cotton farm near Turkey Scratch, Arkansas. My dad and mom are working in the fields along with neighbors and black sharecropping families like the Tillmans and some migrant laborers we'd hired, seasonals up from Mexico. My older sister, Modena, is back at the house watching my younger sister, Linda, and my baby brother, Wheeler. Since I'm still too young for Diamond to sit me on the tractor, my job is to keep everyone hydrated. I got a couple of good metal pails, and I work that hand pump until the water runs clear and cold. I run back and forth between the pump house and the turn row, where the people drink their fill under a shady tree limb. I learned early on that the human body is a water-cooled engine.

It was hard work. The temperature was usually around a hundred degrees that time of year. But that's how I started out, carrying water to relieve the scorching thirst that comes from picking cotton in the heat and rich delta dust.

I was born in the house my father rented on a cotton farm in the Mississippi Delta, near Elaine, Arkansas. The delta is a different landscape from the one you might be used to, so I want to draw you some sketches of the old-time southern farm communities I grew up in, when cotton was king and rock and roll wasn't even born yet.

I'm talking about a low, flat water world of bayous, creeks, levees, and dikes, and some of the best agricultural land in the world for growing cotton, rice, and soybeans. When the first Spanish explorers arrived in the sixteenth century, the delta's cypress forests sheltered Mississippian Indian tribes—Choctaw, Chickasaw, Natchez—who constructed giant burial mounds related to astronomy and magic. I'm descended from them through my grandmother Dolly Webb, whose own grandmother had Chickasaw blood, like many of us in Phillips County.

In the 1790s Sylvanus Phillips led the first English settlers across the Mississippi River into eastern Arkansas. They were mostly immigrants from North Carolina, the Helms probably among them. They laid out the town of Helena, seventy miles downriver from Memphis, in 1820. It grew overnight into a pioneer river port full of keelboats, flatboats, stockboats, and ferries. The river was a mixed blessing, rising and falling annually so that levees had to be built and maintained.

Helena rose in the steamboat age, along with Vicksburg and Natchez, Mississippi, and Memphis. The town earned a brawling reputation early on. In the 1840s Helena was described in the New York press as a notorious den "where all sorts of nigger runners, counterfeiters, horse stealers, murderers and sich like took shelter again the law." An apprentice steamboat pilot named Sam Clemens, later better known as Mark Twain, saw Helena's riverside slums and dark saloons filled with gamblers, idlers, and thugs. Tied to the landings were the boats of slavers, minstrel shows, itinerant doctors, whiskey dealers, brothel keepers, and other businessmen of the American frontier.

During the Civil War, Phillips County was ardent rebel country, producing seven Confederate generals, more than any other county in the South. To me that says a lot about the place. There's a Confederate cemetery atop Crowley's Ridge, overlooking Helena and the river. Union artillery controlled river traffic with four batteries of cannon on top of the ridge there. A few thousand poorly armed rebel farmboys tried to dislodge those Yankee guns during the Battle of Helena in 1863. Charging up the naked hill under withering fire, most of them died trying. I used to visit the quiet, leafy graveyard when I was a boy.

14

Think of endless cotton fields, gravel roads, groves of pecan trees, canebrakes, bayous, pump houses, kudzu vines, sharecroppers' cabins, tenant farmhouses, flooded rice fields, the biggest sky in the world, and the nearby Mississippi, like an inland sea with its own weather system. Think 110 degrees in the shade in the summertime. Cotton country. We were cotton farmers.

Cotton was labor-intensive even after the Civil War, with the result that Phillips County lies in what used to be called the Black Belt, meaning the population is maybe 80 percent African-American. That's why the delta is known for its music. The sound of the blues, rhythm and blues, country music, is what we *lived* for, black and white alike. It gave you strength to sit on one of those throbbing Allis-Chalmers tractors all day if you knew you were gonna hear something on the radio or maybe see a show that evening.

My father, Jasper Diamond "J.D." Helm, was born in Monroe County, Arkansas, in 1910. The Helms were farming near Elaine in 1919 when the famous Elaine race riots broke out. Some black tenant sharecroppers around Elaine couldn't live on low crop prices that amounted to peonage, so they started a union and withheld their cotton from the market. A bunch of Ku Kluxers from around Helena drove over and shot up one of their meetings. Things took off from there, and quite a few people from both races were killed before federal troops from Little Rock, Arkansas, put a stop to it. Someone put out a rumor that all the white farmers and their families were going to be murdered by the rioters. My daddy remembered waiting with his father and brother on the front porch of their farm, pistols and shotguns at the ready. "If they show up here," my grandfather told his sons, "don't shoot till I say so, and we'll fight 'em as long as we live." But the riot never did come down the road that day.

My grandfather Helm died when my father was just a boy, so I never knew him. But I was close to my mother's father, Wheeler Wilson. He was a logger as a younger man, working for the Howe Lumber Company and Plantation. After they cut down that first-stand cypress forest after the turn of the century, there was nothing left except that rich delta soil, so many of the loggers became farmers. Wheeler kind of went back and forth between logging and farming for many years. He liked dirt farming, but he didn't have any education except the kind you get from being pencil-whipped by the mortgage bank. Sometimes he'd prefer to stay in one of the lumber camps and work. There'd be a big corral of mules back in there, some tents, maybe a few small buildings. I'm talking about the *country* now, south of Elaine. The road finally stopped at a little place called Ferguson, where you had to turn around. It was the end of the line, Bubba! But Wheeler liked it in that timber camp. He'd trap and hunt on the side, file saws, make a pretty good living. Then in the spring, when they started turning that dirt over and the air was filled with it, he'd go back to farming.

Wheeler wasn't afraid of anything and took nothing from nobody. One year when he was farming he got in a fight with a local man named Levy Doolittle over a crop. Mr. Doolittle had come to the farm to argue over a field of corn, and Wheeler told him, "There's the damn crop. Go ahead and take it, or d'ye want me to cut 'n' shuck it for ya too, ya damn fool!" Well, they took it a little farther than a cussfight. They done broke it down and started firing at each other. Luckily, no one got seriously hurt. Mr. Doolittle might have been grazed slightly; just a little birdshot from a distance, nothing meant to kill. Meanwhile, Mr. Doolittle was firing back at Grandpaw Wilson, who was standing in his doorway, and splinters and wood chips were flying. I guess it was something of a standoff, at least until Mr. Doolittle saw Grandmaw Agnes hand Wheeler a couple of double-ought buckshot cartridges, at which point Mr. Doolittle ran backward over the levee. They didn't see him again until it was time to go to court, where they all ended up. The lawyers kept it up almost that whole winter. "Well, Mr. Wilson, you say you don't recollect firing at Mr. Doolittle when he had his back toward you; just how do you explain *this*?" They held up some kind of jacket with the back shredded to ribbons by shotgun pellets. And Wheeler said, "Well, the only thing I can think of is, somebody hung it over a bush and shot the hell out of it." Of course everyone hee-hawed, and the judge gaveled 'em all out of there. They'd wasted enough time with that bullshit anyway. So Wheeler told me to never get involved with a lawsuit. Even when you win, you lose.

He hated the Ku Klux Klan. I'm real proud of that. One day when he was farming he heard that some of them were trying to organize in the area. He put his shotgun in the back of his wagon and found a bunch of 'em on the porch of the general store. He went right up and said, "Excuse me, sirs, but have any of you all seen any of them

16

goddamn Ku Kluxers?'' No one said anything, so Grandpaw prompted 'em a little. "Those *sorry* sheet-wearin' sons of bitches." They still didn't say a word. "Well, if you see any of them Ku Kluxers, you tell 'em Wheeler Wilson's looking for 'em, and you can tell 'em where I live."

Wheeler was a scrapper, damn sure was, and I like to think I might take after him a little. He came up just as pure as anyone came up in those parts and always noticed that when he wanted to get a loan for farming, he went through the same door as any black man, any yellow man, any kind of man. And he also noticed the banks would outpencil him every time, and he didn't like it. Because he was white, he stood up to 'em more than once and ended up in court over it.

His attitude, and my mother's, toward people is what gave me a big advantage in life. It saved me from having to wear that whole damn load of racism that a lot of people had to carry. My mom, God love her, she was one of those Bible people. She thought it was wrong to bother anybody, regardless of race, color, or religion. It just wasn't a Christian thing to look down on anybody, and that's what she taught us.

People called my daddy by his middle name, Diamond Helm. In 1932 he was a twenty-two year-old cotton farmer during the week and a musician and entertainer on the weekend. Diamond played guitar in a little band with some friends at house parties that charged two bits a head for dancing. They had white lightning in quart fruit jars—you only needed to inhale the vapors, and it'd make your hair hang down.

Diamond met Wheeler Wilson's beautiful blond daughter Nell at one of these parties. They were married on June 9, 1933, at the Baptist church in Elaine. My sister Modena was born a year or so after that, and I came along in the spring of 1940. I was baptized Mark Lavon Helm.

Not long after that, Nell and Diamond moved to a tiny rural farming community called Midway, because our long dirt road intersected with the hard gravel road about midway between the village of Turkey Scratch and the town of Marvell, all about twenty miles west of Helena. My younger sister, Linda, was born two years after me, with my baby brother, Wheeler, waiting several years after that to make his appearance.

So that's where we grew up, way back off the hard road, miles through the cotton fields, almost all the way to Big Creek. Don't even think about electricity. We might have used a battery-powered radio until I was ten years old. Our nearest neighbors were Clyde and Arlena Cavette and their three girls, Mary, Tiny, and Jessie Mae. Their farm was just a couple of miles away, and our families shared two sets of intermarried relatives, so we were all raised together as closely as possible, and Mary is still my closest friend.

My earliest memories are of my mom. She was pretty, with blond, curly hair and piercing blue eyes. She was fun to be around, always joking and laughing. She was the disciplinarian of the family and kept an immaculate house. "Get out of my kitchen!" she'd yell, usually because she was working in there. She was a great cook, and that's the way she raised us up. She felt the best you can really do for anybody is to set 'em down and feed 'em good. You may not be able to do anything else, but you'll at least have 'em in a good holding pattern so life can go on. Nell (her real name was Emma) was basically a traditional farm housewife. She worked in the fields in spring and fall just like we all did. "Lavon, go bring me some stovewood and a bucket of water." Mom didn't believe in slapping me when I got into trouble, but she did have long fingernails, and if I *really* acted up, she'd drop her hand, fingers pointed down, onto the top of my head. *"Don't do that."* So I learned to cover my head when punishment was imminent, whereas other kids learned to cover their rears.

Her brother Herbert Wilson was a tractor mechanic who lived with his kids—my cousins—down in Crumrod, Arkansas, below Elaine. When I was a toddler we'd stay with them, and Uncle Herbert would clean out a tractor barn on Saturday nights and show movies. I remember those flickering images like it was yesterday: a little fat guy in a hat yelling at a skinnier guy in a suit and mustache. It must have been 1943. Years later I realized that's where I first saw the comedy team of Abbott and Costello.

This was during the war, and cotton production was at its height. All day and night the freight trains carrying bales and cottonseed oil came rolling down the Cotton Belt, and I ran to see every freight that went by. My cousins would hold me down to tease me, and I'd fight 'em off just so I wouldn't miss seeing that freight.

Back at home, we were a musical family. Mama sang in a clear alto voice, and Dad and I sang together as far back as I can remember. He liked all kinds of music and taught me "Sitting on Top of the World" when I was four years old. All us kids remember sitting on his lap in the evenings while he relaxed in his chair. He'd sing to us and affectionately rub our hands with his rough farmer's fingers until we'd get calluses on our knuckles. My father knew so many songs, he was like a fountain of music. He was still teaching me songs when he passed away at age eighty-two in 1992. His mother, Grandmaw Dolly, was the bell cow of our family for a whole lot of years. She had remarried a gentleman named Luther Crawford and would organize family get-togethers at her house in West Helena or at Old Town Lake in Elaine. A beautiful old lady.

If I think back, I can still hear faint echoes of "Blue Moon of Kentucky" on our family radio. We'd have to buy a battery two and a half feet long and maybe eight inches thick; a big, heavy damn thing! I remember my dad pulling our tractor right up to the window of the house one night when the battery was down, and he plugged the radio into the tractor battery so we wouldn't lose the *Grand Ole Opry, The Shadow, The Creaking Door, Amos 'n' Andy*—those were the shows you couldn't miss. *Sky King.* From about four-thirty in the afternoon on, I was so close to that radio that my memories are of the rest of the family behind me. That was our entertainment. My dad and Clyde Cavette would go into town and get two fifty-pound ice blocks that would fit in our iceboxes. You could chip off them for a week. They'd buy an extra fifty pounds of ice, and we'd get together that night and make freezers of ice cream. Mom and Arlena would bake up a couple of big cakes: one coconut, one pecan. On special occasions the two moms would collaborate on lemon icebox pies, their own invention. They'd beat two cans of Pet milk until it was whipped to foam, adding sugar and lemon juice until it congealed. Then they'd freeze it in the icebox. I loved this beyond belief. It was so sweet your mouth would pucker. After I was old enough to work, they'd have to make three pies: one for each family and one for Lavon. And I'd *guard* mine. Then we'd make the radio the main feature, maybe play cards, visit.

Going to music shows was high-level entertainment for our family. They'd set up tents at the edge of Marvell and have a stage, folding chairs, and refreshments. The first show I remember was Bill Monroe and His Blue Grass Boys on a summer evening in 1946, when I was six years old. Boy, this really *tattooed my brain*. I've never forgotten it: Bill had a real good five-piece band. They took that old hillbilly music, sped it up, and basically invented what is now known as blue-grass music: the bass in its place, the mandolin above it, the guitar tying the two together, and the violin on top, playing the long notes to make it sing. The banjo backed the whole thing up, answering every-body. We heard Bill Monroe regularly on the *Grand Ole Opry,* but here he was in the flesh. Lester Flatt and Earl Scruggs were in the band when I saw them.

That was the end of cowboys and Indians for me. When I got home I held the broom sideward and strutted past the barn, around the pump, and out to the watermelon patch, pretending to play the guitar. I was hooked.

After that I made it a point to soak up as much music as I could. I really liked Bill and the Carliles, a famous novelty group that performed funny songs that got into the country charts. My favorite was called ''Knothole,'' the chorus of which went: ''Knothole, knothole, you oughta see what I saw through the old knothole.'' Bill Carlile had his pretty wife playing in a band with stand-up bass and an electric guitar. Who else? Muddy Waters was extremely popular; he had the first real electric blues band and some hit records. We loved Lonzo and Oscar, Onie Wheeler, Homer and Jethro, Noble ''Thin Man'' Watts, whoever we could get on the radio from Memphis, Shreveport, or Nashville.

Whenever one of the big traveling shows came to town, the Helms would be there. Silas Green from New Orleans had a twelve-piece orchestra that we all liked, but everyone's favorite was the F. S. Walcott Rabbits Foot Minstrels from, I believe, Biloxi, Mississippi. Posters and handbills announcing the shows would go up weeks in advance. They'd set up with the back of a big truck as their stage. They had a nine-piece house band down in front of the stage, a fast-talking master of ceremonies, a good-looking mulatto chorus line, blackface comedians, and singers. This was like another world for us kids.

I'd stare at the drummer all night because with those horns and that full rhythm section, the drums always looked like the best seat in the house. The sound of the cymbals and the snare drum popping was synonymous in my mind with Saturday night and good times. F. S. Walcott had a fantastic left-handed drummer, whom I'd study as closely as I could from my seat. This was a problem in those days of segregation, because the audience was split down the middle by an aisle. On the left were the black to light-skinned folks, while the light-skinned to people with red hair sat on the right. The left-handed drummer sat on my right, which put his tom-toms between me and him. So he's working the snare drums in front of him, favoring the band, and as he's getting ready to roll he's coming right around toward me. I'm sitting two rows back at the most. I'm probably in the *front* row, in fact, studying what he's doing for the whole two-hour show. I'm naturally right-handed, but people have always told me that I play left-handed. If I have any technique at all, that's where it comes from.

Our favorite act was "The Lady with the Million Dollar Smile," F. S. Walcott's big featured singer, who'd come on in the third quarter of the show. She was an *armful*. She wore very bright dresses and had all her teeth filled with diamonds! She sang all those real get-down songs like "Shake a Hand." Later on the master of ceremonies would announce, "Ladies and gentlemen, it's been a great evening. We haven't played a show this good since New Orleans! I sure wish every night could be this good. . . .

"Now it's time for what we call the Midnight Ramble. I know a lot of you have to get up early and get to work, a lot of you have your families with you, and we want to thank all of you for coming and wish you well till next year. In the meantime, for those of you who can stay late and have a mind for more sophisticated entertainment . . ." He'd introduce one of the beautiful dancers from the four-girl chorus line and tell us how Caledonia would show us what made her famous down in Miami, Florida, where she hails from.

The Midnight Ramble cost another dollar, dollar and a half. You'd see what in those days was defined as a hootchy-kootchy show. The comedians would do some of their raunchier material, and people'd be holding their sides. The band would get into its louder rhumba-style things, and the dancers would come out in outfits that would be right in style today but were bare and outrageous back then. The master of ceremonies might get caught up in it and jig across the stage like a chicken or anything familiar from the barnyard, which always set the crowd off. That was the Midnight Ramble, so called because it usually ended at twelve o'clock.

Today, when folks ask me where rock and roll came from, I always

21

think of our southern medicine shows and that wild Midnight Ramble. Chuck Berry's duck walk, Elvis Presley's rockabilly gyrations, Little Richard's dancing on the piano, Jerry Lee Lewis's antics, and Ronnie Hawkins's camel walk could have come right off F. S. Walcott's stage.

We got our supplies from A. B. Thompson's grocery store in Turkey Scratch. Mr. Thompson was also our amateur country doctor; he'd bandage you up if you fell off your bicycle or stepped on a thorn. There was a one-room school at the Turkey Scratch church called the County Line School, with all the grades together. Our teacher, Miss Stella Harris, lived with the Thompsons during the school term. This is where I started my education.

Just getting to the bus stop on the hard road could be a problem when the fields were flooded. Sometimes Mary Cavette and I would be covered in mud from our trip by wagon and mule to that bus stop. Mary would be crying and I'd be laughing. Sometimes a tractor had to pull the bus through a mudhole. This went on for a couple of years until my father went before the school board and demanded a little panel truck so we and the Cavette sisters could be driven up to the hard road, where our neighbor Anna Lee Williams was usually waiting for us.

I loved school when I finally got to it. I met up with my right-hand man, Charles "Mutt" Cagle, whose family lived a stone's throw from us. Mutt was my first pal, and we've buddied together ever since. I especially loved those school lunches, which changed every day, unusual for a little boy used to the routine of the farm. Things went pretty well for a couple of years until I hit the second grade. That's when I got put off the school bus for fighting. I don't remember the specifics, but I got into it with some older kids who went to the bigger school back in Marvell. After that I walked the few miles to school for a year or so. When that old yellow bus passed me on the road, I didn't look at them, and they didn't look at me. It was a standoff.

One of my most vivid memories of childhood is the sultry summer night in the late forties when they inoculated all the children for measles or diphtheria; whatever they were doing that night. Oh, God, that was a mess! The kids had gotten wind of it, and we were scared to death of those big glass syringes with the thick steel needles. They hung an old tarpaulin around the pump house. That was ugly. Us kids *knew* we were in trouble now. It was usually wide open, a nice place to sit and have your lunch. All of a sudden it was dusk, and the pump house was hidden by this tarpaulin lit by yellow kerosene lanterns inside. It was like a slaughterhouse, with farm folks holding their terrified children. I tried to hide out, but someone caught me and threw me in the wagon, and the mules pulled up to that pump house. It took a fight, but they eventually got us all.

Tornadoes were my other main childhood fear. We had two tornado seasons, spring and fall, but tornadoes could breed any time the warm breezes coming up the Mississippi Valley from the Gulf of Mexico collided with the cooler winds coming from the west over Oklahoma and Kansas. The storms would move east from there on a north/south axis with the Cotton Belt in the center—Tornado Alley. We all grew up with horror stories about brooms stuck into trees, straw end first, and baby chickens blown inside Coke bottles, and people and things simply disappearing forever. So we'd hurry to the storm house when the sky got dark and terribly still, with puffs of hot and cold winds alternating from different directions.

Tornado weather could turn a beautiful spring day into a hellish orange color that led all the way west to the heart of the approaching storm, dark blue and gray, rolling and churning eastward. Lightning bolts zigzagged across the whole mass with a sound like a hundred runaway trains. At night the sky turned blacker than Egypt, and lightning sent fiery bolts slamming to earth, setting big trees afire with a roar like a cannon going off. The lightning struck houses, barns, wire fences, mules—anything that didn't have a lightning rod attached. We lost two coon-hunting dogs chained to a wire fence this way when lightning hit.

A tractor with its plow in the ground is a perfect lightning rod, and this proved fatal to my Big Creek fishing buddy Elmer Snyder. Elmer had more nerve than fear and thought he could squeeze out the last few rows of a cotton field before the rain started falling. He was on his last pass when the heavens opened and threw down a yellow bolt of electricity that hit midway between plow and tractor, melting the plow points, bending the frames, and blowing out the tires. God had called Elmer home.

The Helm family knew all about life in Tornado Alley. One summer night, after a big July Fourth family dinner, all hell broke loose. My older sister Modena was in my father's arms, huddled with my mother, my aunt Geneva, and my cousin Eddie behind our kitchen door. There was leftover pecan pie and fried chicken on the table when the house started shaking. My father was about to tell everyone to run for the ditch when the whole house cartwheeled over and over, ending up in the cotton field as the wood stove, furniture, dishes, and people crashed around in a mess of broken glass and debris. When the house stopped rolling, they climbed out a window and walked over to the neighbors, using the light from the flickering lightning to find their way. The neighbors tried to get them cleaned up, and J.D. always remembered how he couldn't get a comb through his hair for all the pecan pie stuck in it. Mom remembered that one little jar of mustard was smeared all over everyone in a thin film of goo.

After that we always had a storm house on our farm. A delta storm house was about six feet wide by eight feet long, dug into the ground to a depth of five feet. The roof was covered with planks and water-proofing, then mounded over with dirt and sown with Bermuda grass. Floorboards were laid above the seeping groundwater, and a vent out the top and a hand pump kept it dry and breathable. The door faced east, away from the weather. It was a dark, musty hole of a room, but with a tornado raging and a kerosene lantern hanging from the ceiling, it became a safe, bright, warm, and cozy place, friends and family crowded on low benches, the children asleep in the middle on piled-up coats, protected from the wrath of the Almighty. The down side of these excursions to the storm house was walking home barefoot through the mud after the storm subsided. My mom was fussy about her clean home, and before I could slip between my cool cotton sheets, I'd have to pump a washpan full of water and wash my muddy feet. On bad nights in Tornado Alley, when we'd gone home before the storm had run its course, we'd be roused awake and led confused and stumbling back to the storm house. One night I had to wash my feet four times!

[Sound of a dinner bell over an old forties radio]:
"Clang! It's *King Biscuit Time,* so pass the biscuits!"*

It's high noon on our farm, any day of the year, and the radio's tuned to KFFA, 1250 AM, for our daily dose of the blues.

"King Biscuit Flour presents Sonny Boy Williamson and His King Biscuit Entertainers every day, Monday through Friday. Now friends, the King Biscuit Entertainers want to play your favorite song, so you can have a special request. Just write it down on a postcard or letter and mail it to *King Biscuit Time,* Post Office Box 409, Helena, Arkansas."

Then Sonny Boy would play his harmonica and let it fly. He was the king of the delta blues in our area, a friend and disciple of the late Robert Johnson, though Sonny Boy was older. (His passport gave his birth date as 1909, but 1899 and 1894 have also been suggested.) Sonny Boy had traveled with Johnson during Robert's brief delta stardom in the 1930s. They were regular performers on street corners and in the juke joints of Helena and Elaine, where Robert's hit records like "Terraplane Blues" were well known, and passed through Marvell on the way to Helena. Robert lived there with a woman and her son.

After Robert Johnson was killed in 1938—allegedly poisoned by a jealous husband—Sonny Boy teamed up with Robert's stepson, Robert Jr. Lockwood, and kept Johnson's music alive. Around 1941 they began regular broadcasts on the Interstate Grocery Company's *King Biscuit Time* show on KFFA in Helena. Sonny Boy blew harp and Robert Jr. played electric guitar. It was the first time many delta residents—and that might have included Muddy Waters—had ever heard the instrument. Sonny Boy's singing became so popular in Arkansas and his native Mississippi that the company put out a new product: Sonny Boy Cornmeal (still sold in the South). For a while the program was called *The Sonny Boy Cornmeal and King Biscuit Show.*

"That was 'West Memphis Blues,' " the announcer is saying. "Now, ladies and gentlemen, it's a fact: To bake up delicious corn bread, you've got to have the freshest cornmeal. All good cooks know this. It's a very simple job to turn out piping-hot corn bread dishes when you use famous Sonny Boy Meal. Just read the recipes on the back of any two-pound, five-pound, or ten-pound bag of Sonny Boy Meal and pick out the one you like; whether it's corn muffins, corn sticks, hush puppies, or just plain skillet corn bread. So why not pick up a bag of Sonny Boy Meal and see all the delicious corn bread dishes you could bake up? And now, Sonny Boy is going to play 'Crazy 'Bout You Baby.' "

"Thank you very much, my man," Sonny Boy says. "This one is going out for Miz Pearly Mae and her husband. That's down on Franklin Street, yassir!"

And they'd tear it up, raw country blues, while we sat listening to the radio at dinnertime.

Sometimes Sonny Boy and the band played in Marvell on Saturday afternoons. They'd set up on the loading dock behind the depot. It had a tin roof that created a good band-shell type of sound. Their old school bus had KING BISCUIT TIME written on it, and the logo with Sonny Boy sitting on a corncob, playing the harp. The first thing you noticed about Sonny Boy was his size: This was a *big man.* He'd lay out a tarpaulin on the ground and set his mike on it. Then he'd open the back door of the bus, and there'd be an upright piano. (Mutt Cagle and I would watch this carefully from a respectful distance, ever mindful of Sonny Boy's notorious reputation as one tough son of a bitch.) His drummer, James "Peck" Curtis, would set up his cymbals, a big wooden snare, and a wooden bass drum hand-lettered KING BISCUIT TIME/KING BISCUIT ENTERTAINERS/J. P. CURTIS/KFFA/MONDAY THRU FRIDAY. Sonny Boy and the guitar player would set up some amplifiers and microphones, just plug in, and have a show and street dance. They knew all the big hits of the day, like "Eyesight to the Blind," "Do It If You Want To," and "Mighty Long Time." They played what they knew their audience wanted to hear.

Sonny Boy in person was a powerful, extremely impressive man, in overalls and a straw hat. His huge mouth had calloused lips from years of playing the harp. When I first saw him, I noticed he sang *into* his harmonica. Sonny Boy's voice passed through the metal harp and came out sharpened like a straight razor before it hit the microphone, giving the song an extra metallic jolt of energy. I remember the feel of that music vividly. It had a twang to it, a whip, punching straight ahead. Sonny Boy overpowered you with his amplified open-air country R&B.

When I was a little older, maybe ten or eleven, I'd make it my business to catch a ride on a farm truck into Helena whenever I could. First stop was Habib's Cafe, where I'd buy three doughnuts for a dime. Then I'd run down Cherry Street to the KFFA studio, where they knew me as a young entertainer from 4-H Club shows. They'd let me sit in the corner and watch the King Biscuit boys do their show. Robert Jr.

Lockwood might stop in, or Memphis Slim, or Robert Nighthawk, all from our area. I didn't bother them, so I got to sit in that studio quite a few times. I'd try not to stare at Peck Curtis, but it was hard because he was a hell of a drummer. Between numbers, while the announcer was selling cornmeal, I'd watch Sonny Boy run the band in a raspy, low voice. " 'Stormy Monday' in C," he'd say. Peck or the guitar player couldn't quite hear what he said, so Sonny Boy would whisper hoarsely, "C, goddamn it! I said *play it in C, motherfucker!*" (You just didn't want to mess with Sonny Boy.) Or he'd call a tune but change the tempo at the last second as the commercial was ending: " 'Come Go With Me,' in the same beat, same key—no, we'll do it in eight; *do an eight.*" The band would scramble to adjust as the announcer turned the mike back over to Sonny Boy, who'd in turn pitch that evening's show in nearby Clarksdale, Mississippi, before crashing into "Come Go With Me"—as a rhumba.

Boy, that was about as good as it got. I'd be buzzing all the way home to Turkey Scratch after one of those sessions. Sonny Boy Williamson—our local musical hero.

I was nine years old in 1949. That was the year I got my first guitar and started farming with my dad.

The land was our legacy. Most of my father's generation spent a good part of their lives building levees just to keep the high water off us so we could farm. Most of the farm houses we lived in were raised up on stilts. My dad started me on the tractor that spring. I'd been riding with him for years, and now I got to drive it. We started in April, turned the fields over with the breaking plow, and then got on top of it again with a disk. Some years, if your soil demanded it, you went back and disked it over again into fine-tilled soil. Just before planting, you'd work the ground with a section harrow, a flat, metal-toothed rake that furrowed the ground, smoothed it, and broke up any clods of dirt. Clouds of birds whirled overhead and around the tractor, searching for worms and insects in the freshly plowed earth. Eventually you'd have big fields of fine delta soil in rows about four inches high.

Then we'd hitch a cotton planter to the tractor. It had a wheel that cut into the dirt and a spout that dropped the right amount of seed. The wheel rolled on an angle and pushed the dirt back on top of the cottonseed. You planted two rows at a time, and you needed to be done by the end of April, weather permitting, because the summer heat would follow you right into the shade. If your cotton was up by the middle of May, you wouldn't have to be out in the field replanting on a tractor when it was 110 degrees.

We cultivated and chopped the cotton all summer. You went in with a hoe and thinned the crop from one solid row of plants to a lot of little mounds with maybe two stalks each, six to eight inches apart. Got the grass out of it, blocked out those extra plants; *backbreaking* work. We worked one row at a time with ten to fifteen choppers in a field.

You had to water those folks and keep 'em hydrated, or they'd all just drop. My first job on the farm was waterboy, but I wanted to hang with my dad and all that machinery, those tractors: Ford, John Deere, Allis-Chalmers. Dad would buy 'em through the bank. Each farmer had a connection with the John Deere distributor. By the time I was nine, I'd rode so many rounds I could cultivate on my own.

The cotton blooms into big yellow and purple blossoms in June. By the end of July you want to be "laid by." That means all your cultivating is done. When the cotton loses its bloom, it's left with a boll, which grows all summer and starts to pop open in September, bursting into four locks of snow-white cotton. Now it's September, early October, and time to pick the cotton. The work was too much for the local people, so we'd hire Mexicans to help chop the cotton. There were always three or four big farmers who'd be farming 1,500, 2,000 acres of land—big sections of 640 acres each. They'd get together and hire a Texas contractor to bring up a load of workers, maybe sixty to eighty people. We'd go through one of the big farmers and subcontract a crew of laborers. They'd be with us for three or four weeks chopping and picking, then go pick cherries in Michigan. One of my first jobs off the farm was working at Vic Thompson's grocery store in Marvell on Saturdays. I had to learn a little Spanish so I could help the Mexican customers with eggs, butter, and milk. They all wore their standard white shirts and big white hats, and a few of them were funny as hell. I liked 'em because they were just so interesting.

All of us—black people, white people, Mexicans—worked together in the fields. Our family worked side by side with the Tillmans, black neighbors who were important members of our little farm community.

Our families were so close that Sam Tillman gave me a spanking when I needed it. My mother might cook dinner for as many as six or eight people working in the fields. If we had a truckload of Mexicans, Dad would round them up and take 'em to the grocery store or bring in bread, cheese, sandwich meat, some cold Pepsi-Colas, and maybe some apples. Then he'd gas up the tractor while we found some shade in the tree brakes. The older I got, the more I enjoyed those shade trees.

All this old-fashioned agriculture has vanished, of course. My youth in Arkansas was really the last of it. In the 1950s field hands were replaced by the big mechanical cotton pickers and choppers they came out with. That whole world of tenant farmers and sharecroppers, field hands and waterboys, is ancient history now. It exists only in the long memories of those of us who lived it.

For a kid like me, looking to have fun and raise a little hell on a cotton farm, resources were somewhat limited. You had to work with what you had. For my purposes, this proved to be my daddy's Allis-Chalmers tractor. I'd take that old three-wheeler with the disk cutter on the back of it, put it in high gear, and had a hell of a lot of fun running tractor wheelies across a cotton field. That disk brought the tractor's front end up in the air, so if you popped your clutch *just right* you could run for acres out there on two wheels.

High gear, wide open. You'd see that drainage ditch coming, so you picked up that disk nice and smooth. The side of the drainage ditch was the closest thing we had to a hill, and you'd hit it with that front end and force it in the air, bounce it up, run twenty yards on the back wheels. It couldn't turn over because the disk was there.

I'd stand up during these stunts, just to make my dad crazy. I'd be coming around the corner, about to hit that turn row on two wheels, and I'd see J.D. jumping and waving by the gas tank, trying to get me to stop. Wide open: Hit the clutch, hit one of the brakes, and start skipping up to that gas tank where old J.D. is having a fit, and at the last moment flop that disk. *Fooomp!* All stop.

Bad things could happen too. You could hit that turn row and catch the axle of your disk on a fence post—there wasn't much margin for errors of judgment—and find yourself heading into the thicket with your chains dragging so you couldn't pick up the disk. If you weren't careful, the chain could hook onto your back wheels, and you had an accident, Bubba. Throw that section harrow right on top of that tractor. In our area, a lot of people got hurt or killed outright in those days.

We were pretty fortunate in our section, because we had only one accident that I can remember. It was a late, wet spring, before I was old enough to work. The tractors had lights on them by then so they could work at night when it was cooler. One night they were refueling at the tank, a fire started, and one of the tractor drivers burned his leg pretty bad. There was a downside to farming, like anything. It was damn hard work. The tractors didn't have umbrellas when I started, so we were out in the broiling sun. As soon as school let out, my dad made me get out there every day. I hit the fields in the morning and didn't come in until late in the afternoon. There it is. A country childhood isn't all running around barefoot and trips to Big Creek.

A few years later, when my dad was buying Allis-Chalmers equipment from the Helena dealership owned by my friend Eddie McCarty's dad, I started to drive for Allis in tractor contests. Eddie's dad would put out a WD for me, a big tractor circa 1945. Hand brakes, hand clutch, left-foot plunge; good tractor. The WD45 had a single wheel in front, and you'd turn that thing, hit your brake, and you could spin it right around. By the time I was a teenager, I was one of the tractor-driving champions of Arkansas.

Thank God you didn't have to pick cotton until September. My folks insisted I get an education, so we had an understanding that as long as I stayed in school, my dad wouldn't keep me home to work in the fields.

In September 1949 I started a new school. All the little country classrooms had been consolidated, so in fourth grade we were bused to Marvell to go to school out there with forty in a class. This was too scary, since I'd already been put off the bus for fighting with some of those kids. To us Marvell was the big town, and there were some real tough guys. Mutt Cagle and I had to stand back-to-back a couple of times and just fight 'em off. But there I met my lifelong friend Edward "Fireball" Carter, with whom I got into all sorts of trouble over the next nine years. You have to pity the poor souls who tried to teach us through high school, because if any two people didn't know the answer, it was me and Ed.

Ask Mary Cavette if you don't believe me.

She was a year ahead of us in school and remembers me well. Call her up; she lives in Tennessee.

"Oh, my word, was he a big tease," she'll say. "Lavon *lived* to pull jokes. He'd tease the girls until they'd cry. He was the worst! It was his whole life if he could pull a joke on you. He loved it. He'd get everyone involved, and everyone knew about it except you. Lavon was so good at it. He'd laugh and laugh, and you got so mad at him, but then he'd always come and hug you, and it would be all over.

"He was always in the back of the school bus, fidgeting and drumming on things, playing the Jew's harp, or beating pencils on his books. This continued in the classroom, and he was always being reprimanded because he laughed all the time. He loved the sound of people laughing. It was infectious; Lavon would laugh, and the whole class would start. You couldn't help it. He'd get tickled, and everybody'd get tickled.

"Well, Lavon quickly became the center of things. Wherever he was, that's where the crowd would gather. Lavon may have been a big tease, but he was also very kind and would let you laugh at him too. I remember one May when we were kids, it rained all month. The water came up, and the Helms' farm was isolated. Diamond got a boat, and they all stayed over at our house for a week. When the rain stopped, everything was clear and beautiful, and the flooded fields between our farms had become a temporary lake.

"Lavon wanted to take me and my sisters out in the boat, and Momma said, 'You kids aren't going out in *that*!' But when no one was looking, Lavon got the boat and took his sister Linda and me and my two sisters for a cruise. My little sister had cerebral palsy, so just getting in the boat took a lot of doing. Lavon had a paddle, which he somehow lost in the middle of this huge lake. The wind started to ripple the blue water, so it looked *very* deep. My little sister started crying because she was scared. Lavon's maybe ten years old and can't swim real well. 'Don't worry, sister,' he said. 'I'm gonna swim for help.' Lavon looked at the expanse of water and gulped. He rolled up his pants and said, 'If anything happens to me, just tell Momma that I died tryin' to save y'all.'

"Well, he jumped in, and the water came to his knees. He towed us home, and we're still laughing about it."

31

* * *

By the end of October we had picked our cotton, so we all had a little money. On Saturday afternoons we'd go into Marvell for the movie matinee at the Capitol Theater, next to the pool hall. We'd watch Zorro, Roy Rogers, Johnny Mack Brown, Lash La Rue, Hopalong Cassidy, whatever they had. I always sat in the front row and stayed through all the shows, until 11:00 P.M. ("That's true," Mary Cavette agrees. "Nell would have to go into the theater and get Lavon so we could go home.")

Marvell had two drugstores, Anderson's and Ford's, and two department stores, Hirsch Company and Davidson's. The Rawley Salve man parked between them. He had a little panel truck with RAWLEY'S SALVE painted on the side. It was an ointment you could put on cuts, bruises, anything. People bought a lot of his tonics, cure-alls that came in little bottles. For all we knew, it was mostly alcohol and nearly pure morphine. Back then it could've had damn near anything in it. It damn sure made you feel better, though, and he did a lot of business, I know that. He'd diagnose you and prescribe right on the street.

There was a darn good guitar player named Ralph DeJohnette, who played at the pool hall with Bubba Stewart on drums (the first time I ever saw a drummer use brushes) and some of the local boys. They were real good, and inspired me to ask my daddy for a guitar. He went over to Morris Gist's music store in Helena, bought me an inexpensive Silvertone, and began to teach me a few chords and runs. It was my good fortune that Ralph DeJohnette happened to be our RFD mailman, because the Silvertone wouldn't stay in tune. I used to meet Ralphie at the mailbox up on the hard road every day so he could retune my guitar. I'd hope it would stay in tune till Ralph came by next day with the mail.

That's how I started out. I was nine years old when I knew I wasn't meant to be a cotton farmer.

Like many farm families, we were dependent on the elements for our survival, and some years we had better luck than others.

I'll never forget one summer night when I was maybe ten. The whole family was at a ball game I was playing in when someone came and told us our farmhouse was on fire. We all piled into our pickup

32

truck. Diamond was driving *fast*, and the truck was so full I was sitting on Mary Cavette's lap. We rounded that old turn in the road and saw our house had burned completely down. There was nothing left. I started to cry with relief when I saw my dog Cinder running around. I couldn't help it. ("That was the only time I ever saw Lavon cry," Mary remembers.) Anyway, Diamond moved us into Gotze's store nearby, which was empty because the owners had moved away. We put in a kitchen and lived there until we got another house built up. This was the first of several trials by fire I've had in my life.

In 1950 I won first place in our school's talent contest with my hambone act, slapping my hands against my legs and rapping out "Little Body Rinktum Ti-mee-oh." This routine came right from home and the family musicales around the supper table at the end of the day. I had my little guitar, J.D. had a mandolin, and everyone sang. When I was about twelve I made my sister Linda a string bass out of a washtub, a broomstick, and some cord. Right from the start Linda could really hold a bass line, and I slapped my thighs, played harmonica and Jew's harp, and we both sang old songs we'd learned at home and new songs from the hit parade. Soon we started winning junior-high contests and county-fair talent shows. After a while I started playing my guitar, and soon "Lavon & Linda," as we billed ourselves, started getting attention on the local music circuit. Between 1952 and 1955 Linda and I probably entertained every Kiwanis Club, Farm Bureau, Lions Club, Rotary Club, Future Farmers of America, and 4-H Club meeting in Phillips County. She'd sing "Dance With Me Henry," and I'd do "No Help Wanted" or something by Chuck Berry or Muddy Waters.

It was the Arkansas 4-H circuit that really helped us take off. Just about all the farm kids I knew were in the 4-H Club because it was the way country kids got to travel around. We'd raise livestock (I grew and shucked my own corn to feed to my projects) and take them to shows and fairs and get to meet other kids like ourselves. I'd usually bring a steer or a hog that I'd raised, and enter the tractor-driving contest and the talent show with my sister. By the time I was maybe thirteen we had our names painted on Linda's tub, and we almost always won. One of the rewards from this was the chance to attend the 4-H summer camps in some of Arkansas's cooler hill country.

Mary Cavette remembers us from those days, the early 1950s: "Lavon and Linda were unusual, and everyone loved them. They were blond, they were cute, and they were immaculate. Lavon was Jack Armstrong, the All-American Boy, with a Marvell Junior High letter sweater, slicked-down hair, all starched and ironed. Their momma, Nell, would use Faultless starch on Lavon's blue jeans and hang them on the line till they could stand alone. Then she'd press 'em with a flat iron, and they stayed stiff. Linda was always smiling and would wear a crisp dress. They were exciting because Lavon had the natural ability to get everyone in the room going to his rhythm. It was like magic, that incredible talent. After ten seconds he had everyone clapping in time, and by the end of the song everyone'd be smiling and laughing. That was Lavon and Linda: personable, polite, good-looking, always well received."

When I was fourteen my daddy took me back to Mr. Gist's music store in Helena to get a real guitar. It was late on a Saturday afternoon, and the streets were packed with people in from the farms, migrants, and local people. Phillips County used to be the tenth most populous county in Arkansas, and you'd see all kinds of folks. When most people think of the Mississippi Delta, they think in terms of black and white, Anglo-Saxon and African-American. But it wasn't completely like that. From its earliest days the area around Helena was more like a melting pot. Chinese families had grocery stores, Jewish families were in the cotton business, Lebanese people kept stores. Mexican farmhands meant you always heard Spanish. The delta was positively multicultural. Morris Gist's music store was one of the places where all the various cultures met. Mr. Gist supplied instruments to several generations of musicians, maintained the jukeboxes in our area, and was then involved in distributing records cut by a hot young Memphis disc jockey on WDIA named B. B. King. Mr. Gist was also Sonny Boy Williamson's landlord.

Daddy and I went up to the counter, greeted Mr. Gist, and I heard J.D. say, "Morris, we'd like to see the Martin guitar there for my boy Lavon."

That was the day my credit history began. I got to take that nice little Martin home on a layaway plan. It was three-quarter size and all brown, and I just about slept with the thing. There was no stopping

Lavon & Linda after that. When I was beginning high school we won the Phillips County Fair talent show, performing "Chattanooga Shoe Shine Boy." Then we won at the Arkansas Livestock Exposition in Little Rock, which gave us a shot at the big Mid-South Fair in Memphis, where we somehow managed to win again.

I wish you could have heard that audience whoop it up that night in Memphis when the judges made their announcement. Words can't express how proud my sister and I felt.

I think it was at one of these shows that we met the man who first put us on the road. I remember seeing J.D. talking to a well-dressed man, whom he introduced as Bob Evans. Of course I'd heard of him by reputation. Mr. Evans was a cotton farmer and buyer who had been a big-band singer with Fred Waring and His Pennsylvanians. He was a sophisticated guy; probably the only person in Helena who had actually been to New York. Being an entertainer and knowledgeable in the music business, Bob would usually be the one to hire local talent like us to represent Arkansas at various events such as beauty pageants or political campaigns. (He eventually served as the director of the Arkansas Publicity and Parks Commission.)

"You kids don't know how lucky you are," Diamond told us after a show one night. "Mr. Evans thinks you're great. He wants you to be part of the Bob Evans world!"

Bob managed a couple of novelty acts—people who pantomimed to records in crazy costumes, a pretty girl who could sing—and a circuit he booked in Arkansas and Louisiana. So Lavon & Linda found ourselves appearing at Miss Arkansas pageants and the Miss Louisiana contest, and campaigning for Democratic politicians Bob Evans supported. Here's the scene: afternoon barbecue in West Helena on a Saturday afternoon in the fall of '54. Linda and I do a couple of songs and get a real nice hand. Then Bob Evans announces that Orval Faubus, running for governor of Arkansas, is going to say a few words. After we'd done a few of these with Mr. Faubus, I began to listen to what he said. He was calling for hot lunches in the schools, raising taxes to support better education, better care for the handicapped and the retarded, and an end to crooked elections. Well, he won the election and did all those things he said he would. I can attest to those hot lunches, and the rest is history. You could look it up.

35

We made a little money (which is how I probably got the down payment for that Martin) and got a lot of experience playing shows all over our delta area.

Our early career coincided with the birth of rock and roll. We literally watched it happen in our part of the country. Traditionally, white people played country music, and black people played the blues. But in the thirties white musicians like my dad began to sing the blues with a twang, and it became something else with a different bump to it. That was the seed. Then in the late forties and early fifties Muddy Waters came out with the first electric R&B band and a string of R&B hits—"She Loves Me," "I'm Your Hoochie Coochie Man," "I Just Wanna Make Love to You," "Got My Mojo Working"—that appealed to black and white people alike where we lived. Over at KFFA, the radio people noticed that telephone requests for Sonny Boy Williamson were as likely to come from the ladies at the white beauty parlor as from the black.

Cut to the chase: 1954 and seventy miles north in Memphis, where Sam Phillips, owner of Sun Records and Sun Studios, is looking for a white boy who can sing and move like a Negro. Within the space of two years, Elvis Presley, Carl Perkins, Johnny Cash, Roy Orbison, and Jerry Lee Lewis had all recorded at Sun Studios, and a new era began. It was country music, all right, but it had that good black backbeat in there as well.

I'm pretty sure it was late 1954 when we first saw Elvis perform. Since he was from Memphis, we felt he was one of us. Everything stopped when his early record of "That's All Right Mama" came over the radio. He'd appeared on the *Louisiana Hayride* radio show by then, and we'd all heard that audience screaming and shrieking when Elvis started to move to the rhythm with those suggestive, rubbery dances of his. Just the excitement of him coming to Helena was almost too much for some of our young ladies to bear.

I think Bob Evans took us to the Catholic Club in Helena to see Elvis's show. It was just Elvis, Scotty Moore on guitar, and Bill Black on stand-up "doghouse" bass. No drums. There was a law that said you couldn't have a drummer in a place where drinks were served. Well, it was just a madhouse. Johnny Cash and Carl Perkins and his band were also on the show, and they were great, but when the kids saw Elvis they went crazy. The girls were jumping up and down and squealing at Elvis in his pink jacket and jet-black hair, and he was wiggling and dancing during Scotty Moore's electric guitar solos, played with thumb and finger on the bass strings while his other fingers picked the melody with lots of echo and reverb. It was fantastic, early rockabilly, always circling and real bouncy, with an almost jazz feel to it. The kids around us were screaming so loud it was hard to focus on what the musicians were doing; all I remember is they were rockin' *down*. It was hot. It was crackin'. Bill Black was playing the downbeat on the pull of a bass string, then double-slapping the strings against the fretboard to hit the backbeat. At a break in the music he'd spin the bass and Elvis would kick out his leg as he delivered the punch line of "Good Rockin' Tonight." I remember Scotty's grin as he helped Bill bring the song back in while my own feet were tapping the deck with a life of their own. Elvis was absolutely great. The only thing wrong was that it was over too early.

"Jesus," Bob Evans remarked on the way out. "Those boys could get really big, you know that?"

Elvis came back a few months later, much changed. I think this must have been early 1955. We drove over to Marianna, Arkansas, where he was playing the high-school auditorium. Only this time Bill Black was playing an electric bass and D. J. Fontana was on drums. Boy, D.J. just about knocked the lights out. People wanted to dance, but they were sort of chained to their chairs, so they jumped up, rocked a few beats, sat back down, and stamped their feet.

This was about the best band I'd heard up to that time. D. J. Fontana planted those drums down and started stacking verses against one another with his fills, building up to the solos, riding the solos in and riding them out again. He had incredible technique and fast hands, so he could deploy those Buddy Rich press rolls whenever he wanted to. He played like a big-band drummer—full throttle. Now Elvis had a real foundation, some architecture, and he made the most of it. D.J. set Elvis *free*.

At the same time, that electric bass changed the whole rhythm section. Those two electric instruments really nailed that music down. Up till then, when Scotty wanted to bend his guitar strings to make them cry, the whole bottom fell out of the music. But with that electric bass carrying the load, Scotty could reach up and fill the gap during the solos. The effect was devastating, the birth of rock and roll. The other reason the electric bass caught on pretty quickly was that you didn't have to tie that doghouse bass to the top of the Cadillac anymore. And suddenly your bass player wasn't a cripple from trying to play that damn stand-up!

Later in 1955 Elvis left Sun Records to sign with RCA. Our opportunities to see him locally diminished as his growing fame took him farther afield. But there was no shortage of great bands to fill the gap. On any weekend you might have your pick of Jerry Lee's band, Billy Riley, or our own Phillips County hero Harold Jenkins, before he was known under his stage name: Conway Twitty.

I met him for the first time in 1956 when I ran a grocery store in Midway for a friend named Mary Phipps, who became ill and let me manage the place while she recuperated. At the time, the Interstate Grocery Company was helping us renovate the store with a new counter and register, and after I painted the interior they hired our best local band, Harold Jenkins and the Rock Housers, to play for our grand opening. We set up microphones and speakers on the store's front porch, and everyone in our area came by. Lavon & Linda opened with a couple of our songs. Then the Rock Housers played some rockabilly. They had a terrific guitar player, Jimmy Ray Paulman, whom everyone called Luke. Soon people were dancing, and our grand opening was judged a big success.

For me the best part came afterward, when I went over to thank the musicians for coming. "Son, I like what you're doing," Mr. Jenkins said, referring to our little opening number. "Why don't you come by some night and sit in with us for a tune?"

I told him he could count on it.

Diamond was more than supportive of Lavon & Linda's career, but as we got a little older Momma was less and less sure about the propriety of her younger daughter appearing in public with her bare leg hitched onto an upside-down washtub. One night after we'd performed, Momma told me, "Lavon, honey, your little sister is retiring from show business." When my mother had a certain tone in her voice, you just didn't argue with her, and I knew I was on my own.

But I didn't mind that much, because I had a secret weapon: Thurlow Brown.

Thurlow was a cotton farmer and guitar player from down near Elaine. He was maybe ten, twelve years older than me. Thurlow was short of stature but so tough he could whip any man around. And take my word for it: He was the best electric-guitar player we had, an incredible musician. Whistle a tune to Thurlow, and he'd play it back in harmonies for you. Play it once, and he'd know it by heart forever. He was the first guitarist I knew who could run up the neck and hit all those bar chords and augmented and diminished chords. He could have been famous, but he didn't like leaving his farm, so he never broke out of our area. But he backed up me and Linda on some of our contest victories, and by the time our mom made Linda quit, I was just about ready to see if Thurlow might form a little rock and roll band with me.

I went to see Thurlow about this possibility sometime in 1957, when I was a junior. My friend Fireball Carter and I drove down to see him, listening to "Great Balls of Fire" and Bo Diddley rap out the words to "Who Do You Love" on the car radio.

I drummed on the steering wheel to that unbelievable Bo Diddley jungle beat as we tried to find Thurlow's hangout, Virgil's Store, set behind a couple of levees in the southern part of the county. Virgil's was a place where the regular rules just didn't apply. You could always find a game of chance or ladies of the night if you wanted, and if moonshine interested you, step right up.

We got to Virgil's, and Thurlow Brown was there, all right. He had his guitar plugged in, and he was playing along with the jukebox, one of his favorite pastimes. I had my guitar, and I asked him about Chuck Berry's "School Days," a current hit that I liked a lot. Thurlow played that intro lick perfectly; he had that augmented chord just from hearing it once or twice on the radio. I came in with the first line, and he played the answer line on his old Fender Broadcaster—solid body, no levers, no gears; just tone and volume knobs and that beautiful sound.

We got together with our two guitars, a kid from Marvell named Jennings Strother, who had a stand-up bass with a pickup and an amplifier, and a drummer we found at the high school. We called ourselves the Jungle Bush Beaters and proceeded to raise a little hell around Marvell and environs. It wasn't much, but we played loud and had a hell of a lot of energy.

Thurlow was different from you and me. He was the only person I knew in Arkansas who owned a monkey. He'd ordered it by mail, and it arrived one day down at the Missouri Pacific Railroad depot on Missouri Street in Helena. Thurlow liked to bring the monkey over to the pool hall in Marvell so they could drink beer together. After two or three, one or both of 'em might get mad, and they'd have a fistfight. That should give you an idea what Thurlow was like. Another time he was called to the depot because he'd ordered a huge South American python, and it had arrived in a broken box. No one wanted to even touch that crate. Thurlow collected his snake and became quite close to it. He liked to visit the taverns with the snake wrapped around him, under his jacket, and introduce people to it. Surprised a lot of folks with his reptile, Thurlow did.

The Jungle Bush Beaters were a fairly typical high-school band, except that Thurlow could really play. We played Bo Diddley and Chuck Berry songs wherever we could, but didn't work that much because you were supposed to be eighteen to play local joints like the Delta Supper Club in West Helena, or the Rebel Club in Osceola, or the Silver Moon in Newport, Arkansas.

In 1957 the rock and roll craze was at its explosive peak. In January we all watched Elvis sing "Don't Be Cruel" on *The Ed Sullivan Show*. They let him be seen only from the waist up, but it changed America anyway. Elvis was tame compared to Little Richard or Jerry Lee Lewis, who had come up to Memphis from Louisiana as a piano player and emerged a rock and roll star. I'll never forget the first time I heard that snare drum on "Whole Lotta Shakin' Going On." Jerry Lee's drummer, Jimmy Van Eaton, had taped a cigar box to the top of the snare; he carried the backbeat and played his fills right on the cigar box without any metallic overring. That was Memphis tuning. If you tuned down that snare, you could play it loud without sounding like someone dropping a damn stove. It sounded so good, it made me want to start playing drums.

I was riding in a truck with Mutt Cagle and Fireball Carter the first time I heard Little Richard's "Keep a Knockin' " on the radio. I almost drove off the road to Turkey Scratch because I was beating on the steering wheel so hard. That rhythm knocked me flat, and still does. The Jungle Bush Beaters were major Little Richard fans, and we had to learn all his hits—"Tutti-Frutti," "Long Tall Sally," "Rip It Up," "Good Golly, Miss Molly," "Ready Teddy," "Jenny, Jenny,"

"Lucille," "Slippin' and Slidin' "—because we got so many requests for them.

The most serious and conscientious member of my boyhood gang was Fireball. Tall and lanky, very strong, his task throughout high school was to try keeping me and Mutt out of trouble; not easy because my attitude at the time was: The goofier and funnier it is, the happier everybody'll be. At all costs, let's laugh. *At all costs.* If we'd driven up to Memphis to hear some music on Beale Street, Fireball would be the one to say that we'd better hit the road or we'd miss the last ferry across the river to Helena and be stranded in Mississippi with the mosquitoes all night. Sensible.

Ed came by his nickname via the gridiron. We'd been playing football together since junior high, when there weren't enough cleats to go around, and they let little slotbacks like me run barefoot. In high school we played under the lights, usually in front of two whole towns. The entire population would turn out, seven or eight thousand people at a night game. The Marvell Mustangs' bitter rivals included Elaine, Barton, the West Helena B-team, and Marianna, which had a Chinese quarterback named Fong who nearly bit off my thumb in a game one time.

One night we were playing the Hughes High Blue Devils. They had a hell of a good team, but we held 'em off pretty good. When it came time for them to punt, Ed Carter broke up the middle, and the punter kicked the ball right into Ed's head. This knocked Ed down, but we recovered the ball and maybe even scored. Their punter, that old boy, said to Ed, "You're gonna get your damn head kicked off!"

We were on this kid like dogs on meat.

"What the fuck do *yew* care? Do your goddamn job and shut your mouth! Mind your own fuckin' business!"

Then we had a fistfight with 'em.

After the game Coach Leon Sharpe looked at Ed Carter in the locker room and said, "Son, you were a *fireball* out there today. Never seen anything like it in my life."

That's how Fireball got his name. Everybody forgot his real name. We'd cut school to meet willing young ladies down on the levee, and we'd make Ed come with us. He'd be off with his girl, kissing behind a bush, and we'd hear her yell, "*Fireball*! Where the *hell* do you think you're goin' with that hand of yours?" We be laughing so hard we couldn't stop.

We had a nice school and some good teachers in Marvell, but my mind was usually elsewhere. I wanted to play music, and that's it. It didn't matter whether I was in class or driving a stinking tractor in one-hundred-degree heat after school let out in May. I knew that playing for people was a lot healthier than inhaling gasoline fumes to get high after a brutal day in the sun.

In the dark of night I'd lie in my bed and listen to the train whistles in the distance. I wanted—I needed—to go. To me the prettiest sight in the world was a '57 Cadillac rolling down the road with a doghouse bass tied to the top. That looked like the car I wanted to be in.

Soon I'd get my chance. My day would come.

Chapter Two

THE HAWK
(OUT FOR BLOOD)

I must have been fifteen when I started going up to Memphis to see the musicians who were inventing rock and roll. It wasn't long after that I became one of those kids that *had* to stay out all night, who just *couldn't* go home. One night I managed to sneak into the Delta Supper Club in West Helena, which was the local watering hole where everyone played. You could see Conway there, or Sonny Burgess and the Pacers. The ceiling was a little low, but it wasn't too bad a place to play. It had a stage like a little band shell, and Mutt Cagle always insisted it had the best dance floor in the South. Air conditioning was a No. 3 tub and a block of ice set in front of a big window fan. They'd set up a couple of those on a hot Saturday night, and people'd stand the sweltering heat for the high quality of the music and the good time that came with it.

The Delta Supper Club was one tough place. It had a big seam running down the middle of the bar where it had been glued back together after an ejected customer stormed back in with a chain saw and cut the bar in half. As rowdy as the place was, I've seen rowdier times playing fraternity parties in Oklahoma. You could still go in and out of the club without a fistfight, although if you wanted that kind of action someone would certainly accommodate you. It had a good jukebox and was just a regular dance-hall kind of bar, a bottle bar like all the bars in the South. You bring your bottle, and they provide the ice, glasses, and food.

One night I'm in there listening to Conway Twitty and the Rock Housers, who were the best band around. Oh boy, were they good. Conway was from Friars Point, Mississippi, but moved to Helena when he was about ten so his daddy could pilot Charlie Halbert's ferryboat. His first band was the Phillips County Ramblers, a country-style group, but that changed when Elvis's "Mystery Train" inspired young Mr. Jenkins to begin writing rockabilly songs. He went up to Memphis and worked with some of the Sun musicians, like Elvis, Carl Perkins, and Jerry Lee, and often came through our area with a series of good bands.

So I'm in the Delta Supper Club, and Conway's doing "Jenny, Jenny," and the place is just going *nuts*. He had all the rockabilly moves—the stutter, the twitches, the strut—and the band, led by Jimmy Ray Paulman on guitar, provided a raw rockabilly jolt. The girls loved Conway's big, heavy-lidded good looks and long hair that reminded 'em a little of Elvis. The dancers are jitterbugging and working up a sweat, and I take a swig of my beer and work up the courage to ask to sit in for a song, since Conway was known for giving the young ones a shot.

"Sure, son," he said between sets, after I'd reminded him of the time my sister and I had opened for him on the porch of our little store in Midway. "Last song of the next set. Just come up and do whatever you want." So I got up and probably did one of Sonny Boy Williamson's things, and that might have been my debut as a singer in front of a band. I can't tell you what a feeling it gave me to be up on that stage. I was in *high cotton*! After the show, I said, "Mr. Jenkins, thanks so much for the experience. Do you think I could come by and try another one some time?"

"Sure thing," he said, "but we're headed up to Canada tonight, and it'll be a little while before we're back."

Canada?

"Ontario. They love rockbilly up there. Got a whole circuit; good bread to be made. You oughta come on up and see for yourself."

I thought this was a great idea, but J.D. and Nell had already told me in no uncertain terms that I had to finish high school before they'd cut me loose to play music. After that I sat in with the Rock Housers whenever they'd let me, although I was happy just to be there, observe, and be amazed by the pure power they were putting out.

In September 1957 Governor Orval Faubus tried to stop the integration of Central High in Little Rock. This caused a big scene, as President Dwight Eisenhower sent in federal troops and Faubus was branded an arch-segregationist. We knew it wasn't true. He'd been a progressive governor, but it would have destroyed his career in Arkansas politics if he'd been branded pro-integration. The way it happened, the Arkansas schools integrated pretty quietly after my senior year in high school, and Governor Faubus won four more terms, which was just fine with us. Orval dragged Arkansas into the twentieth century by the scruff of its rough red neck.

One night that fall I was in a bottle club in Forrest City, Arkansas, with a half-pint of Ancient Age bourbon in my back pocket. Guitarist Jimmy Ray Paulman's brother George was playing bass with a bunch of ol' boys from West Memphis. I don't remember how it happened— I think the drummer was either drunk or didn't show up—and I volunteered to play the drums. It didn't matter that I was a guitar player. I hit that Bo Diddley beat and watched it just jungle-up that dance. We had a lot of fun that night, and I thought that maybe I ought to start playing drums.

Meanwhile, Conway Twitty was about to lose Jimmy Ray Paulman to a young rocker from Fayetteville in northwest Arkansas: Ronnie Hawkins.

The Hawk was born in 1935. His dad was a barber and his mother taught school, and by the time he was twenty-two Ronnie had already enjoyed a checkered career. As a teenager he had run bootleg whiskey from Missouri to the dry counties of Oklahoma in a souped-up Model A Ford. Sometimes he'd make three hundred dollars a day. By the time he was eighteen he'd invested some of his profits in part-ownerships of various bars and clubs in Fayetteville. There he attended the University of Arkansas, which generated turn-away crowds every weekend.

Ronnie never learned to play an instrument, but soon he was entertaining in his clubs by opening for the bands that came through, like Sonny Burgess's band or Harold Jenkins's Rock Housers. The Hawk was famous for his camel walk, a funny dance step he'd learned from a black musician named Half Pint, who shined shoes in his dad's barbershop. It was like Chuck Berry's duck walk; you looked like you were standing still, but you were moving. Older people who had seen vaudeville shows knew it as the camel walk. Soon Ronnie was forming his own bands, usually known as the Hawks. While in the army, he had an all-black backup band called the Blackhawks. Things being the way they were in the South then, Ronnie soon discovered that an integrated band was more trouble than it was worth.

When he got out of the service, the rock and roll craze was exploding. Chuck Berry was the king of R&B, and Bill Doggett's 1956 hit "Honky Tonk" was just the kind of music that interested the Hawk. Ronnie packed a pair of jeans and his record-hop suit into his army duffel, checked his spit-curl hairdo in the mirror, and lit out for Memphis to become a rock and roll star.

I was still in high school at this point. I had the Jungle Bush Beaters with Thurlow to keep me busy on weekends when we weren't farming. I also played drums with the twenty-five-piece Marvell High Band (until summarily relieved of duty for continually playing in double time). I also helped stage a senior-class musical that people enjoyed so much we took it around to other high schools, split the money with 'em, and put our share in the senior class trip fund. I was dreaming of being a rock and roll star too, making it my business to check out every good band that came our way, like Roy Orbison's Teen Kings from Texas, who played the Malco Theater on Cherry Street in Helena one night to promote Roy's first big hit, "Ooby Dooby." I loved that band because it was a country-R&R hybrid: electric mandolin, drums, doghouse bass, Roy playing electric guitar and another Martin flat-picker. They made a country sound, with a lot of good bottom to it. I saw that band and wanted to be up there with it.

In 1957 some musicians in Memphis offered Ronnie a hundred dollars a week to front their band. The guitar player was Jimmy Ray "Luke" Paulman, who had met Ronnie when Conway's band played up in Fayetteville, and Luke had sat in with the Hawk's band. Ronnie told everyone in Fayetteville that he was leaving to be a rock and roll star, and next time they saw him it would be on prime-time TV. When he arrived in Memphis the group had already broken up over who would run the band for ten dollars extra per night! Ronnie Hawkins found himself stuck; his pride dictated he couldn't return to Fayetteville until he had a band that could outdraw every other group around.

So Luke invited the Hawk down to Phillips County to try something else. Hawk and his friend Donny Stone came down to West Helena with Luke and moved into Charlie Halbert's Rainbow Inn Motel. Charlie owned the local ferry and was one of our most important music promoters. He loved musicians and enjoyed helping them out, including Elvis, Conway, and me.

Anyway, Ronnie Hawkins began to put together a band with Luke on guitar, George Paulman on bass, and their cousin Willard "Pop" Jones from Marianna on kamikaze rockabilly piano. Charlie called a friend at KFFA, who let Ronnie and the boys rehearse in the station's basement, where Sonny Boy Williamson kept his amps and gear.

Now they needed a drummer, but all the drummers around our area were already working. George Paulman told them about a seventeen-year-old high-school kid from Marvell who'd sat in with him and a bunch up in Forrest City. That evening I was just coming in from doing some chores when I noticed a Model A Ford moving fast up our road, leaving a tornado of yellow dust in its wake. The car backfired once or twice as it pulled into our yard. Out stepped Luke and a big ol' boy in tight pants, sharp shoes, and a pompadour hanging down his forehead.

"I like that hairdo," I told him.

"Why, thanks, son," the Hawk rasped in his nasal Ozark twang. "I call it the Big Dick Look."

I took the boys up into the house to meet the family. Hawk got right to the point. "Lavon, we're startin' a band, and there aren't any drummers around. They tell me you're a good guitar player and you play a little drums too. Do you wanna join the band?"

I thought I'd died and gone to heaven. "Yes sir!" I said. "I am *ready*. Let's *go*. Just say *when*. Where do we *start*?"

Then reality hit me. "Do you know where we can get a set of drums?" I asked the two musicians.

At the kitchen table, my dad cleared his throat. Momma didn't look too thrilled. The Hawk sought to reassure them. "Mr. Helm, sir, we got it all planned out. We can play clubs around here and then go up to Canada. Conway—uh, Harold Jenkins—knows a guy up there that can keep us working half the year. Luke here goes up there with Conway all the time, ain't that right, Luke?''

Jimmy Ray nodded. He was kind of quiet.

"Mr. Helm," the Hawk continued, "Conway's making good bread in Canada. Real good bread, and he says there ain't no reason not to go. He says they're *starving* for a good band up there."

Diamond hemmed and hawed a little. "*Canadia,*" he said. That's what he called it. "You ever been up to Canadia, Mr. Hawkins? It's cold all the time. They've got ten months of winter up there, and two months of bad sledding. Canadia—I don't know . . ."

The three of us and my brother, Wheeler, worked on my folks for a couple of hours. I think we had my daddy convinced at one point, but Momma wore us all down in the end. We reached an agreement that while I was still in school I could play with the band locally on weekends. Then when I graduated in May, they'd give me their blessing, and I was free to go up to Canada.

Well, we got some drums—I think I borrowed a set from Bubba Stewart in Marvell—and rehearsed for months until I got out of high school. We booked our first gig on a Friday night at the Rebel Club in Osceola. "It's a rough place, son," the older and wiser Hawk advised me on the way over. "In fact, you have to puke twice and show your razor just to get in." I must have gulped. The Hawk spat out the car window and reminded me that if anyone asked, I was twenty-one, not seventeen. "Better grow some whiskers if you wanna go to Canada," he'd say. "I don't know how the hell I'm gonna get you into those clubs up there if you keep looking like a damn choirboy."

That first gig was great. Ronnie Hawkins could really work a crowd on a Friday night. I mean, he had 'em where he wanted 'em. He was big, good-looking, funny, and had a good voice. He was an entertainer rather than a musician. He had an instinct for crowd psychology and could start a rumble across the room if he wanted to just by flicking his wrist. It was this power he had over people. We'd hit that Bo Diddley beat, Hawk would come to the front of the stage and do his kick, that camel walk, and the thing would just take off. Ronnie had been a professional diver as a teenager, so he could execute a front flip into a split that would astonish you. Then he'd dance over and pretend to wind up Will Pop Jones, a big, strong kid who hit those piano keys so hard they'd break. God, that rhythm was awesome! I didn't really know what I was doing on the drums, so I just kept time. People danced, so I figured everything was on target. After the show Ronnie gave me fifteen bucks, and I was in heaven.

"Stick with me, son," he advised, " 'cause this is just hamburger money. Soon we'll be fartin' through silk!"

Things continued like this during my senior year. I went to school during the week and ran off with Ronnie for the weekends. Toward spring, when our house was surrounded by high water and we had to come out by boat, Hawk would drive over Thursday night if it looked rainy. I'd pack some clothes and a suit and stay at Charlie Halbert's so I wouldn't miss the show. Sometimes we opened for established musicians like Narvel Felts or Carl Perkins, who was the king of our circuit. Carl had a left-handed, right-footed drummer, W. S. Holland, who I watched and learned from whenever I got the chance.

Our band got better every time we played, and soon I got up the nerve to do a couple of songs myself. Ronnie'd hold the mike up to my mouth while I kept time and shouted out the words to "Short Fat Fannie" or "Caledonia." I'd been teaching myself to drum by playing along to old Sonny Boy Williamson records and soon realized my primitive gear was holding me back. The old snare I was using had calfskin on it and was a bit ragged; after each set I put it in the oven to tighten it up again. What I needed were new drums.

We also needed to join the musicians union, Charlie Halbert told us, if we wanted to play the Delta Supper Club, the Silver Moon, or Pop Warner's club up in the Missouri bootheel. So one day in early 1958 Charlie, Hawk, and I drove up to Memphis in Charlie's Lincoln. I was at the wheel, as usual. We pulled up to the union hall, Memphis Local 71, and I got out. Ronnie stayed in the car.

"Ain't you coming?" I asked him.

"Naw," Hawk said. "I can't play anything. What do I want to join the union for?"

I didn't argue with him. I went in, signed up (Charlie loaned me the first year's dues), and for the next six years all the Hawk's professional gigs were booked under my name.

Charlie Halbert, bless him, then took us over to the Hauch Music

Company and put a down payment on a brand-new set of red-sparkle Gretsch drums for me. We may have also ordered our red lamé band suits on this trip. Charlie was our guardian angel. As we sped out of Memphis that evening, he fell asleep in the seat beside me. To reward his kindness, I pretended to stall out his Lincoln on the train tracks at a crossing in West Memphis and woke Charlie just as a freight rounded the bend, heading straight for us.

Meanwhile, my academic career was winding down fast. Fireball and I disgraced ourselves on the senior class trip to Washington in the spring of 1958. First we all went up to Memphis and boarded our own train car, which we rode all night to DC. We got into a nasty poker game with some Oklahoma kids, harassed any poor soul that tried to get some sleep, teased the homesick little farm girls until they cried, then snuck off and got lost in Washington and raised some more hell on the way home—enough so that ours was the last senior class to make that trip. There are still people in Marvell who blame me and Fireball for ending that tradition.

Yet when we finally graduated, I had somehow fooled enough of my classmates to be voted Most Talented, Friendliest, Best Dancer, and Wittiest in our class. At our senior prom, the song we played over and over would soon be the No. 1 record in the country: Conway Twitty's "It's Only Make Believe." Harold Jenkins had been biding his time for years, and it finally paid off for him.

We left for Canada when school let out in May. My dad was all for it—he was impressed by the good money we were making on the weekends—and Momma gave me her blessing as well. I was a fairly independent kid, and I was lucky she let me just be that way. I remember watching her waving good-bye in the rearview mirror as I drove the Hawk's car down our country road, away from the life I'd known in Turkey Scratch, toward a whole new world a thousand miles north.

There were only four of us going to Canada: Hawk, me, Luke, and Will Pop Jones. Hawk thought that George Paulman was too "rural" to be in the band, meaning that George would just as soon fight the customers as play for 'em. We hadn't hired his replacement yet, so we drove away as the Ron Hawkins Quartet in a '55 Chevy sedan that the Hawk borrowed from his sister Winifred for the trip north.

The Hawk always let me drive, but he was funny about his cars. Ronnie wanted those Cadillacs driven a certain way and parked right, with the brake locked so the weight of the car was off the transmission. I'd been driving a tractor for nine years, so it was the most natural thing in the world for me to pull in with the tractor, stop, lock the brake, drop the plow to the ground, kill the engine, and gas it up before any condensation had a chance to form in the tank. Those simple tractor-driving rules suited the Hawk just right. He didn't even like the other boys to drive. "Dammit, son!" he'd swear at Luke. "You gotta lock that brake, give the tranny a little rest!"

From the beginning, I was the Hawk's right-hand man. To this day he's a good friend and a great leader, with an uncanny ability to pick the best musicians and build them into first-rate bands. He was immediately likable, trustworthy, and just naturally an entertainer; one of the funniest guys I ever met. The Hawk had been to college and could quote Shakespeare when he was in the mood. He was also the most vulgar and outrageous rockabilly character I've ever met in my life. He'd say and do anything to shock you. Meeting a woman for the first time, he might drop to his knees and pretend to eat her. She had to either laugh or run away. I'd grown up on crude country jokes, but Hawk's sense of humor was unbelievable.

"See here, son," he said deadpan as we headed out of Illinois. "You ever fuck a goat?"

"Uh, no, Hawk—not yet."

"Well, I have—good pussy, too. Only problem is you have to stop and walk around to the front when you want to kiss 'em."

Rockabilly humor. Luke winked at me. Later we were talking about going down on girls, and Hawk told us he kissed 'em down to the belly button and then developed amnesia.

None of knew what to expect from Canada. My dad had told me the Eskimos were violent and would kill us if they had the chance. We thought we were going to igloos and dogsleds. We were just country boys, but the Hawk had gone through the university and even *he* didn't know what to expect. "Canada," Ronnie assured us, "is as cold as an accountant's heart." Instead we found ourselves driving through southern Ontario in the summertime, a lush, green landscape of farms and lakes, prosperous towns, and above all else Toronto, the cultural capital of Canada and our future home base.

Our Canada connection was Harold Kudlets, a booking agent in Hamilton, Ontario. Soon we started to call him "Colonel" Kudlets; the Hawk insisted that if Elvis could have a colonel, he could damn well have a colonel too! Harold was a colorful guy who'd started in the big-band era, but now he had a system going: He booked bands from the South through Conway Twitty to play a circuit in Ontario, Quebec, and U.S.-Ontario border towns like Buffalo, Detroit, and Cleveland. He also turned it around: If he found a good band from Toronto or Buffalo, he'd book them into our Missouri-Arkansas-Louisiana-Oklahoma circuit. The Colonel basically ran a transnational rockabilly interchange. The same type of music was popular in both areas in the late fifties, and we were the beneficiaries.

We went over to the Colonel's office. He took one look at me and blanched. "Tell me, sir," he asked. "How old are you?"

"Eighteen, sir."

"Well, you look about twelve years old to me. Don't you boys know you have to be twenty-one just to be in the places we're booking you into?"

The Hawk explained that in Arkansas I'd gotten by wearing dark glasses to make me look older. The Colonel looked dubious. We survived our initial jobs by sneaking me into the taverns, hiding me in the kitchen between sets in case the police came by (as they often did), then sneaking me out when the band was finished for the night.

The first place we played was the Golden Rail Tavern in Hamilton. We rehearsed all afternoon, speeding through our material, with the Hawk as wild as an ape. When the bartenders saw what Ronnie was up to and heard our music—Bo Diddley in overdrive—they all threatened to quit. Opening night looked like a disaster: People were lining up to get out. But eventually word got out that rock and roll had really hit town and that this band was *hopped up*! We played "Ooby Dooby," "Hey! Bo Diddley," "Lawdy Miss Clawdy," and some Chuck Berry as loud and fast as we could. The Hawk really worked that crowd, dancing and doing that camel walk. They loved our speed and power, and our red suits with the black satin lapels. The Ron Hawkins Quartet was an immediate hit. The bartenders stopped complaining when they saw how much business we brought in. We were even held over for a week. The next gig was at the Brass Rail in London, Ontario, where we were held over for three weeks.

Finally we played the Le Coq D'Or on Yonge Street in Toronto's honky-tonk downtown entertainment district. This was the big time in Canada, and they loved it. The Le Coq D'Or was soon jammed with every "rounder" in Toronto. From the beginning, the Hawk attracted a rough crowd: racket guys, pool hustlers, off-duty cops, tobacco farmers, gamblers, hookers, and their pimps. Ronnie used to yell, *"It's racket time!"* to start the show. It was our good luck that our music attracted these people, since they befriended and helped us in many ways, many times over the years.

Our recording career also began during that first visit to Toronto. An A&R (artists and repertory) guy named Dan Bass from Quality Records came to the Le Coq D'Or and liked our version of "Hey! Bo Diddley," which Mr. Diddley himself had recorded in Chicago for Chess Records the year before. Soon we found ourselves in a little studio on Kingston Road. There we cut a primitive "Hey! Bo Diddley," which later in 1958 was released as a single (both 45 and 78 rpm discs) in a pressing of maybe five hundred copies. It didn't go anywhere because we didn't have a record deal yet.

We said good-bye to Canada after maybe three months. We were all homesick, and anyway Hawk's friend Dayton Stratton had booked us into the southern circuit of taverns, dance halls, roadhouses, and frat parties. This would help sustain us as we shed layers of skin, eventually emerging as Romping Ronnie Hawkins and the Hawks, then as Levon and the Hawks, then just the Hawks.

But when we got back down south, we almost immediately got homesick for Canada again. A lot of the honky-tonks we played at home were run by gangsters. They weren't supposed to have liquor licenses, so these places were under someone else's name. It was often hard to get paid after a night's work. Times were rough, and money was so scarce we had to carry what the Hawk called an Arkansas credit card: a siphon, a length of rubber hose, and a five-gallon can. The only way we could get from one date to the next was by siphoning off our customers' gasoline while they were still inside drinking. The Hawk told people he was the only rock and roll singer to perform every night with chafed lips from sucking gas.

The Hawk also liked to carry "the difference" in the glove compartment. We almost never took it out. But it was a rough circuit, as I said. Some of those places we had to play our way in and fight our way out. There were a number of times things got out of hand. The Hawk had to tag a couple of people. Ronnie was fearless and didn't mind tempting fate, and there were nights we were amazed to be alive. One time some guy in Alabama got too close down front, and he and the Hawk made a negative connection. The Hawk always felt it was his microphone and his stage. The next thing we knew, he'd dived into the crowd after this guy. We all jumped in after him. Well, there was a brawl, but it didn't last long because Willard grabbed this one guy and smashed him against the wall. Then we jumped back onstage and started to play "Who Do You Love" again. This kind of thing went on until we became familiar on the circuit. It was like leaving County Line School for Marvell. We were uptight for a couple of months until we fought our way into the system.

After a few weeks, we were happy to go back to Canada. There the circuit was tough but less violent. The places we played in Ontario were mixed-drink clubs. The hours were better, we played fewer sets a night, and last call was at midnight rather than whenever they shut down for the night like at home. The best part was that a Canadian tavern booking might last as long as a month. You could make friends and have some fun instead of living on the highway.

So as soon as he could, the Hawk put a down payment on a pink and white '57 Cadillac four-door Sedan deVille and bought some new equipment and a teardrop-shaped trailer to haul it. We painted a hawk on the side of the trailer and lit out for Canada again with Jimmy "Lefty" Evans to play electric bass. Lefty was a real pro; he'd played with all the Memphis boys, including Conway and Billy Riley, and was doing sessions when he decided to come on the road with us. Ronnie gave me a couple of greenies to stay awake, and we made it from West Helena to Toronto in under twenty-four hours. It was a fast life, and we had a policy of going with speed. When we had a destination, we didn't just idle around. We drove fast. We were a blur.

We were thrilled to be back in Toronto. I remember thinking it was the best place for live music I'd ever seen, outside of Memphis. We realized that down south we were just one of several good bands playing a rockabilly style that was already becoming dated. But in Canada we were unique and exotic, playing the most uninhibited, wildest rock and roll that hip Torontonians had ever heard. They loved the band and did everything they could to make us feel at home. We joined the shady clientele at the very down-market Warwick Hotel, not far from the Le Coq D'Or.

On a typical Friday night in late 1958 the intersection of Yonge and Dundas streets became Canada's equivalent of Times Square. Leather-jacketed hoods in greasy ducktail hairdos drag-raced down Yonge in their tail-finned Pontiacs. Garish neon signs advertised the bars and taverns, little boys with dirty faces charged a dime to shine your boots, and the local hookers, most of whom became our friends, waited for customers on street corners when the tough Toronto cops weren't looking.

Ronnie Hawkins became the king of this scene almost immediately. He turned the upstairs room of the Le Coq D'Or into his private studio and "gymnasium." He told people, "I got the only gym in the world where you come in feeling OK and leave a total physical wreck." After the Le Coq D'Or closed at midnight, he'd move the band upstairs to rehearse all night. Soon invitations to these after-hours affairs were eagerly sought, since a few of them turned into legendary parties.

"Let's not call them orgies," the Hawk would say. "Let's just say it was seven or eight people in love."

Ronnie liked to tell people we had parties that Nero would have been ashamed to attend. I'd wink and tell them not to believe everything that came out of Ronnie's mouth, but most people realized that where there's smoke, there's fire. Anyway, the Hawk assiduously cultivated the worst reputation he could for us. He felt it was part of the promotion of the show.

We usually played from Thursday through Saturday nights. To pick up a little extra money, on Sundays we played out-of-town clubs like Pop Ivy's down in Port Dover. One night at Krang's Plaza, in the west end of Toronto, a little kid named Freddie McNulty came in and started to dance by himself. He was short, with curly red hair and a loony smile, and he loved the Hawks beyond all reason. He was a show all by himself, right down in front; one of the wildest rockabilly dancers you ever saw. Freddie could shake it down! He was a character, the first person who ever gave me five. He came across the stage, and I stuck out my hand. He said, "I dig ya style, man," and *whack*! He didn't play anything, but he had a genius for music, so we'd let him sit in on gigs and sneak him in with us when we went down to Port

Dover on Sunday. Hell, they were still sneaking *me* in because I was underage. Freddie became our mascot. He followed us back to the hotel, got us coffee, went to the movies with us, whatever.

We'd brought our red band jackets with us up from Arkansas, but soon they began to disintegrate. We worked up a terrible sweat when we played, so our suits had to be dry-cleaned almost every day. Across from the Le Coq D'Or was a tailor, Lou Myles, who became the Hawks' wardrobe coordinator. He made us a new set of black suits—pinched waists, skinny lapels, and pegged pants worn over pointy black boots—that we wore with fresh white shirts and narrow black ties. That was our look: cool, lean, and mean.

One night our agent, Harold Kudlets, came over to see our show at the Brass Rail. The Hawk was out for blood that night: We had popped some pills, and Ronnie was doing somersaults on the edge of the stage. The customers almost went berserk when he unchained Willard on Chuck Berry's ''Thirty Days,'' and he started hitting those damn piano keys so hard the hammers started popping out of the old piano. When the Colonel saw the pandemonium we were generating, he called a New York agent who booked a circuit of nightclubs on the Jersey Shore. That's how we got to Wildwood, New Jersey, in the spring of 1959.

The clubs on the Shore drew rock and roll fans from New York and Philadelphia. Soon we were doing turn-away business, drawing almost as well as some of the biggest acts in those days, including Sammy Davis, Jr., Teresa Brewer, and Frankie Laine. That got the talent agents all stirred up, and soon we were being courted by New York record companies who saw Ronnie as the Next Big Thing. After all, that year there was a huge void in rock and roll: Elvis was in the army, Chuck Berry was in jail, Jerry Lee was in disgrace for marrying his thirteen-year-old cousin, Little Richard had joined the ministry, Conway had gone country, and Buddy Holly was dead. Some people were saying that rock and roll was dying, but that Ronnie Hawkins might be able to save the patient.

Mitch (*Sing Along With Mitch*) Miller over at Columbia Records wanted to sign us real bad, but Ronnie was more interested in an agent that had been sent to see us by Morris Levy, the head of Roulette Records. We went into Manhattan to see Mr. Levy at Roulette's office on West Fiftieth Street. As we were going up the elevator the Hawk leaned over and whispered to me, "Be polite to Mr. Levy, son. He's Mafia up to his eyeballs."

Morris was one tough cat, and he practically owned Broadway back then. He knew all the big boys, and nobody messed with him. He'd come up owning famous New York jazz clubs like the Royal Roost and Birdland, and started Roulette in 1956 in partnership with deejay Alan Freed, who had moved his famous *Moondog Rock 'n' Roll Party* show from Cleveland to New York's WINS two years earlier and changed its name to *Alan Freed's Rock & Roll Party*. The Hawk explained that Freed was no longer part of Roulette, but that Morris *owned* the disc jockey, who liked to gamble and accepted cash—hundred-dollar bills in a brown bag—in exchange for playing songs on his show. In 1957 *Variety,* the show-business paper, called Morris the "octopus" of the music industry, so far-reaching were his tentacles. His acts on Roulette and about five other labels eventually included Count Basie, Frankie Lymon and the Teenagers, the Harptones, the Crows, and Buddy Knox, whose "Party Doll" had been Roulette's first single. With Alan Freed's help it went to No. 1 in five weeks.

"We can't miss with these cats behind us," the Hawk said.

In addition to his labels, clubs, and restaurants, Morris was also a major song publisher and a partner with Freed in his successful rock and roll stage shows at the Brooklyn Paramount and Fox theaters. (Many years later, after Morris was said to be worth $75 million, he would be referred to as the "Godfather" of the American music business.)

Whatever his reputation, Morris treated us like royalty. He took us to his new restaurant, the Round Table, a classy steakhouse on Fiftieth Street, where he introduced us to Frankie Carbo, the so-called underworld commissioner of boxing in New York. That was the first time I ever ate one of those big New York–cut steaks, bacon wrapped around it, twice-baked potatoes, all the trimmings. Morris told us he wanted us for Roulette, spent a lot of money wining and dining us, and convinced the Hawk. We signed to Roulette in April 1959 and began to record almost immediately.

On April 13 we cut a version of "Ruby Baby" and "Forty Days" at Bell Sound, produced by veteran A&R man Joe Reisman on a two-track tape recorder. What a feeling of joy that was! I'd seen KFFA's studio back in Helena with Sonny Boy Williamson and the King Biscuit

Boys, but this was *Bell Sound*! All of a sudden there we were. "Forty Days" was Ronnie's rewrite of Chuck Berry's "Thirty Days," and boy, we took it fast. You can pick up a smidgen of what that band was all about when Willard speeds through the piano solo and lifts the song right off the ground. Roulette released this as a single in May, Morris Levy put his big guns behind it, and it spent eight weeks on *Billboard*'s Hot 100 chart, eventually reaching No. 45. At the end of April we were back in New York recording eight tracks, including "Red Hot," "Wild Little Willie," and "Odessa," Hawk's tribute to a famous black madam whose house on Yazoo Street in Helena was well known to us. The first time he took me to visit her he said, "Son, I've been coming to see Odessa since the Dead Sea was merely sick!" Ronnie liked to maintain that he knew every hooker between Helena and Toronto.

We also cut our next single, "Mary Lou," which had been written and cut by Young Jessie Obie in 1955. Hawk learned the song from Roy Orbison, and our version was a hit, reaching No. 26 during the wonderful, hot summer of 1959.

We just about lived in the Cadillac that summer. During one of our breaks we went back to Arkansas, and Ronnie picked up a new white '59 Sedan deVille and got a trailer to match. While we were checking on the Hawk's business interests in Fayetteville (he owned the Rockwood Club with Dayton Stratton), we went to the local car dealer. Ronnie signed for me—I was *barely* nineteen—and I drove a new Cadillac of my own out of there. Now we had a little fleet.

We started pushing our records right after we recorded "Forty Days." The hottest TV program on the air back then was *The Steve Allen Show,* and of course Morris Levy got us an audition. By then all the rockers had been on TV, so it wasn't any big deal, but for us this was the big time, and we were all a little nervous as we rode up in the elevator to audition for Steve. It was the Hawk, me, Lefty, Luke, and Willard. Luke and Lefty had their amps, I lugged the bass drum and the tom-tom, and Colonel Kudlets carried my sock cymbal. We got off the elevator, clattering and banging, and found ourselves in the rehearsal hall. Everyone turned and looked at us like we'd just come from Mars. Dayton Allen and Tom Poston were up on the podium, reading from a script, and everybody was laughing. Steve Allen and his wife, Jayne Meadows, sat on folding chairs, talking to the producer and director, and I don't think they noticed us at first.

We waited in the hallway until the cast finished rehearsal, then suddenly we got a green light. Everyone watched as the Hawk announced, "Folks, this is the one that took us from the hills and the stills and put us on the pills!" We started playing "Forty Days," but a little too fast. Actually, it might've been a *lot* too fast. I guess we were scared, because we came out of that gate like fuel dragsters. There was no turning back, so we kicked it into high gear: the Hawk doing backflips; Willard playing flat on his back, his clothes popping open; Luke on his knees; and Lefty running straight at him with his bass. Shit! I thought everyone had gone crazy. All activity in the studio stopped. They stared at us in shock, like they'd never even seen *monkeys* act like this. We'd put a fiddle pickup in the studio piano, which made it sound ten times louder than an ordinary piano. It didn't sound electric, just loud. Steve Allen was a musician, a big-time composer and piano player. He watched aghast as Willard banged those keys and the hammers started flying out of the piano like it was a popcorn machine.

Somehow we crashed to a finish. An assistant murmured they'd call us, but of course they never did.

Next we went down to Philadelphia to do *American Bandstand,* which Dick Clark broadcast over the ABC network. This was the MTV of the fifties: Every weekday across the country millions of kids tuned in to watch Dick's teenage dancers do the latest steps and to catch the newest acts. Since they figured we were from the country, the set was dressed like a western saloon. They also put garters on our sleeves, gave us cowboy hats, and plastered us with makeup. What the hell, we were gonna be on TV, that's all we knew. (The other act on the show besides us was actor Chuck Connors, star of TV's *The Rifleman.* Dick and his kids thought they'd seen it all by then—Jackie Wilson, James Brown—but they appeared stunned when Ronnie began to do double backflips as we lip-synched our way through "Mary Lou" and "Forty Days." Lip-synching had tamed a lot of acts on *Bandstand,* but it didn't stop the Hawk. He went wild anyway, and "Mary Lou" went on to sell 750,000 records.

We were back in New York in September 1959 to appear on Alan Freed's huge Labor Day show at the Brooklyn Fox. We did two or three shows a day, and there were so many stars I hung out in the wings watching between sets. Jackie Wilson headlined with his latest release, "You Better Know It." Jimmy Clanton did "My Own True Love." Several up-and-coming acts were on the bill: Dion and the Belmonts, the Skyliners, the Crests, the Mystics. Fifteen-year-old Johnny Restivo did his hit, "The Shape I'm In." The Tempos, from Pittsburgh, did their huge hit of that summer, "See You in September," after which Bo Diddley, a Freed road-show regular since 1955, came out and killed everyone with "Crackin' Up" and "Say Man."

Bo Diddley's band had only three pieces: Clifton James on drums, Jerome on maracas ("Bring it on home, bring it to Jerome"), and Bo on guitar. Without a piano, Bo tuned his guitar by ear, which always gave problems to bandleader Sam "The Man" Taylor. (Mr. Taylor took Lloyd Price's band and augmented it with his own, going up to thirty instruments sometimes. This was the first time I ever saw two drummers on a stage, sitting side by side. Lloyd's man played his snare drum turned on a sharp angle between his legs and swung his sticks like hammers, mallet style. Sam's drummer played in standard cross-sticking style. Spider, the bass player, played a stand-up bass right at the drummers' shoulders. When the three of them bore down, it didn't swing, it *swung*.) While Bo Diddley and the band were working the house, Sam searched for the key they were in. When he found it, he'd adjust the mouthpiece of his saxophone to sharp or flat to allow for Bo's "by ear" tuning. Then he signaled the band, holding up two fingers and one across in the shape of an *A,* then gave a thumbs-up to tell them it was on the sharp side. Now they were ready for the big final chord. On Bo's last *chop t' chop chop,* the whole outfit meshed with Bo's band, and the drummers roughed it up and crashed out on Clifton's downstroke. It was a lot of power, a big chord blasted out by everybody, and it made my hair stand up. (One night I overheard one of the horn players tell his buddy, "You never know what key lurks in the heart of Bo Diddley.")

That show was an education. We did our songs and watched the kids go nuts as Ronnie camel-walked and did his backflips. Afterward, on the way back to Canada, we realized we were the only rockabilly-style act in the show. Dion had drawn the biggest response. The writing was on the wall, and we read it. The music we were playing was on its way out.

That September our third single, "Wild Little Willie," was released, and Morris Levy sent the band off to do promotional tours, playing record hops. We'd go to Detroit or Cleveland and pile into a station wagon with an electric piano, a set of drums, and a couple of amps. There'd be five hundred kids dancing in a high-school gym, where we'd set up and play three or four quick songs. Then we'd throw all the stuff back into the car, and dash off to another record hop on the other side of town. Sometimes we did several of these a day. This was how you promoted yourself back then, but after a while it stopped being exciting to the Hawk or any of us, especially since we weren't paid for these dates. (After one of these shows, the local promo man suggested we go out for a pizza pie. "Hey, Levon," whispered Willard in the backseat, "what the fuck is a pizza pie?"

"Shut up, Willard," I hissed. "D'you want him to think we're a bunch of hicks?" But that was indeed when we Arkansas boys had our first pizza.)

Right there was when things began to change. Luke, our guitar player, had a wife in Arkansas who wanted him home, and he started to talk about leaving the band. But we kept pushing all that autumn. We ran back to Toronto to play the Friar's Tavern, then down home for a swing through Fayetteville, a couple of frat parties at the University of Oklahoma in Norman, then over to Little Rock to play the Club 70 and a dance at the National Guard Armory, where things could (and often did) get out of hand. In mid-September we were back on the Jersey Shore around the time Roulette released our first album, *Ronnie Hawkins*. On September 16 the Hawks, without Ronnie, were booked into Bell Sound in Manhattan to record a couple of instrumentals under our new producer, Mr. Henry Glover.

Henry was an old-time record man and an Arkansawyer to boot. He had helped Syd Nathan build Cincinnati's King Records into America's first major independent label, becoming the first black record executive while producing early sessions by James Brown, Little Willie John, Hank Ballard and the Midnighters, Lulu Reed, and the Delmore Brothers. Henry wrote songs as well: "Honky Tonk," "Drown in My Own

Tears," and later "California Sun" and "Peppermint Twist," after he'd cut Hank Ballard's original Twist dance records.

Something clicked between Henry and me. I tried to put myself under the wing of this A&R genius (he'd talked Little Willie John into cutting "Fever"), and for the next twenty-five years we would depend on his counsel and advice.

So we were at this session alone, working on tracks without vocals. After we'd cut a couple of instrumentals on his new four-track machine, Henry came into the studio and said, "Lavon, you know you've got a hell of a band here. If you boys ever decide you want to do something by yourselves, I hope you'll come talk to me about it first."

This meant the world to me at the time, because Henry wasn't just a rock and roll maven. Since coming to New York to work with Morris Levy at Roulette, he'd been involved with jazz artists like Sonny Stitt, Lockjaw Davis, Sarah Vaughan, and especially Dinah Washington. Henry knew good music when he heard it, and if a veteran music man like him thought we could cut it on our own, well, maybe we could someday—if the need arose.

We were back in Wildwood, New Jersey, that weekend when something funny happened. Playing nearby was Ronnie's cousin Dale Hawkins, best known for the 1957 hit "Suzie-Q." Dale's band had an incredible guitar player from Louisiana, Fred Carter, Jr., who played as well as Luke and maybe even a little better. Well, Ronnie and Dale had a little reunion—"Shor good to see ya agin, cousin; how many years has it been anyway?"—but as soon as Dale left the room, Ronnie tried to hire Fred Carter, Jr.! "How much ya makin' with Dale, son?" he asked. Ronnie knew Luke's days in the Hawks were numbered, so he offered Fred more money, and besides, Ronnie had a couple of hit records. Dale wasn't too pleased, but Fred showed up in Canada shortly afterward. For a while, before Luke went home for good, we had a two-guitar attack that I thought was incredible. Where Luke played classic rockabilly style, Fred had developed a plectrum/finger-picking technique that became known as the Louisiana funk sound. Check out "Suzie-Q" to see what I mean. It wasn't easy to hire Fred, though. We might have had to pay him $150 a week.

We spent most of October 1959 in Toronto, playing the Le Coq D'Or and the Concord Tavern and working out songs for Ronnie's next album, which we would cut later in the month back in New York.

This was when we began to notice a local kid hanging around our bandstand. He was young, maybe fifteen at the most. He'd do anything to make himself useful—haul amps, help set up, run for coffee—and after several weeks of seeing him every day, I noticed he usually had a guitar case with him. He didn't cause any problems, so it was OK by me, I guess. His name?

Robbie Robertson.

Chapter Three

TAKE NO PRISONERS

Rosemarie Crysler was a beautiful Mohawk Indian girl from the Six Nations reservations above Lake Erie. After World War II started she came to Toronto to live with an aunt and met a guy named Klegerman, with whom she had a son in July 1943, Jaime (pronounced Jamie) Robert. Mr. Klegerman was a professional card player and gambler, as his son later described him. He was killed while changing a tire on the Queen Elizabeth Way between Toronto and Niagara Falls when his son was a baby. Robbie's mom married a Mr. Robertson, and they both worked in a jewelry-plating factory while Robbie was growing up.

The boy spent his summers on his mother's reservation, surrounded by cousins and uncles who played fiddles, mandolins, and guitars and laughed a lot. His great-grandfather would grab the boy with the crook of his cane as he ran by, tell him stories and lore, trying to make a Mohawk out of him. His mother took Robbie for guitar lessons when he was ten; the Hawaiian instructor laid a guitar on his lap and taught him to play it flat, Waikiki style. It was the only training the boy ever had. Meanwhile he stayed up all night listening to WLAC out of Nashville, a fifty-thousand-watt clear-channel station with a thousand-mile range. Deejay John R. played blues all night in the 1950s. It was the underground radio of the day. There was also George "Hound Dog" Lorenz, a rock and roll disc jockey in Buffalo whose show was influential for a lot of young Canadians.

Robbie liked school until he caught the rock and roll bug. At thirteen he was in a band called Little Caesar and the Consoles, playing New Orleans songs like "Blue Monday." Then he formed Robbie Robertson and the Rhythm Chords around the time the now-classic sci-fi movie *Forbidden Planet* came out, featuring Robbie the Robot. So Pete Traynor, one of the Rhythm Chords, drilled some holes in Robbie's Harmony guitar, installed some antennae and wires, and they renamed the group Robbie and the Robots. Then there was Thumper and the Trambones. At fifteen Robbie Robertson was a tall, dark street-smart punk living with his mom in Toronto's Cabbagetown neighborhood and hanging out on Yonge Street, catching the bands that came through town: Bo Diddley, Carl Perkins, Ronnie Hawkins. That's when we met him.

Robbie, Pete Traynor, and a piano player named Scott Cushnie had this little band, and they opened for the Hawk one night at Dixie Arena. The Hawks, Robbie told an interviewer, "played the fastest, most violent rock and roll I'd ever heard. It was exciting and exploding with dynamics. The solos would get *really* loud, Ronnie would come in and growl, then it would get quiet, then fast and loud again. It was these cool-looking guys doing this primitive music faster and more violent than anybody, with overwhelming power.

"It was also the way they looked, how young they were. They weren't as young as me, but they were still pretty young. There was this little kid playing drums. You couldn't believe this guy was the drummer, but he was *terrific*. Terrific to look at and terrific to hear. . . .

"I knew the majority of the music I liked and felt connected to was from the South," Robbie continued, "and they kind of represented that to me. And Levon didn't let down my fantasy of what this thing was. He was real, authentic, and had such a love for music. To me it seemed he came right from Mecca."

The Hawk took a liking to this kid. One afternoon I came into the club, and Robbie was auditioning for the Hawk, playing him a couple of songs he'd written. That night Ronnie said to me, "Son, y'know that kid who's been hanging out? He's got so much talent it makes me sick! Maybe we should take him on."

I pointed out that we already had a couple of guitar players.

"Yeah," the Hawk said, "but Luke's going home soon, and this kid can write a little. Besides, I know his mom. She's worried about him, and maybe if we take him on, it'll keep him out of jail. Let's think about it."

We didn't hire Robbie right away, but the Hawk took him along to New York when we cut our next tracks at Bell Sound. He sat next to me in the Cadillac and talked my ear off as I drove down the "Queen E." Jesus, this kid really wanted to be in the band. I got the impression he'd kill for a permanent seat in the Cadillac. Of course, I would've too.

One reason the Hawk took Robbie to New York was that he trusted Robbie's ears. Robbie was opinionated about hit records, and Ronnie figured since the kid was still a teenager, what Robbie liked would also appeal to the teenager rock and roll market. We were looking for that big hit, right? So while I went over to the Metropole Cafe on Seventh Avenue to check out Cozy Cole or Gene Krupa, Hawk and Robbie went over to the Brill Building on Broadway and met some of rock and roll's biggest songwriters—Doc Pomus and Mort Shuman, Jerry Leiber and Mike Stoller, Carole King and Gerry Goffin, Otis Blackwell—and auditioned a hell of a lot of songs. "That wasn't bad," the kid told Mort "Save the Last Dance for Me" Shuman. "You got anything else?"

The Hawk cut two of fifteen-year-old Robbie Robertson's tunes with Henry Glover on October 26: "Hey Boba Lou" and "Someone Like You," as well as "Baby Jean" (cowritten by me) and nine other tracks. These came out on the Hawk's second album, *Mr. Dynamo,* which Roulette released in January 1960.

The Hawk told anyone he could that this kid Robbie was going to be one of the biggest stars in the business some day. Ronnie had us all convinced. Nevertheless, he told Robbie he was too young to be in the band.

Late in 1959 Willard wanted to go back to Arkansas for a while; not quit the band, just take a leave. The Hawk replaced him with Scott Cushnie from Robbie's band, who finished a gig we had at the Brass Rail in London, Ontario. Luke went home, deeply mourned by the Hawk, who maintains to this day that Jimmy Ray Paulman was the best rhythm guitar player in the history of rock and roll, bar none.

Then Lefty Evans quit while we were working down in Arkansas. As a going-away present for him, I picked up two cherry bombs for a dollar. While Lefty was asleep in the Cadillac, I lit the fuse of one of the big firecrackers, tossed it in the backseat, and shut the door. The hissing fuse woke him up, and Lefty tried to stomp it out, but the fuse kept burning. I could see Lefty's fingertips just reaching the door handle when it went off. Then he tumbled out of the car amid thick smoke and flying bits of paper.

We were cruel to one another in the band.

Fred Carter, Jr., took over lead guitar, and Robbie Robertson was called down to Arkansas to play bass. It might have been Scott who suggested Robbie.

The Hawk called Robbie at his mother's house from his nightclub in Fayetteville. "Son, can you play any bass?" he asked.

"Yes sir," Robbie lied.

"Start practicing. I'll call you next week."

The Hawk didn't call. A few weeks later Robbie reached him at the Rockwood Club. "OK, come on down," Ronnie told him. "I'm gonna put you in training. Maybe we can break you in."

Robbie begged, pleaded, and lied until his mom let him go. There was no money for bus fare, so he pawned his '57 Fender Stratocaster. He took one bus from Toronto to Buffalo, than another to Chicago, then a train to Springfield, Missouri, and another bus up winding Ozark roads to Fayetteville. When Robbie got off the bus, Ronnie and his friends simply laughed at this city kid wearing a long overcoat. It was *hot* in Arkansas in December. "You look like an immigrant from Albania," the Hawk told him. Ronnie took the kid to the barber, got him cleaned up, bought him some new clothes, and explained that he and I were going to England to be on TV, and if Robbie practiced real hard while we were gone, he *might* have a spot in the band when we came back. "Nobody knows if you'll be good enough," he told the kid. "We'll see how it works."

Then he put Robbie on a bus to Helena.

Up in Fayetteville, the Ozark mountain air was clear and fresh. As Robbie's bus came out of the mountains, down through Little Rock, he saw the landscape flatten. The light changed as it filtered through the delta dust. Everything was low and wet, with rice growing in fields of water. "People walked in rhythm and talked this singsong talk," he remembered. "When I'd go down by the river in Helena, the *river* seemed to be in rhythm, and I thought, *No wonder this music comes from here: The rhythm is already there.*"

I picked Robbie Robertson up at the bus station and drove him out to Turkey Scratch. "How come your house is up on stilts?" he wanted to know. Diamond was still farming cotton on some land he owned and some he leased. Linda was still at home, and my brother Wheeler was only about ten. Momma made Robbie supper, and he told her it was the best meal he'd ever had. I bet it tasted good, after ten hours on that bus. Diamond told some funny stories, and Robbie about split his sides. Then Diamond got out his mandolin, and we all might have sung a little, with Robbie playing my guitar. Later that night we drove back into Helena, and Robbie looked around with his mouth open.

"It's like being in another world," he said. "I never saw so many black people in my life. It's like Africa." I explained that down here in the delta there were eight black people to every white. Robbie didn't say anything. He sat in the passenger seat and stared into the darkness of the night.

In January 1960 Morris Levy flew Ronnie and me to London. Rockabilly hadn't died in England like it did back home, and Ronnie had a following, especially, we heard, up in Liverpool. Before we left, the Hawk gave Robbie a hundred dollars to live on, and he and the rest of the band moved into Charlie Halbert's motel. Fred Carter, Jr., was supposed to teach Robbie a few things while we were away; instead Fred took him up to Memphis, to the famous Home of the Blues record store on Beale Street, and Robbie spent his allowance on blues and R&B records. Fred also took Robbie to Sun Records, where Jerry Lee Lewis was recording. *I'm here,* Robbie said to himself. *I made it.*

In England we appeared on an early BBC pop-music show called *Boy Meets Girl* and got to hang out and jam a little with Eddie "Summertime Blues" Cochran, who was also big in England and touring at the time with the Shadows, a good British band. I was astonished by Eddie's ability to chord a guitar using his little finger as a bar. It was something else! Eddie Cochran was a hell of a rocker; we were saddened a short time later when we heard he'd been killed in a car accident over there. (I almost got killed myself in London when I stepped off the curb after looking the wrong way for oncoming traffic. I'd forgotten the British drive on the left!)

Meanwhile, back in Helena Robbie was picking apart Howlin' Wolf records for their bass and guitar parts. He practiced twelve hours a day until his fingers were hard as nails. Robbie remembered the Hawk pumping him up, telling him how good he was. He thought about Ronnie's mercenary, out-for-blood attitude toward the music business, and realized that Fred Carter wasn't exactly killing himself as a guitar teacher. Robbie realized he was fighting for his life. "There was no way," he remembered, "that Ronnie was gonna come back and say, 'This ain't working out.' "

The Hawk and I returned home and couldn't believe the progress Robbie had made in two weeks. We started rehearsing and would sit up all night deciding what to do with the band.

Charlie Halbert had a big mansion up on a hill, and he let us rehearse in his living room, which had a good piano. Robbie watched Fred work his Fender Telecaster. He had replaced the two bottom strings with steel banjo strings, a trick that gave his sound a real bluesy twang. Robbie picked up all this stuff and absorbed techniques from everyone, even transposing some of Ray Charles's piano licks for electric guitar. One night we sat down and played Ronnie's big 'numbers—"Mary Lou," "Hey! Bo Diddley," "Who Do You Love"—and Robbie was pumping the bass lines. Hell, *I* wanted to get up and dance, it sounded so good.

When we finished rehearsing that first night, the Hawk looked at me and said, "This cat's a genius." He turned to Robbie. "Son, you got the job. Stick with us, and you'll get more nookie than you can eat."

In the winter and spring of 1959–60 Ronnie Hawkins reached a turning point. Morris Levy wanted him to stay in New York and take over rock and roll, maybe go to Hollywood. "You can't go back to Canada!" Morris shouted at us in his office. "You've got it all to yourself. Elvis is in the fuckin' army, and you're better than him anyway now. Buddy Holly, Eddie Cochran—dead. There's a vacuum here, and you're the only one around who can take advantage of it. You're on the goddamn verge! You can't just vanish on me."

But the Hawk wasn't as sure as Morris was. If you watched *Ameri-*

can Bandstand that year you saw who was taking over: Dick Clark's new teen idols, like Frankie Avalon, Fabian, Bobby Rydell. Italian kids from Philadelphia with big hair. When the big payola scandal hit the front pages a few months later, Alan Freed's career was over, and with it the rock and roll business we'd come up in. Hell, the fifties were over. Meanwhile, the Hawk had been investing. He owned a couple of clubs in Fayetteville and had bought two farms in the area. These required cash flow. We'd worked for almost two years building a lucrative circuit in southern Ontario and Quebec. Hawk knew that in Canada he could work seven nights a week all year and be guaranteed a living that the changing American music business might no longer provide.

I felt the way the Hawk did. By then my dad had quit farming, and Momma was working in a department store. I'd been sending money home every week since I went with Ronnie, so my own family was dependent on the Hawk's working steadily. There were so many bars between Windsor, Ontario, and Montreal that I knew we could work every night of the year. Unlike Luke, Lefty, or Willard, I didn't have a girl back home. In fact, I was getting extremely infatuated with the Canadian girls. By all means, I agreed with the Hawk, let's get back to Toronto and be the big fishes in the littler pond.

Morris Levy couldn't believe it. "Hawkins moves better than Elvis," he told me. "He looks better than Elvis and sings better than him too, if you ask me. Why don't you talk to him?"

I had tried. So had Henry Glover. Even the Colonel. Morris was mystified. "He keeps saying how much he loves Canada," he told me. "It's breaking my heart."

We went back to Canada with Robbie in the band, playing bass. He told me later his whole outlook had changed in Arkansas. "I'd hear something at night and not know whether it was an animal, a harmonica, or a train," he remembered, "but it sounded like music to me. And every day the radios would go, 'Pass the biscuits! It's *King Biscuit Time!*' and you'd hear this harmonica—'waa, waaaah'—and it was Sonny Boy Williamson. The jukeboxes were like being in heaven, but what blew my mind was that in the places we played, the audiences weren't just a bunch of kids, it was everybody. Old people too, from the richest to the poorest, checking it out and getting crazy. I'd never even seen a beer flow like this."

71

Back at the Warwick Hotel in the hooker district, we were happy to be home. That's when the great Stan Szelest from Buffalo came into the band. Ronnie thought we sounded thin when Luke left, so he hired seventeen-year-old Stan to play piano. (The Canadian bar owners didn't like hiring Canadian musicians. Rock and roll came from the States, and that was all a tavern owner in Simcoe, Ontario, or Quebec City wanted to know.)

Stan was a Memphis-style musician with that full muscle in his playing. His group, Stan and the Ravens, *were* rock and roll in Buffalo, and Stan had made his bones on the road playing behind Lonnie Mack in Pennsylvania's mining and steel towns. Stan was young, but he was already a star-quality musician. He was big and good-looking, and I was happy because Stan and Robbie were closer to my age than Luke and Lefty, who were closer to the Hawk's advanced age of twenty-five. We took Robertson and Stan over to Lou Myles and bought 'em a couple of black mohair stage suits. Once Lou made your suit, you were officially a Hawk.

With rockabilly a dying form, Ronnie tried to stay even with the changing times, which led to some funny things happening. Rock and roll was still good business in Canada (we were making five hundred dollars a week, top money for a band in those days), but the younger kids were being converted to the folk-music revival sweeping North America in the wake of the Kingston Trio. Canadian folkies like Ian and Sylvia and Gordon Lightfoot were drawing to the coffeehouses in Toronto's Yorkville district crowds as big as the ones we were bringing to Yonge Street.

So in March 1960 we were back in Manhattan recording folk songs for Morris Levy. Ronnie sang "John Henry," "Motherless Child," and "I Gave My Love a Cherry." He even cut a protest song, "The Ballad of Caryl Chessman," about the condemned killer whose rehabilitation in prison stirred up those against capital punishment. Henry Glover brought in jazz bassist George Duvivier to back Ronnie, and Roulette released *Folk Ballads of Ronnie Hawkins* in May 1960.

Spring and fall were the times we went back to Arkansas. Working out of Fayetteville, we made our rounds. At the Club 70 near Little Rock they did a heavy trade in amphetamines in the parking lot. The place, torched and repeatedly rebuilt like so many Arkansas honky-tonks, was between the city line and the Air Force base at Jacksonville. Inside you'd get a volatile mix of northern kids from the base and locals from Little Rock, and soon chairs would be flying over our heads. After the show we'd head into the Ozarks to play a college dance in Fayetteville or a frat party in Norman, Oklahoma, where we'd have to wade through a knee-high river of beer cans to get to where we were set up.

We had a friend there named Dayton Stratton, who co-owned the Rockwood Club with the Hawk. Dayton was also a manager and a booking agent, and he helped us with security. If we were putting on a dance in Norman, he'd hire some wrestlers from the University of Oklahoma to keep things relatively peaceful.

Dayton was the ultimate southern gentleman—until you riled him. I'd see him beg people to stop fighting and just sit down and enjoy the music, but sometimes they wouldn't listen. If they took a poke at Dayton, oh my God. He'd hit 'em with both fists and kick at a well-defined area between the head and the groin. I've seen people try to fall when Dayton was working on them, and they couldn't because the rain of blows was that intense. They'd eventually go down, and Dayton would keep it up until they hit the floor. He would clean house! One night I had to stand between Dayton and a friend of mine. *That* was scary.

During this period we played a week at the Canadian Club in Tulsa, after which the owner gave us a check that bounced as soon as we tried to cash it. Well, that made us angry. We'd heard this guy had stiffed a lot of other musicians, including Ray Charles just a month earlier. I hated that particular place because it had a low, spackled plaster ceiling. Whenever I got up from the drums, I'd always hurt my head on the little "stalactites." Jimmy "Pork Chop" Markham, who played drums with Conway Twitty, told me he had the same problem. All drummers hated the joint.

The Canadian Club's owner had gotten away with ripping off musicians because he figured no one had enough money to hire a lawyer and go after him. So Ronnie, Dayton, Donny Stone, and I decided to take matters into our own hands. We went back to the club that night after closing. Leon Russell had the house band, and we tenderly moved his equipment out to the parking lot, because Leon's gear wasn't paid for yet. Then Hawk and Dayton went in, broke the beer machine, and generally wrecked the place. Then Ronnie poured fifteen gallons of gas on the floor, running a line of gas out the back door to the parking lot. That's the way they did it in the movies.

Well, I lit the match, touched the line of gas, and it all blew at once! The force of the explosion knocked us all down. The Hawk was blown through the back door of the club, and his eyebrows got burned off. There was nothing left of the Canadian Club except smoking rubble. We were too dazed to leave the scene and were still there when the cops arrived.

They let us go! Told us the owner was a lowlife who was always causing trouble. "Hell, boys," they told us, "you done us a favor. We'll just say we couldn't find the arsonists. Now get out of here and don't come back."

Later, Dayton and Donny returned, found out where the club owner lived, wrecked the Cadillac parked in front of his house, then went in and got the money he owed us. We heard this guy took out a contract on us, but we never heard from the hired killers and are still laughing about torching the Canadian Club to this day.

Instead of going straight back to Canada, we stopped in Nashville to record Ronnie's next record, *Ronnie Hawkins Sings the Songs of Hank Williams*.

The two worst things a musician can say to his producer in Nashville are "I've been thinking" and "I'd like my band to play on the record." Country records were all cut by a clique of studio musicians, and the artist's wishes never entered into it. Well, we arrived at Bradley Studio, an old Quonset hut, ready to cut "Jambalaya," "Hey, Good Lookin'," and Hank's other songs, and the Hawk floored 'em by demanding that we all play on the record. The producer said no, and Hawk read 'em the riot act. The Nashville session people were sitting around and didn't like this. They looked at us, we looked at them, the Hawk was shouting, and it looked like our Nashville debut was going to end in a fistfight. Meanwhile, downstairs in studio B, Bobby "Blue" Bland and his orchestra were recording "Turn on Your Love Light." I could hear the music leaking out of the studio; Blue Bland was a hero to me, and I was itching to go downstairs and listen.

The Hawk won eventually, and his Hank Williams LP was released in November 1960. I didn't enjoy Nashville and got out as soon as I could, but Fred Carter, Jr., saw the light when he realized a studio guitarist could earn twenty times what a musician could earn on the road. Fred kept talking about it, and we could see his days in the band were numbered.

Sure enough, he soon carried out his plan to move to Nashville. There Fred quickly became one of the elite studio guitarists and then a record executive with his own studio.

There's a period in here where the Hawks' guitar players were all jumbled up. For a short time Fred was replaced by Roy Buchanan, a brilliant and moody player who definitely had his own mystique. He had a beatnik look, complete with goatee, which both Ronnie and I adopted for a while. Roy had strange eyes, didn't talk to anyone, and looked real fierce. Ronnie always reminded us to smile, move, and dance when we played. We had to look like we were having a better time than anyone. It was show business, those little leg kicks that fellas in bands had to do back then.

Not Roy. He didn't believe in putting on a show. He just stood there and played the shit out of that guitar. Roy played a *Louisiana Hayride* style like Fred and James Burton, who was playing with Ricky Nelson then. We loved how good Roy was, but he was too weird for the Hawk. One night Roy tried to convince us that he was a werewolf and destined to marry a nun. Not long after that, Robbie took over the lead guitar.

The Hawk was thinking about me playing second guitar. I wasn't a lead guitarist, but I did play a decent rhythm guitar. "Do you know," he asked, "how powerful two guitars could be?" I remembered Luke and Fred together just a couple of months earlier: It was a hell of a sound. Pork Chop Markham came up from Arkansas for a look but decided he was better off with Conway. We also thought about Sandy Konikoff, the drummer in Stan Szelest's former band, but then the Hawk decided to stay with one guitar.

So we hired Rebel Paine from Buffalo to play bass. He must have come in with, or just after, Stan. Rebel was a Seminole, originally from the Florida Everglades, and a hellacious character and a great bass player. Willard was back in the group, and Stan was playing keyboards, with Robbie on guitar and me on drums.

To me, Stan was the demon in the Hawks. I was in awe of him, not only for his musical ability (which bordered on magic) but because he actually kicked the shit out of me a couple times when I got on his nerves. Stan was a big, strong rocker, and he didn't take any shit from anyone—especially me, who liked to give it out. One time he said to me, "Levon [by then the boys had changed my name from Lavon because it was easier to say], for two cents I'd kick your ass."

I said, "Hell, Stan, I'll give you a goddamn dollar bill."

The Hawk says, "OK, best man spits over my finger" (an old Arkansas way of starting a fight), and Stan and I started swinging at each other in the hotel room, knocking over lamps and breaking things. The Hawk made us finish it in the parking lot. I kneed Stan in the gut; then he punched me in the forehead. I felt stunned, like a hog staring at a wristwatch. Stan was throwing up. For the next month it was like sitting next to a rattlesnake in the Cadillac.

Robbie Robertson had a Steve Cropper rhythm-section style of playing. He was an ensemble player, like we all had to be. He had a serious side, but he was just a kid like the rest of us, so he was a good laugher and fit in pretty well. Eventually, after Stan and Rebel went back to Buffalo, Robbie and I got to be close friends.

"The one who really saved my ass was Levon," he once recalled. "He was my best friend, my big brother. He taught me the tricks of the trade. Ronnie taught me the sexual tricks; with Levon it was the angle, the inside scoop on style and southern musical things."

This is true, if you don't mind my saying so. I took Robbie under my wing, and we roomed together on the road for some time afterward. It was me and Robbie against the world. Our mission, as we saw it, was to put together the best band *in history*.

Realigned, the Hawks took to the road.

The Hawk's trailer was made to match his car. We had the Cadillac of trailers. It was like a little teardrop-shaped ice-cream wagon back there, but wasn't a lot higher than the Cadillac itself, so you had to give it a little extra room, coming around people. The trailer was white, and had a hawk painted on the side. I mean, you couldn't miss us. Years later Dr. John told me he'd seen us go by in Louisiana in the early sixties. He said we were going at a pretty good clip.

I was at the wheel. Always. The Hawk knew I'd push it up and we'd get there faster. My tractor-driving experience came in handy one night when we lost the trailer on the northeast side of Mount Gaylor, where the Ozarks peak. Late at night, I'm doing maybe eighty, eighty-five, and that damn thing hits a rock and comes loose. The safety chains had enough slack in 'em to hold the turn, about three inches off the road. "Son," the Hawk says, while the boys are hollering in the back, "if that son of a bitch is goin' off the cliff, we're goin' with it."

To stop the thing I had to pop the brake and stab maybe twelve inches of '59 Cadillac tail fin through the window of the trailer. It looked awful. I lived through that twice, and it scared the hell out of us.

Our first roadie was a skinny, very funny guy from Scotland who managed one of the all-day movie theaters on Yonge Street. He let us in anytime in the afternoon. His name was Colin McQueen, but the Hawk called him Bony.

He unloaded the trailer and set up our gear until he ran afoul of the Cadillac. The Hawk was strict about that car and could spot a dent from a hundred yards. One day he saw a little nick about the size of a quarter in the bumper, inches from the steel post the car was parked against. Bony had the keys because the Hawk had told him to get the car washed. So Bony had a short career with the Hawk, who was always a stern taskmaster.

For a while we had to cart our own stuff, set it up, try to clean up a little bit. Then we met Bill Avis, from Lake Simcoe, Ontario, and the Hawk hired him to be our road manager.

"I met Ronnie and the band in early 1961," Bill remembers, "when they were playing at the Le Coq D'Or in Toronto. I'd quit school due to hard times and was hanging out, looking for work. I tried to see Ronnie when he was in town because it was simply the best band anyone had ever heard—country rock and roll. Hawk did that camel walk and people went nuts. And there'd be Levon, dead center, stage rear, twirling his drumsticks and singing 'Slippin' and Slidin' ' and 'Short Fat Fannie.' Robbie was already in the band, with Will Pop Jones, Rebel Paine on bass, and Stan Szelest on keyboards.

"The first thing you noticed was how good-lookin' this band was. Clean-cut, tall young men immaculately dressed in hip suits, cuff links, good haircuts. They just looked *sharp*. Stan Szelest looked incredible. Ronnie called Stan 'Lon Chaney on helium.'

"The next thing you noticed was that everyone looked up to the band. All the rounders—hoods, hookers, night people—would do anything for them. These people weren't that nice to other musicians, who noticed this. So other bands—local guys like Larry Lee and the Leisures—copied our music, our clothes, our style. There was no question about who were the kings of the hill.

"When I got the nerve to ask Ronnie for a job, he said, 'Son, I'll give you fifty dollars a week and all the nookie you can eat.' That was all I needed to hear. So I was the roadie: set up the mikes, mix the sound, do a little PR on the side. They took me to Lou Myles the tailor and got me a black mohair suit like theirs. They had a big Cadillac, and later two of 'em, and we drove those suckers a million bloody miles over the next six years.

"Like most people, I got to be friends with Levon, and we roomed together quite a bit on the road. In Toronto we lived with Mama Kosh—that's what the band called Robbie Robertson's mom—in her house at 193 First Avenue. We rented rooms from her when we were in town playing the Le Coq D'Or, Concord Tavern, or Friar's Tavern. She's a lovely lady, and she genuinely loved the band.

"Her son, meanwhile, was just coming into his own as a guitar player. Robbie was too young to legally get into most of the places we played, but he could stretch those goddamn strings, man, until you'd think they'd pop. He was a player, a showman. He'd raise that right arm over a sustained note, and the place would go ape! He'd make those strings *hum*.

"I was so happy to be part of this gang. The Hawks were like a permanent stag party with an entourage of the most beautiful girls in Canada. We were a hot band, and we knew we were going places, even if we weren't quite sure where we were going or even how to get there. To us back then, the sky was the damn limit!''

Nineteen sixty one was a big transitional year for us. We started it out playing a dance Dayton Stratton was putting on in Dallas the night of the Cotton Bowl. The University of Arkansas was playing Duke University, and unfortunately the Blue Devils beat us 7–6, and the Razorbacks in town for the game felt more like getting drunk than dancing. We were playing the show with Conway's band, which had a real good drummer, Jack Nance, who I'd looked up to ever since he'd taught me how to twirl the sticks. Nobody was in a good mood that night, least of all the Hawk, who pointed to Jack and whispered to me, "You're gonna cut Jack's ass tonight, cut him so damn bad he's gonna *bleed*. He's gonna want to *quit* when you get through with him, OK?" Because it was *war* with the Hawk. That's how it was. He was known for taking no prisoners.

Ronnie's band was pretty much in flux. Willard had been going like fire for three years and wanted a change. Rebel's wife wanted him home after a year on the road with us. One Sunday afternoon that spring we were in the Cadillac heading toward our weekly job at Pop Ivy's in Port Dover. "If we don't get some new blood in the group this year," the Hawk said, "it's gonna be all over. But it ain't a big problem because there's so much goddamn talent here in Ontario, I can't even stand it."

I was a little more skeptical.

"What about that big kid over in Simcoe?" Ronnie suggested. "What's his name—Danko? Nice-looking boy. He'd bring in the girls, and he plays guitar in that little group of his."

"Yeah," piped up Robertson from the backseat, "but he only knows four chords."

"That's all right son," the Hawk joked. "You can teach him four more the way we had to teach you."

"My family lived in rural Ontario," Rick recalls. "I'm from Greens Corner, near Simcoe, in the southern Ontario tobacco belt. My grandfather, Joseph Danko, came from the Ukraine and bought a huge farm in Manitoba to grow wheat, long before they had tractors. My dad, Maurice Danko, was born on the farm but came to Ontario when he married my mom, whose family was there. I was born at home in 1943, the third of four brothers.

"We were a musical family, all of us. My dad played mandolin and banjo. So did Uncle Spence, who married my mom's sister. My earliest memory is pretending to play music so I could stay up to watch those people party. Dad played country music with some older people at barn dances. Those were the first times I saw people play music, people dancing—a hundred fifty dancing in a big old barn. To this day, it's weird for me to look at people at a concert, and they're not dancing.

79

"I'm like Levon. We didn't have electricity till I was ten years old. We listened to the *Grand Ole Opry* on a windup Victrola and battery radios. I had a crystal set that brought in WSM and WLAC in Nashville. I could even get Wolfman Jack coming out of Nuevo Laredo. I was a bit of a showman as a kid because I was allergic to dust. I'd get these red blotches if I worked in the garden. I'd be gasping for air! So my mother got these songbooks that came out every couple of weeks, and I learned songs on the guitar. I'd get 'em from the radio too, country songs from Nashville: Kitty Wells, Red Foley, Ernest Tubb. Uncle Spence had been in Nashville and said he knew 'em all, and that really impressed me. He took me to Toronto one summer, and we got to meet [singer-banjoist] Grandpa Jones, then in his thirties!

"I was one of those kids who was basically out of the house by the time he was ten. I was playing publicly from age twelve on. The drummer was my seventh-grade teacher, Mr. Titmouse. He had a set of drums, but no cymbals. I fired him the moment I got out of public school—the only person I ever fired in my life!"

"At fourteen I realized I could rent a hall in January, Uncle Rollie would put up posters, and two hundred people would show up because there was nothing else to do. We'd be Rick Danko and the Starliners on Friday night in St. Williams, and Rick and the Roxatones on Saturday in Walsh. In Delhi we had seventeen different ethnic clubs. This was where the tobacco farmers moved after they'd turned the farms over to their kids. We'd play the Slavic club, the Belgian club. At the fairgrounds in Delhi they had a famous guy who weighed six hundred pounds. He had a hot-dog stand. To this day Levon remembers him: Alfonso Cook. The Hawks used to stop in Delhi on the way to Port Dover. Levon'd buy a few dogs and stare at Alfonso for *hours*.

"I quit school at fifteen. I knew I'd be playing music, but I was a serious kid and didn't want to be dependent if I could help it, so I apprenticed myself to a meat cutter and learned how to cut meat. Not butchering, where you go for the throat a thousand times a day, but dividing it into quarters, cuts, and so on. There was an art to it, like any craft.

"I was seventeen the first time I saw the Hawk. This was at Simcoe Arena in late 1960. Conway Twitty was headlining, with Fred Carter, Jr., on guitar, after Fred had left the Hawk. The Hawks were Levon, Rebel, Stan, and Willard. Robbie was just learning guitar. The Hawks were wearing these tight black suits, and the music was more than powerful. It was *unbelievable*. Ronnie was doing backflips. Will Pop was playing so hard when the Hawk danced over to the piano the buttons of his clothes were ripping open. Everyone was covered in sweat. They were *irresistible*. Levon would just laugh into the microphone and make the whole audience laugh. They had routines, comedic timing. Mostly, Ronnie tore the place up. I never saw anything like it. He was doing James Brown steps, only faster!

"Next spring, when the Hawk came back to Simcoe, I arranged to have my band—maybe it was Ricky and the Rhythm Notes that night—open for him. That happened maybe five times. On a rainy Sunday night in May 1961, Ronnie comes up to me after the show at Pop Ivy's in Port Dover—I couldn't believe this—and he rasps, 'Son, what do we have to do for you to get in that Cadillac over there and come with us *tonight*?'

"They had two Cadillacs. I got in with the Hawk. Bill Avis was driving. We made two stops. At the meat cutter's I said good-bye to my boss. 'Don't make any rash decisions,' he advised. When I told him I was going to Toronto with a famous rock and roll band, he shook his head and said, 'You'll be back.' Then we went home to get some clothes. I told my mom I was leaving town for a couple of weeks and parked my '49 MG convertible in the garage because it had a few holes in it. I kissed 'em good-bye and that was it. I was *on the road*. Hawk was telling me that I was gonna play a little rhythm guitar, but that Rebel was coming out of the band later that summer, and I'd be playing bass after that. I'd never played either in my life! Meanwhile I noticed that Bill Avis has us cruising down Highway 3 at maybe seventy-five, and all of a sudden I saw car lights coming on fast behind us. I thought it was the Mounties. But no.

" 'Pull over, son,' Hawk said to Bill. 'That's Levon—give him plenty room!' Sure enough, in ten seconds Levon blows by us at one hundred ten, windows rolled down with bare legs sticking out. Young girls' legs. He had a beautiful '54 two-door: dark green on top, light green on the bottom, first year of the rock-ground windshield. Filled with young women! This was Levon on his way to Grand Bend, where the Hawks were playing next. Yaa-hooooo!!!! Away we went!

"We got to Grand Bend, where the Hawk was playing a hotel on Lake Huron. They put us up in a loft over the beer storeroom, a place where they'd put in a hallway with Sheetrock, with three bedrooms on each side. I didn't know what to expect because these guys had terrible reputations as sex perverts—orgies, gang bangs, everything. I was just a kid from Simcoe and didn't know anything about this life they were living, this *existence*.''

We put young Rick Danko in one of these rooms. The Hawk gave him a couple of greenies and told him to practice while we were playing. Between sets we sent Bill Avis to peek at him through a hole in the wall.

"How's he doing?" Hawk asked.

"Practicing like hell and chewing his teeth," Bill replied.

"He's too green," Robbie said.

Hawk looked at me. I had to be honest. "I don't think he can cut it," I observed wisely.

"That boy's a *hell* of a musician," the Hawk said. "Take my word for it. He's gonna play bass when Rebel goes home."

Eventually we let Rick out of his room, and the Hawk told him to watch the band and learn that way.

"They were basically playing Ronnie's records," Rick says. " 'Mary Lou,' 'Odessa.' Levon would get a big slot, and he'd yell out 'Lucille' or 'Short Fat Fannie.' It wasn't hard, but I had a lot to learn. Levon and Robbie started to work with me, teaching me about the bass and the bass feeling. I rehearsed for maybe two months off the stage before they'd let me on. Rebel stayed around, but he was taking a lot of speed, and I couldn't pick up much from him. So I used to copy Stan Szelest's left hand.

"Every piano player who ever worked with Ronnie asked for as many tapes from Stan as they could, to study him. He was a living fountain of rock and roll piano, a one-of-a-kind player. His presence, the way he could pound a piano, was overwhelming.

"So I tried to play what Stan was doing with his left hand. I wasn't stealing, I was learning. One night Stan gave me a look while I was copying him. He stared at me with a super-conscious look in his eye, and—magic!—all of a sudden I got better at doubling his left hand. He had transmitted some powerful force to me. Stan could just *give it to you*, if he wanted to.

"By midsummer 1961, Rebel was out, and I was in. Stan and I became roommates on the road, and he let me drive his '59 Buick convertible, the 'Ragtop.' He wrote his rockabilly classic 'Ragtop' about that car, so I was honored.

"The other thing that I both recognized and respected was the bond of friendship between Levon and Robbie. It was very strong, a brotherhood, almost a family thing. It was one of the strongest relationships that I ever felt, and the energy was so good that it was fun to be around it."

There were a couple of other developments while we were at Grand Bend. Ronnie liked to keep the pot boiling, and still hadn't given up on the two-guitar idea. So Roy Buchanan came back for a few days, and he and Robbie had a kind of duel. Call it a showdown.

Robbie had been playing for eighteen months and was acquiring a hell of a reputation. There just weren't many guitar players in Ontario who worked as hard as Robbie, bending strings, screaming like Jimi Hendrix would years later. The whole band was incredibly tight because Ronnie literally worked us all the time. If we played until midnight, the Hawk would let us break for "lunch" and then rehearse us till four in the morning. Whether we were in Canada or Arkansas, it didn't matter.

Robbie had actually learned a lot from Roy, whose technical accomplishments as a blues guitarist were without peer back then. (Once I asked him where he learned to play so good and he explained in all seriousness that he was half wolf.) But Robbie was playing with total excitement and raw teenage disturbance. That's what it boiled down to: Roy Buchanan's tricks and technical skills versus Robbie's ability to really rock a good dance party. I'm told there are a lot of people in that part of Ontario who remember those nights when Robbie and Roy went at it. When it was over, Robbie still held the guitar chair in the Hawks. Roy Buchanan, a true master of the electric guitar, went his own way.

Instead of a second guitar, Ronnie hired Jerry Penfound to play horns. Jerry was from London, Ontario, and played a mean baritone saxophone. It sounded low, powerful; really what you wanted to hear under what we were playing. That horn added another dimension; now we could play "Turn on Your Love Light" and soul-type songs, a direction that the band, if not the Hawk, wanted to pursue.

We called Jerry "Ish," short for Ish Kabibble, an old radio character. He was a funny cat who was a really good cook. He'd inherited some money, could fly a plane, wore a big blue diamond ring he liked to flash at the girls. He fit in right away, and when Willard left the band at the end of the summer, Ish stayed in. People were always coming and going.

The Hawk called Will Pop Jones "Caveman." Sometimes he called him "Bungawa." It meant the same thing. He was a hellacious character, the living embodiment of rockabilly. He was a big, raw-boned Arkansan; maybe 185 pounds, with not an ounce of fat. His untutored country manners and habits were so crude they revolted even the Hawk, who was usually beyond embarrassment. Willard would pile white bread, mashed potatoes, and chicken gravy in ascending layers on a big plate until the food was nine inches high and dribbling over the side. He would then take this and a couple of Cokes up to his room to eat by himself, in exile. His table manners were so bad that Ronnie didn't like to eat with him.

Willard would show up onstage very shiny, with everything in order, but he played with such ferocious energy that after one song he'd be rumpled, then totally disheveled: sweaty jacket, shirttail out, collar open, tie and hair askew, loafers half off, exposing one green sock and one purple sock. All this and hammers sailing out of the piano. Few who saw him perform ever witnessed anything like it.

Willard was unbelievably cheap. The Hawk used to say he could squeeze a nickel so hard the buffalo would shit. On the road he'd sleep in the Cadillac unless someone let him crash on the floor of his motel room. If we were all in the car, Ronnie would say, "Willard, *please* don't go to sleep; you know how awful you look when you wake up." This was because Willard had a lazy eye; one eye looked one way, the other eye went the other way. No one back home in Marianna ever thought about getting Willard the simple operation to straighten this out, and for years the Hawk ragged on him about it until we were finally able to get him to the doctor in Toronto. Willard had the operation, came out of the hospital, and was so strong he did four or five sets with us that night, wearing a patch.

After he had his eye fixed, Willard started getting dates. We all remember one famous one that didn't work out, when Willard met a working girl during a booking at the Concord Tavern. She took him home, and it was going along pretty smooth until the subject of money came up. The lady wanted to be paid, and Willard didn't want to hear about it. They got to shouting at each other, and Willard noticed she had a couple of hamsters in a cage. He grabbed one hamster and said, "I'll pinch his goddamn head off! I ain't bullshittin' ya, girl! I'll pinch him right now in front of you!" Willard was about to sacrifice the hamster, when the lady relented.

We were living at the Warwick Hotel at the time. A sign outside said ENTERTAINERS WELCOME, so the clientele consisted of musicians, strippers, and hookers. That address ended a lot of dates for us before they even started; killed a lot of parties. "The *Warwick*? Are you *crazy*? Forget it!"

The day after his date, Willard went downstairs to get some breakfast over at the Wilton Restaurant: two bacon cheeseburgers and a couple of cartons of milk, please. As he was walking back to the hotel, the girl's pimp and a buddy stepped out of an alley. Willard quickly sized up the situation. These weren't the friendly, familiar pimps that came to hear us play, like "Russian Wally" or "Ralph the Frenchman." These guys were there either to collect or to slap Willard around a little.

"Wait just a minute," he said, and gently laid the paper bag containing his meal against the wall. Then he whirled around, grabbed the pimp by the arm, and smashed him face-first against the side of the brick building. Willard let go of the arm, and the pimp just . . . faded. He fell down the brick wall like water and lay unconscious in the street.

Willard calmly picked up his sack and disappeared into the Warwick to eat by himself.

So Willard was a terrific, funny character, and I was sad to see him leave the Hawk when we went back to Arkansas in the fall of 1961.

The Hawk kept talking about getting Garth Hudson to replace Willard. Garth played the organ and some horns for a band in Detroit, and everyone kept saying he was the best musician on our circuit. Others said that Garth would rather play Bach than rock.

Hawk had tried to hire him as early as 1959, but Garth Hudson wasn't interested in joining us. He was a little older than us, a trained classical musician who was only playing rock and roll to make a little money in his spare time. His family was very conservative, and Garth didn't think they would approve of him joining any rockabilly band on a permanent basis. Somehow Ronnie had talked him into coming to the Le Coq D'Or to see us. It must have been December 1960.

"Aw, I finally told Ronnie I'd look at his band," Garth remembers. "There was Willard with his pounding left-hand technique. I'd never heard anyone amplify a piano that loud before. He was a big guy with tremendous thrust, played those wild glissandos like Jerry Lee Lewis, with incredible stamina. Stan Szelest was a close second in terms of sheer power. I thought, *I can't play this music. I don't have the left hand these guys do.*"

"Then I looked a little closer. Stan Szelest's fingers were *bleeding* from pounding the keys. I looked at Willard and saw hammers actually flying out of the piano. The whole thing was too loud, too fast, too violent for me." Six months later he came to see us a second time, and again left without joining.

We all knew that if Garth Hudson joined the band, it would put us up a notch, and we'd be unstoppable. But he said no again. So Ronnie reached down into a little Stratford, Ontario, band that he was managing (he'd sent them down to Fayetteville to play the Rockwood Club) and pulled out Willard's replacement.

Richard Manuel was a whole show unto himself. He was hot. He was about the best singer I'd ever heard; most people said he reminded them of Ray Charles. He'd do those ballads, and the ladies would swoon. To me that became the highlight of our show.

Richard already had a small following when we met him. He was born in Stratford, Ontario, in 1944. His father, Ed, was a Chrysler mechanic, and his mom taught school. Richard sang in his church choir with his three brothers and started piano lessons when he was about nine. They ended when Richard played a note that wasn't on the sheet music. It wasn't a wrong note, he insisted. (Later he realized it was a different voicing of the same chord.) The piano teacher slammed the lid on his fingers because she thought he wasn't paying attention.

But the Manuel family piano soon became a hangout where Richard and his friends would get together and rehearse. "The Beak," as he was nicknamed because of his prominent nose, was into the blues real early—Ray Charles, Bobby Bland—which he'd pick up on WLAC's *The John R. Rhythm & Blues Show* after midnight. He ordered records from Memphis and Nashville by mail, and friends remember him arriving at junior high school with fresh Jimmy Reed and Otis Rush albums under his arm.

In 1960, when he was fifteen, Richard, John Till, and Jimmy Winkler started a band called the Rebels, which soon changed to the Revols in deference to Duane Eddy and the Rebels. Soon the Rockin' Revols were the best teenage band in Stratford. Hell, even we heard about 'em. Richard, of course, was the singer. He did teen-idol songs like "Eternal Love" and "Promise Yourself" and played a mean rhythm piano on a boogie-woogie version of Franz Liszt's "Liebestraum" that was broadcast over CKSL in London, Ontario.

We first ran into the Revols when they were opening for the Hawks at Pop Ivy's place in Port Dover. "See that kid playing piano?" Hawk said. "He's got more talent than Van Cliburn." After their show, Ronnie told the Revols they were so good they were making us nervous. Richard blushed. "Thanks, but you don't have to worry. You guys are the *kings*," he told us in reply.

Next time we saw them was at a battle of the bands in the Stratford Coliseum in 1961. The Stratatones opened, we were next as headliners, followed by the Rockin' Revols. I remember them watching us from the wings as the Hawk went wild at the edge of the stage, working the crowd. Robbie was rumbling on guitar. Nobody else was playing that good that I knew of. The Hawk was a hell of an act to have to follow; he didn't leave you much to work with after he had exhausted an audience.

But when the Revols came on, Richard sang Ray Charles's "Georgia on My Mind" and brought down the house. That did it, as far as the Hawk was concerned. Rather than compete with the Revols, he hired 'em. He sent them to Dayton Stratton, who booked them into the Rockwood Club and other stops on our southern circuit. The Revols lived in a house trailer in Fayetteville, which they nearly demolished, they were so wild. One time they took the Hawk's Cadillac to Memphis to clear up an immigration problem—none of the band's six members was much over sixteen—and got themselves arrested at three in the morning and spent the next day in the Memphis city jail until they could prove the Cadillac wasn't stolen.

While we were in Arkansas, Stan Szelest left the band to marry his high school sweetheart, Caroline. Ronnie had a policy of discouraging us from having steady girls. Our life-style, he insisted, was *not* to fall in love. Ronnie only hired good-looking guys to draw girls to the places we worked. The boys were sure to follow the girls, and we'd all have a party. But if you had a girlfriend, you'd sit with her between sets instead of mingling at the bar. Ronnie figured that if you weren't prowling around, you weren't doing your job.

When Stan went back to Buffalo, the Hawk called Richard and told him to come on down to Arkansas. Richard turned him down because he had a pact with Jimmy Winkler: One couldn't leave the Revols without the other. At a band meeting, Jimmy told him, "Beak, this is your chance. You better take it."

So Richard called back, and he was in the band. His younger brother took his place in the Revols, who drove Richard to the airport for the flight to Tulsa, where we would pick him up. They bade the Beak farewell, but not before taking out a flight-insurance policy on him—just in case.

Rick Danko remembers: "Richard's first night was a baptism because Ronnie was real drunk, and he just pulled the curtain back, showed Richard the crowd, and told him, 'Let it *ride,* son!' Richard had never played lead piano, only rhythm piano, but he could really sing. He reminded me of Ray Charles, James Brown, and Lee Marvin! That's what he sounded like. I knew at once that Richard and I sounded great singing together. He brought a lot of powers and strengths to the group. He brought in gospel music from his church upbringing. Plus, he loved to play and just come up with new things. It was like having a force of nature in the band."

The piano was a rhythm instrument in the Hawks, like the drums and the bass. Solos, when they happened, were played by the guitar and the horns, and later the organ. The piano was there so the rhythm didn't drop out. Richard fit into that slot right away. Energy piano, we call it. At the same time, he gave the Hawk a rest when it came to singing, because Richard could scream a rocker or croon a ballad and make you believe it. I'd been singing only because someone had to sing when Ronnie didn't. Having Richard's voice put us on a higher level musically.

Richard settled in quick. He was instantly likable and extremely funny. He liked to drink a little with the rest of us; he was seventeen when we met him, and he told us with a sheepish grin that he'd been drinking for ten years. He really missed his parents when we went out on the road. In fact, we all missed our folks. We were young and away from home, and we would spend hours sitting around hotels talking about our parents, and families, and the funny things they said and did. That loneliness was a fact of our lives, and in retrospect we know it took a toll on Richard.

We spent a good part of that fall of 1961 working in the South, breaking in Rick and Richard, who'd been hired within just a few months of each other.

Usually that time of year we'd live at the Iris Motel in Fayetteville and do the frat parties, college dances, and roadhouses in Arkansas, Oklahoma, and Texas. It was a helluva circuit back then. We played places on Oklahoma Indian reservations where we felt we wouldn't get out alive if they didn't like us. Other places people didn't come to hear the band; they came to steal our gear, throw coins and lit cigarettes at us, test us a little. If we got past that, *then* they'd listen to us. (There was a little Indian boy who used to come see us in Tulsa back then. He'd watch Robbie very carefully from down in front of the stage. You couldn't miss him. This was Jesse Ed Davis.)

One week we played a gangster club in Fort Worth that had been robbed and firebombed so often they didn't bother locking it at night. We had to take turns strapping on guns and guarding our equipment when the joint closed. One morning at dawn the cops burst in with dogs, and there was almost a showdown before we got it sorted out. The next night the club was teargassed by a bounced customer. These kinds of places often didn't pay us at the end of the week, and we'd find ourselves stealing steaks from supermarkets to survive.

Just being a professional musician in that part of the country was like being a gunfighter. The younger ones wanted your reputation, and if we were a new band in town we made our last set an open session, or else. People down there all knew music, and the local guitars would come up with a smile, plug into your amp, and try to run you off the stage. They'd happily make you look like a chump, if they could.

But eventually we got that respect we were after. Despite our unsavory rep throughout the Midwest and Canada as pill-poppin', whorevisitin', gas-siphonin', girlfriend-stealin' reprobate musicians, we'd hear our competition—good bands, too—and they'd be playing our arrangements, our turnarounds, stuff we invented. That's how we knew we were so good.

I had been bothering Ronnie for months about trying to hire Garth Hudson again. We'd seen him play with his band and in little jazz clubs, and he was a phenomenon to us because of the scope of his musical knowledge. He was as interested in good polka music as he was in J. S. Bach. He could play with Miles Davis or the Chicago Symphony or the Grand Ole Opry. We felt we had to have Garth.

When we got back to Canada the Hawk agreed we needed Garth in the band at any cost. "This guy's a damn genius or I'm Jack Kennedy," Hawk fumed. "I don't even understand what he's doing musically, but I know it works. You don't have a great band unless you have him or someone like him, someone who's been to school, knows how to arrange. You need him to teach the other guys."

"Why don't you just pay him what he's asking," I suggested. "How much could it be?"

"Son, Garth doesn't just wanna get paid to play. He wants me to buy his time when he *ain't* playing," Ronnie explained. "I told him he could have anything he wanted. I told him he could give you guys *music lessons* when we ain't onstage."

"What did he say?"

"He thought it was funny. He said he would think about it if we'd throw in a new Lowrey organ as part of the bargain."

Garth grew up in London, Ontario. "My dad, Fred James Hudson, and my two uncles were farm people from around London," he recalls. "Not tobacco farmers. They told jokes about tobacco farmers and complained about their methods—no crop rotation, and they bleached their soil with chemical fertilizers. But Dad left the farm and went to work for the Canadian Department of Agriculture as an inspector. My mother, Olive Louella Pentland Hudson, had me in 1937, and I was her only child. I was raised in the Anglican Church, Diocese of Huron. There was a strong English tradition in the farming community, and

London had some magnificent stone mansions, built with English money. I dated a girl who lived in the gardener's house attached to one of these estates. I took her to a dance and hit a stop sign at a T intersection with a '49 Pontiac Tierback Straight Eight. That was a dark day. I couldn't sleep that night. In the morning I heard my folks in the kitchen. My father hadn't seen the bumper yet. That's when my heart problems started. I was probably sixteen.

"My mother played the accordion. She had a good ear and played the piano too. We had a player piano in the house when I was little. I guess I learned something from watching it, because I could play 'Yankee Doodle' by ear before taking lessons from Miss Milligan on Richmond Street. I think I was five years old. Her brother played first violin with the Hart House Symphony, an old Toronto institution. My first record—I still have it—was a 78 with a chip in it: 'Wild Old Horsey' with 'Gee It's Great to Be Living Again' on the other side. It was kind of country swing put out by a political-religious movement of the late 1940s called MRA: Moral Rearmament of America.

"My dad played flute, drums, cornet, saxophone, and triangle. Dad had a C-melody silver saxophone. He'd get it out every year or so, put a handkerchief in it, and play sweet band music like the Lombardos, Guy and Carmen, who were from nearby London. They had the Royal Canadians. All my uncles played too, and they were good musicians. My uncle Austin played trombone. He had great tone and worked at the London Arena four or five nights a week with various bands. Sometimes they played the Stork Club in Port Stanley, thirty miles south of London on the shore of Lake Erie. It had the largest ballroom floor in Canada. Later I played there myself with dance bands.

"I sort of grew up with country music because my father would find all the hoedown stations on the radio, and then I played accordion with a little country group when I was twelve. My parents sent me to study piano at the Toronto Conservatory. I had a good teacher who used older methods and older pieces. That's how I learned to play the Bach preludes and fugues, material like that. I loved Chopin, and Mozart amazed me. But I found I had problems memorizing classical annotated music. I could do it, but not to the extent that is necessary. So I developed my own method of ear training and realized I could improvise.

"Another uncle of mine owned a funeral home. That was where I

91

started playing in public. They had a good organ, and I played hymns from the Anglican Church, but usually it was Baptist hymns: 'What a Friend We Have in Jesus,' 'Jesus, Keep Me Near the Cross.' When we played 'Abide With Me,' that was the signal for the minister to come in.

"I had a high-school guidance counselor who laughed when I told him I might like to be a professional musician. He told me music was a hobby, and I ought to think about going into agricultural research, which is what I thought I was going to do. But I also had a teacher who played in a big band, who saw I was interested in transcribing music. He asked me to do something for him, and I used a record player and wrote down what I heard. Then he played the transcriptions with his band.

"My first group was the Three Blisters, and we backed up the high-school variety shows and the choirs. Then we had the Four Quarters. I played the accordion, still one of my favorite instruments. Then—either 1952 or 1953—I started to tune into Alan Freed's *Moondog Matinee* from Cleveland, from 5:05 to 5:55 every day. He played great rhythm and blues, and I remember him talking about the first Moondog Coronation Ball, where they had thousands of people who couldn't get in. It was almost a riot. That's when I realized there were people over there having more fun than I was.

"There was a little rockabilly band in London called the Melodines. They did Bill Haley stuff, pretty well too. So some friends and I formed a group called the Silhouettes. We played around town and then went to the Windsor-Detroit area, where there was more opportunity to work. We hooked up with a young singer and called ourselves Paul London and the Kapers. I guess my professional career began at Aybar's Island View Tavern in Windsor, Ontario, with Paul London.

"We played teen hops and similar things. I originally wanted to play piano in the band, but it turned out to be more fun to play the saxophone. Our repertoire was Little Richard and Larry Williams. We did 'Long Tall Sally,' 'Hoochie Koo,' and 'Ready Teddy.' I think I moved to piano when we played an afternoon dance party on CFPL-TV. To learn what to play, I listened real close to Johnnie Johnson, Chuck Berry's piano player. I wanted to play organ, but I couldn't afford the one I wanted. Other bands in Detroit used organ, but one group had a Lowrey, and it sounded great. I went to a music store and tried one out, and the Lowrey had certain things a Hammond couldn't do.

"One night we all went to the Brass Rail in London to see the Hawk at a dinner show. Everyone I knew thought that Ronnie was the best rockabilly performer with by far the best band. Nobody could follow the Hawks, including Elvis, as far as being an organic unit that could get up there and *shake it up*! He was great and funny. To begin the set Ronnie'd yell, 'It's orgy time!' and that would get everyone laughing and in the spirit of the thing. I remember we were nervous because we were mostly underage, but we got in. Boy, the Kapers were impressed by the power and speed of the thing. The Hawk was billed as 'Mr. Dynamo' and more than lived up to the label. They had Willard Pop Jones, with that left hand going *all the time*. He was breaking the keys! That's where I met Levon and Robbie for the first time.

"Then we saw the Hawks again, at the Legion Hall in Ingersoll, Ontario. They played 'Mary Lou' and Ronnie's other hits, and I recall a Marty Robbins–style song called 'Hayride' that would rear its ugly head. I think that was when they invited me into the band, after Hawk sent Levon and Robbie over to check me out. I met with Robbie in Grand Bend, and we talked about it, but I told them no. I wasn't interested in that kind of music at the time. I liked chord changes and music that was a little more 'uptown.' Our band was playing rockabilly, but I didn't have the left hand for that pounding technique that Willard and Stan Szelest used. My family also thought 'rock and roll musician' was a déclassé occupation, especially after my conservatory back-ground, and they were already upset with me for dropping out of college after only a year. So I decided to stay local with Paul London and the Kapers.

"Later in 1961, Willard left the band because he couldn't stand the pace. He went home and got married. Then Rebel Paine and Stan Szelest left, and Ronnie kept trying to get me into the band. The Kapers had made a couple of records in Detroit—'Sugar Baby' and 'Big Bad Twist'—and we were promoting them (one went to No. 8 on the local chart), but we couldn't get it on *American Bandstand,* we were told, because of two negative words. That was the way it worked.

"I saw the Hawks were making the big money because they worked seven nights a week, every week. I told my parents about Ronnie's offer to join the band, but they still disapproved of my playing music in bars and taverns. Finally I had Ronnie talk them into it.

"'Mr. and Mrs. Hudson,' Ronnie told them in his most earnest and straightforward manner, 'I have a band of talented young men who are being held back by their lack of musical education. I want to hire your son Garth to come along and teach them music. I want them to learn how to read notation properly. I've offered Garth a higher wage than anyone else, a cash bonus to join us, and we will pay him an extra ten dollars a week for the lessons he gives the boys. We'll also buy a new organ so Garth can be heard at his best. Now, how about it? Do we have your blessing on this?'

"My parents, God bless them, finally said it was OK. This was in late 1961, around Christmastime. It was Levon, Robbie, Rick, Richard, and Garth for the first time.

"That's when I went to organ. Richard not only had the voice, he had this great rhythmic feel, so I never had to play that heavy left-hand stuff. We bought a Lowrey organ, which nobody else was using except that guy in Detroit. I played it for the next fifteen years."

I understood the qualms Garth's family had. We all did, because back then being a professional musician wasn't something you'd brag about. It wasn't something your girlfriend could go tell everybody. Actually, it was a strike against you. I was almost twenty-two years old and making pretty good money, but I could barely get car insurance. They'd cancel you if they found out you were a musician. We were on their back page, along with athletes, jockeys, and race-car drivers.

With Garth and that organ, we sounded like a rock and roll orchestra. We felt so enriched it was ungodly. He had sounds no one else had. He liked that pedal-steel-guitar stop on the Lowrey; it sounded like a fire-breathing dragon. He had a horn like a car horn hooked to the top of his Leslie speaker cabinet. He'd hit a frequency that sounded that horn, and it was *wild*.

Garth was a serious musician. He spoke slowly and deliberately, and whored around less than us. Just having Garth as a teacher was an honor. He'd listen to a song on the radio in the Cadillac and tell us the chords as it went along. Complicated chord structures? No problem. Garth would figure them out, and we found ourselves able to play anything. Our horizons were lifted, and the thing became more fun. It was like we didn't have to guess anymore, because we had a master among us. That's how it felt.

Garth also brought a second saxophone to the band. With Jerry Penfound's baritone and Garth's alto, we had a soul-band horn section when we needed one. That really changed our sound toward a more R&B feel from the rockabilly we'd been playing for almost four years.

The main thing was, we were back to that double keyboard, Richard and Garth. That's what we built on until we really thought we were the best band in the world.

Nineteen sixty-two was the first full year of the new band. It was also the year that everything began to change for us, especially when the Hawk got married.

Up till then, we were laughing all the time. Ronnie made sure that we had the worst reputation in North America. Richard always had a lot of girlfriends. He even chased girls that I was dating. If Robbie or Rick had a pretty girl, Richard might go after her too. "Son," the Hawk used to say, laughing with paternal pride, "that Richard is a damn *home wrecker!*"

"This was a good-looking group," Bill Avis recalls. "When we came into a room, people looked. The women stared. We did everything with class, and there was nothing to worry about but a case of the clap and maybe the crabs. It was a much different era."

Yet I also can't help but remember all the nights there weren't wild parties, when we'd rehearse until dawn and then worry about where we wanted to go and how we were gonna get there. All those nights when Ronnie yelled, "It's orgy time!" and Garth and I would wink at each other and try to stay focused on what we could do with the band if we had the chance.

No one loved women more than the Hawk. You'd walk into Ronnie's suite at the Frontenac Arms Hotel, where we were living by then, and there'd be girls on every couch, every chair, waiting to get into his room, where he'd be holding court in bed. But the Hawk's attitude changed after he met gorgeous Wanda Nugurski, who showed up one day on the "Coke side" of the Concord Tavern in Toronto. That was the nonalcoholic part of the Concord, where all the young musicians would come to watch us and learn. The Hawk was really smitten with Wanda ("Dammit, Levon, she's the only woman in the world who's got a dildo with two gears!") and married her on March 15, 1962. I had the honor of serving as best man. Ronnie had nominally fought the marriage all the way down the aisle, but he was twenty-seven years old and wanted to have a family. Actually, he wanted it all: the family *and* the life-style of the rock and roll star. Damn if the Hawk didn't have it all, at least for a while.

If Friday nights were hot for us, then Sundays were our downtime. We'd sleep late, play casino, drink Red Cap beer, and watch television. It was the only time in our lives things were quiet and we weren't moving. Soon it seemed like Ronnie was more interested in Sundays than in Fridays, especially after Ronnie, Jr., was born a year after the wedding. That's when things began to change.

Of course, we were on the road a lot that year; one of the last of the old-time rock and roll bands. We played the middle of North America in a vertical arc from Molasses, Texas, to Timmins, Ontario—so far north it was only a couple of hours from the arctic tundra. We logged thousands of miles in Ronnie's '62 Cadillac, all of us crammed in there. One night the Hawk was sleeping, and Richard stubbed out a cigarette on Ronnie's hand, which must have been resting on the ashtray. Oh God, the Hawk was mad! He didn't smoke himself, and it was always an issue among the band. There might be some ash on the carpet, and he'd say, "See *that*, son?" He thought it was a nasty habit, and he said he was scared for us. Eventually the Hawk offered us a hundred dollars each if we'd quit, and the boys took him up on it. So when it was cigarette time, I'd eat one of those little boxes of raisins—six for a nickel. I'd pass some to my buddies in the backseat. Next thing you know, someone had dropped a raisin in the back of the car, so the sun would hit it just right. When we were unloading or going into a restaurant, the raisin got stepped on and smeared like a flapjack. The Hawk was displeased when he saw that. "Goddamn," he growled, "I gave you guys a hundred to get off cigarettes. I'll give you *two hundred* to get rid of these damn raisins!"

It was around this time that Robbie and I bought our own Cadillac. Everyone in the band treated it like it was their car, and it was trashed in eight months. I think we got a Volkswagen bus after that.

As usual, we went home that spring to play our southern circuit.

Lavon Helm, age thirteen, hamboning at a 4-H Club talent show in Phillips County, Arkansas, circa 1953
(TURKEY SCRATCH ARCHIVES)

Thurlow Brown, Linda Helm, and Lavon Helm at a show at Marvell High School, circa 1955
(COURTESY C. W. GATLIN)

Sonny Boy Williamson and His King Biscuit Entertainers at radio station KFFA, Helena, Arkansas, circa 1943 (COURTESY KFFA/DELTA CULTURAL CENTER)

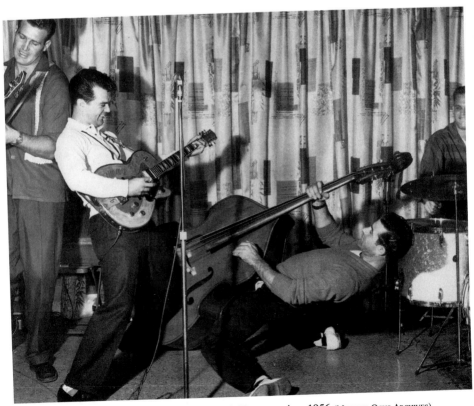

Conway Twitty (*second from left*) and the Rock Housers, circa 1956 (MICHAEL OCHS ARCHIVES)

Ronnie Hawkins and the Hawks when they arrived in New York in 1958. *From left:* Levon Helm, Ronnie Hawkins, Jimmy Ray "Luke" Paulman, and Will "Pop" Jones. (MICHAEL OCHS ARCHIVES)

Ronnie Hawkins and the Hawks, circa 1960. *From left:* Stan Szelest, Rebel Paine, Ronnie, Robbie Robertson, and Levon Helm. Kneeling in front is band mascot, Freddie McNulty. (COURTESY RICHARD BELL)

Ronnie Hawkins and the Hawks at the Brass Rail in Hamilton, Ontario, circa 1963. *From left:* Rick Danko on bass, Richard Manuel on piano, Ronnie (note the beatnik goatee), Levon on drums, Robbie Robertson on guitar, and Garth Hudson on Lowrey organ. (TURKEY SCRATCH ARCHIVES)

Levon and the Hawks in New York, 1964. *From left:* Jerry "Ish" Penfound (who played saxophone), Rick Danko, Levon, Richard Manuel, Garth Hudson, and Robbie Robertson. (TURKEY SCRATCH ARCHIVES)

Levon and the Hawks were headlining Tony Mart's big nightclub in Somers Point, New Jersey, in August 1965 when they were "discovered" by Bob Dylan. (Turkey Scratch Archives)

Bob Dylan, Robbie, and Levon go over Bob's song lyrics backstage at Forest Hills, New York, on August 28, 1965. (Photo © 1967 Daniel Kramer)

Bob Dylan, Harvey Brooks, Robbie, and Levon onstage at Forest Hills, August 28, 1965

(PHOTO © 1967 DANIEL KRAMER)

Clockwise from top: Garth, Levon, and Richard playing football at Big Pink, Woodstock, New York, spring 1968 (ELLIOTT LANDY)

Richard and Levon at Big Pink,
spring 1968 (ELLIOTT LANDY)

Just as photographer Elliott Landy
was shooting The Band for the
Music from Big Pink album sleeve,
a friend of ours took off her clothes
in an attempt to get us to lighten up.
(ELLIOTT LANDY)

The *Big Pink* group photo was taken at a house Levon and Rick were renting at nearby Wittenburg, New York, spring 1968. Our dog Hamlet, a gift from Bob Dylan, was present at the creation. (ELLIOTT LANDY)

Garth Hudson instructs Levon in the finer points of dowsing, spring 1968. (ELLIOTT LANDY)

The Band and their next of kin at Rick's brother's farm in Ontario (ELLIOTT LANDY)

Robbie and Levon writing songs at Rick Danko's house on Zena Road, early 1969

(Elliott Landy)

The Band posing for the brown album in Rick's basement, early 1969 (ELLIOTT LANDY)

Band rehearsal at the house shared by Garth and Richard on Glenford Road, 1969
(ELLIOTT LANDY)

The Band in the kitchen of Big Pink (ELLIOTT LANDY)

Recording "Rag Mama Rag" in California, winter 1969. Producer John Simon leans over keyboard at left. (ELLIOTT LANDY)

Richard, Robbie, and Levon work on lyrics for *The Band* in California, winter 1969.
(ELLIOTT LANDY)

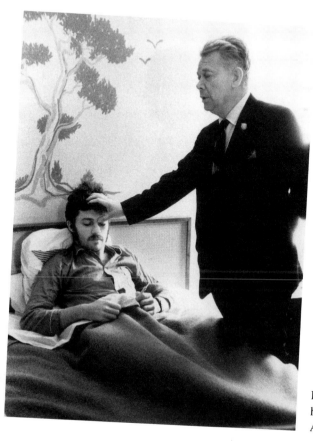

Robbie Robertson and the hypnotist, San Francisco, April 1969 (ELLIOTT LANDY)

Robbie, Levon, John Simon, Rick, and Albert Grossman before The Band's first show at Winterland, San Francisco, April 1969 (ELLIOTT LANDY)

The Band at the Fillmore East, New York City, May 1969 (ELLIOTT LANDY)

Ronnie had his club and his farms in the Fayetteville area, and I bought a house for my folks in nearby Springdale. Friends of ours were putting in a development, interest rates were around 4 percent, and they lent me the down payment as well. My dad had stopped farming by then, and the family was ready for a move out of cotton country. I continued to send a little money home every payday—the band was making maybe $2,500 a week by then—and it was a better situation because the family could be together when the Hawks came down to touch home base every few months.

Tension filled the air that summer and fall of 1962 because of the Cuban missile crisis. President John F. Kennedy found out that the Russians were building missile sites in Fidel Castro's Cuba, a mere ninety miles from Florida. In October he went on television to announce he'd given Premier Nikita Khrushchev an ultimatum: Get the missiles out or else face an American blockade of Russian shipping to Cuba. "Naval blockade's an act of war," Ronnie mused one evening while waiting to go onstage. The Strategic Air Command was put on red alert. B-52s were flying overhead, and things seemed pretty apocalyptic. People were nervous. We'd all grown up with those air-raid drills in school, hadn't we?

We were in London, Ontario. "It looks bad, son," the Hawk opined. "It could get into World War III." I got pretty scared. If North America was going to be incinerated by nuclear bombs, I decided I didn't want to die in Canada. I got a road map, and the Hawk and I planned our route in case of war. We could leave London, go through Sarnia, and head down through central Michigan. I wasn't about to drive through Detroit. We figured we could get to Arkansas without hitting any major city on the Soviets' target list.

October 27 was the deadline Kennedy had given the Russians to pull out. That night we were playing the Brass Rail, and everyone was a little tense. Even Freddie McNulty was subdued. There was a feeling of the impending end of civilization. We were right in the middle of a tune when the Hawk got onstage and killed the music with a wave of his hand.

"Ladies and gentlemen," he said gravely, "I have an announcement to make."

I drum-rolled the crowd to a hush.

"This is an *emergency* announcement."

97

Everyone gasped. Ronnie wasn't smiling. He was reading from a piece of paper. From my drum stool I could see people in back grabbing their coats, ready to bust out of there.

"Word has just reached us . . . that we've stopped three Russian ships . . . with our naval blockade in the Caribbean Sea."

Pin drop.

"Our sailors went on board the Russian ships . . . and discovered they'd all been loaded with Vaseline. So they diverted 'em to *The Virgin Islands! Haw haw haw haw haw!!!!!*"

Chapter Four

LEVON AND THE HAWKS (ONE STEP AHEAD OF LAND OF 1000 DANCES)

I too got married late in 1962. I figured if the Hawk could do it, so could I.

My philosophy had always been not to burden any young woman with my presence for too long a time. The life of a musician was nothing to be married to, and I could never envision settling down and having children. I was of the road; it was my life, and I was living it to the hilt and beyond. We may have had a hard time getting credit cards and insurance, but we felt freer than anyone else in the land as we crisscrossed province, prairie, and state. We were in our early twenties, playing and traveling, and didn't have to answer to anybody. It was the kind of life where if you had a problem today, you could be five hundred miles away from it the next day.

At the same time, my draft board back in Helena was determined to selectively service my ass over to West Germany, the way they had Elvis's. Anyone could see how the army had changed him, how Elvis's incredible edge was just gone. I married my friend Connie Orr, a Toronto lady who'd married a man named George, had a son, George, Jr., but was no longer with George, Sr. So I stepped in—strictly platonic, it was—and married her, thus becoming a Canadian landed immigrant. That took care of my draft board, and Connie (loyalty was and is her middle name) is still a great friend of mine.

In February 1963 we all went to New York to cut some tracks with Henry Glover for Roulette. The label wanted new versions of "Bo Diddley" and "Who Do You Love" to exploit the renewed interest in R&B that had surfaced in the wake of the folk-music boom. Although we hadn't recorded in eighteen months, we weren't rusty. Robbie howled and screamed on guitar, the Hawk growled and hollered the lyrics, and the band duplicated the speed-demon rhythms we liked to do in the bars. "Bo Diddley #117"/"Who Do You Love" was released as a single in March.

We were back in New York that May, and by then we were starting to squabble with the Hawk. When I say "we," I mean Robbie and myself. The Hawk was the daddy of the group, who wanted to stick to the old ways (rockabilly), while Robbie and I were the rebellious teenagers who wanted to push the band deeper into R&B. We were always after Ronnie to record blues-type material, so to humor us we cut a few things like "Mojo Hand" and Muddy Waters's "She's Nineteen Years Old." These were, I believe, the last sessions we did with Ronnie. Our last single together, "High Blood Pressure" (with a jazzy organ solo by Garth), came out in June.

One day we were working with Henry at Bell Sound, and after Ronnie had left for the day Henry let us—just the band—cut a version of Bobby Bland's classic "Further on up the Road," just about our favorite number to play. When we finished and had listened to the playback, Henry asked us when we were going out on our own.

This gave us ideas. The Hawk was settling in with his family, and we were getting interested in different things, from "Chicago Green" to Chicago Blues. That night, in our room at the Hotel Forrest in Manhattan, Robbie and I began to talk about wild possibilities. "Levon," he said, "like, do we really *need* Ronnie?"

It was a combination of a lot of things that led us to leave the Hawk late in 1963. But the band really split up because of age as much as anything else. We were younger, and everyone wanted that independence that youth craves. Ronnie had a set of rules, and he'd fine you if you broke 'em. He played the kind of music he was interested in, and we wanted a band where everyone played and had a voice—

100

literally. We were already swapping the singing duties around, working in harmonies as we needed them. With Richard, Rick, and me, we had the beginnings of the voice that became The Band. Three singers on one song; that became our trademark. We were already doing it before we split with Ronnie, because some nights he didn't bother showing up. If we were up in Grand Bend for a week, we'd do the first two or three nights by ourselves. At the end of the week, the Hawk would show up at the end of the night to do a set. He'd wait for the weekend to appear because he was settling down and wanting to be with his family.

So if Ronnie wasn't coming that night, it was up to the three of us to sing and pass it around. Richard carried the main load, so we were home free. (A lot of people who saw us in those days thought it was Richard's band.) Then Rick and I would throw in the extra tunes of the set. I'd sing a Little Richard tune, and I loved doing those Larry Williams numbers: "Boney Moronie," "Short Fat Fannie." So we were all singing and playing instruments, and to our minds that was the basis for a new kind of band—one without a front man.

Around this time Ronnie hired a young singer we'd met in New York to front the band until the Hawk showed up for the last set of the night. Bruce Bruno, from New Rochelle, New York, was a very talented triple threat, because he was a good singer, a good dancer, and a funny comedian who'd do comic bits with the band and keep everyone laughing until the Hawk arrived.

"I met the guys through Morris Levy," Bruce recalls, "because my brother, Buddy Bruno, and I had both cut records for Roulette while we were still in high school. One night I was at Morris's restaurant, the Round Table, working with a nine-piece band called the Orchids. We were all blown away by the Hawks, even though they were only a five-piece group. Morris Levy leans over and growls to me, 'That's the best fuckin' band in America.'

"I stayed with the Hawks for maybe two years, from the end of '63 to early '65, and it was a wild time. I was drunk or stoned every day, trying to keep up with how they lived. We'd smoke a bone like we'd have a cup of coffee. I got to be good friends with Richard, who was gentle and intelligent, always fun to be around. A couple of times he got so drunk he barfed on the piano, but that was all part of this life they were living. They were already legends among musicians when I

101

met them. The only problem I had was that the Hawks were so good, you couldn't sing with anyone else! They were *that* good. When my time with them was over, I decided I had to get out of that side of the business.''

All this time we were leaning ever further away from rockabilly. Richard liked to sing that Bobby ''Blue'' Bland material and those Ray Charles songs, and we all liked Sonny Boy Williamson's songs and anything by Jimmy Reed or Willie Dixon. This was what we wanted to play, but the Hawk continued to be adamant. ''Boys, I know what the customers want,'' he'd say. ''We just can't play that blues stuff all the time. We got to wake that crowd up!''

Another thing that came between us was that the Hawk didn't like to smoke pot. He wasn't a prude, because he liked to drink. But Ronnie was foremost an entertainer, a diplomat, a defender of his rights. He didn't drink onstage and didn't want anyone else to, either. He wanted a good, solid, *sober* show.

When we first discovered the weed, it was a new world. Chicago Green. You'd run into someone just come from a good day at the track, or maybe they'd just gotten out of jail and had a little money. They might have a little extra to share. Chicago Green was the best pot you could get. Or there was Mexican Brown. Wherever it came from, the band loved it. You could find a whole world in a bowl of cornflakes. We laughed like fools and generally had a great time. It didn't hurt us, we figured. In fact, it helped get us through our lives of constant work. But it was also another point of disagreement with the Hawk, who'd fine us twenty-five dollars if he caught us. It wasn't too severe a lashing, and Ronnie was still our comrade in arms, but he thought it was his duty as bandleader. ''I have a certain responsibility to your families,'' he would say.

In the end it came down to Hawk's feeling that more discipline was the best thing for the situation. He didn't want anyone to smoke pot, drink, or smoke cigarettes in the car. How long could we live with that?

Rick wanted out first, because Ronnie had fined him for having a girlfriend at the show. ''Levon,'' Rick said, ''maybe we're reaching the breaking point here; the sheer ridiculousness of this shit. I mean, we oughta get out and see the world. Or at least go to New Jersey and play anyway.''

"So what do you wanna do?" I asked him.

"Let's go see the Colonel about working on our own, man. I mean, what the hell, you're our official leader anyway, if you think about the union."

This was true. I had seniority in the band, and the Hawk had never joined the musicians union, so for all those years the contracts were always in my name. I was beginning to see it now. We divided up the band's money, and it didn't take a whole lot of bookeeping in those days. *Maybe I could actually do it; run the band myself.* Young Rick was insistent. "Why can't we have a band," he asked, "where everybody plays an instrument, everybody sings, everybody does it without some guy out in front of the thing running the show and deciding the way things are gonna go?" This was a radical notion, like communism. But maybe, I thought, for the first time in our or anyone's imagination, the rhythm section could run the band! If we could run the actual show, why couldn't we run the rest of the operation? If we could stack up those verses and choruses, we might also be able to stack up a tour and some records. That was our attitude.

So Rick and I drove over to Hamilton to see Colonel Harold Kudlets, who explained that Ronnie had just fired him, so why didn't we continue playing the same rooms on the same circuit that we'd been playing successfully for years? The Colonel would book us, be our agent, and try to get us a record deal. We told him that sounded OK to us, and we'd talk to the other boys about it, and when it came time to draw up the contracts we never wanted to see the word "sideman" again. That attitude held for the rest of our career, and over the years we've had managers and lawyers tear up a whole lot of paperwork because it had that word in it.

Rick Danko remembers how it went down:

"Ronnie had let the Colonel go because he felt he'd reached his peak with the organization, and he was going down to New York to talk to Morris Levy to see what he could do next. We were playing in Toronto, it was after the weekend, and I had a girlfriend visiting from out of town. The Hawk had a rule that girlfriends were a distraction. We were expected to play for thirty minutes and then go out and mingle for thirty. He thought this was crucial to our success, and that it wouldn't look right if we were romancing our sweethearts. Young guys attract young girls, who attract other young guys. That's how Ronnie thought life was: sex, drugs, and rock and roll. He told me, 'Son, when your dick gets hard, your brain goes soft.'

"I thought this rule was valid, and so I didn't bring the girl that night. But she knew Ronnie was going to New York and thought it was all right to show up. But Ronnie missed his plane. So he came into the club, and there was my girlfriend. He looked at me and said, 'Aw, that's gonna cost ya fifty dollars, son.'

" 'That's bullshit,' I told him. 'You're not fining me for this one.' Because I was already paying off a fine for gambling on the job. I'd won twelve hundred dollars in a card game, and so I had to pay Ronnie fifty dollars a week. He was funny like that. Then a few nights later Conway Twitty came to town, and we were all socializing in Ronnie's studio over the Le Coq D'Or. Ronnie was drunk and mentioned that I hadn't paid my fine, but a little disrespectfully. 'Fuck you,' I said, drunk myself. 'I'm not paying no fine. You missed your plane, it's not my fault, I didn't bring her, she showed up!' Then he got really pissed off.

"I didn't say anything else, but he was on my case now. Next night we were onstage, and the Hawk kept looking at me funny. Between sets he takes me into the stairwell. He was high on pills, and he says, 'Rick, someday Levon's gonna be governor of Arkansas. Robbie's gonna be the fucking road commissioner, and Richard's gonna be secretary of state. And you, son, are gonna be back in Simcoe cutting some goddamn meat because that's all you're good for.' It looked like Ronnie was getting ready to fire me.

"Next break, I grabbed Levon and told him this story. He said, 'Let me handle it, Rick. We'll have a meeting.' He talked to everyone on the next break, and at the end of the night we all gathered downstairs. Ronnie had a smirk on his face, which faded when Levon said, 'You know, Ronnie, nobody's very happy, especially young Rick over there. He's *very* unhappy. So we want to tell you, with all due respect, that we're givin' you two weeks' notice.'

"The Hawk didn't say much. He hadn't planned on this, but we could tell he wasn't that sorry it happened.

"So Ronnie didn't show up the next night or the night after that. I said, 'Levon, let's call up Ronnie and see if he'll give us an extra $100 a week each'—$1,200 as a unit for the two-week gig we were playing at $2,400 a week.

"So Levon went to the pay phone. Me and Richard are listening to him telling Ronnie that since he's not showing up, we needed an extra $100 each. And Ronnie's saying, 'Shit, son, I got a payroll higher than General Motors. I can't afford this. Maybe I oughta go to Arkansas and put another band together . . .'

"Well, Levon told Ronnie he was free to do whatever he thought best. We took hold of the $4,800 the club owed us for the booking and went home that night to the two-bedroom suite we were sharing at the Frontenac Arms. We sat down and did a little budgeting. We could get a couple of Pontiac station wagons, a couple of sets of electric-blue suits each (plus an extra set that Levon insisted we buy for our devoted fan Freddie McNulty because he was one of us), and go out on our own. There might even have been enough left over for a few weeks' worth of dry cleaning and barbers."

We spent the early days of 1964 in Toronto going over our game plan.

First we got Bill Avis back. He'd stopped being our roadie a year or so earlier when he stayed behind to manage the Hawk's Arkansas operation: the clubs and the farms. He'd met Richard when he came down to play with the Revols. Then he went to work for Don Tyson's chicken operation for a while before coming back to Toronto, where he met five girls who called themselves the Female Beatles. He toured them across the country that year, from Vegas to New York, and was working at Tony Mart's on the Jersey Shore when I finally reached him.

"Levon called me," Bill recalls, "and he said, 'We quit Ronnie. We had to part company. Come back and help us out.' I said, 'Levon, I'll be there as soon as I can, because I'm with the Female Beatles, and I can't leave 'em stranded.'

"A couple of weeks later I got back to Toronto. I had a white Pontiac station wagon I'd been using for the Female Beatles, and Levon had a black one, leased from the same company. Salt and pepper, OK? So we pooled our station wagons, and that's when they first played the Friar's Tavern as Levon and the Hawks."

Actually, we started out as the Levon Helm Sextet. I had to endure some teasing over this, but my name went on the band as a seniority thing. The Colonel thought I knew as many people as Ronnie did, since I'd gotten there at the same time. We thought those people who liked Ronnie would come to see us too. It just made business better for everybody. The group was me, Robbie, Rick, Richard, Garth, and Ish—Jerry Penfound. If Jerry was away, Bruce Bruno would come play with us. Soon we turned into Levon and the Hawks, which sounded better to me. Sometimes it was the Hawks. We also got booked into places we'd recently played by calling ourselves the Canadian Squires.

We had a funny beginning because we gave Ish about a grand toward building a new PA system for us. Jerry could do or build anything, from blowing glass to flying an airplane. He had a fantastic imagination. "We were in London," Rick remembers, "and we got to the club early. Me and Levon are sitting at the bar, and these two guys come in, and they're laughing about a pool game they'd just had where they won $800 from Jerry Penfound. Levon looked at me and said, 'Well, there goes the PA system!' Ish Kabibble; he was funny."

Bill Avis recalls: "We did good business from the minute we started playing, because there was no better band in the world; take my word for it. The money was my responsibility. I'd collect from the clubs on Friday and split the money into envelopes. I'd send $150 to Levon's mom and dad, or whatever he could afford that week. I'd send the Colonel ten percent of whatever we earned. I got $100 a week, Ish got $150 (Ish's paycheck was sometimes garnisheed by the family court in London because he had a child and got behind on his support payments); all the others but Robbie got $162.50, and Robbie got a little more because he was making half the payments on our company car, which gave him the right to 'carry the keys,' as Levon put it."

It was a great time to launch a band in Toronto, because the place was jumping. On a weekend night on that Yonge Street strip you could catch Oscar Peterson, Carl Perkins, Ray Charles and his band, Cannonball Adderly, Charles Mingus. You could see a local band like us or one of our competitors, the Paupers. There was a folk-music scene with young singers like Gordon Lightfoot, Joni Mitchell, and Neil Young in the Yorkville coffeehouses. And it wasn't just music. Toronto was also the publishing, fashion, and style capital of Canada. The city was swinging at least a year before so-called Swinging London. (Ronnie swore it was like a replay of the Roaring Twenties.)

Over at the University of Toronto, Professor Marshall McLuhan was formulating his theories on media that would change the way we received information, the way we lived. The medium became the message in Toronto, and out of that came CNN, MTV, and the whole Global Village in which we all live today.

We loved the city in part because we felt very protected. We had some pretty tough people looking out for us. There was one damn guy—he worked at the Pump Room in London—who bit the caps off beer bottles and then chewed them for us.

As Rick Danko remembers: "We were pretty young guys in a tough part of town, and we learned there was a pecking order in people's lives, and if you respected that, you might earn a certain level of protection. If somebody got in trouble, especially over seeing someone's girlfriend (this happened a lot), you took your problem to someone a little older, a little wiser, with a little more clout, whether it be fists, guns, or political—depending on the situation.

"We were lucky because the rounders liked us. They'd want to come to our parties on the weekend because we attracted unattached young women who were appealing to the eye. The rounders didn't have dates; they'd sit in the corner near the ladies' room at the Concord Tavern out on Bloor Street West. Each chick would use the bathroom once or twice a night and have to pass through the gauntlet of rounders checking them out. Some of the ladies really liked this attention, and that's how a good party would start. We'd have a bar full of tough guys—a guy selling nickel bags of pot would be rubbing elbows with an off-duty narcotics officer—and they'd be sending up notes requesting songs. Or, 'Can we come to the party afterward?' They loved music, loved us, so it was like a *Spy vs. Spy* kind of logic.

"We had people like 'Teddy the Hungarian.' He'd run from the Russians in '56 and was so immensely strong he liked to tear phone books in quarters when he was happy. Levon would have to clear a place for him in a restaurant, Teddy was so big. If someone was giving, say, Richard a big problem over a young woman he was dating, Teddy the Hungarian would be called in to settle out of court. Or 'Tony From Toronto,' who had a bigger gun than anyone.

"I had a situation where I was seeing an eighteen-year-old girl who was making me very hard. Her old boyfriend was just out of jail, got a machine gun, and shot out another guy's truck windows for fucking his girlfriend. I thought, *Aw, man! What's he gonna do to me?* So I called Tony from Toronto, and logic eventually prevailed. Nothing criminal happened, but we never wanted to leave anyone with the wrong impression. If someone around us had gotten a little too drunk the night before, he would be straightened out by our people the next day. It took us years to build this protection up; there was an unbelievably long list of people we could call.''

The Cannonball Adderly Sextet came through town in early 1964. They had a hit record, "This Here," and a profound influence on the Hawks. We all went to see them and were impressed by how cool and collected they were, with expensively tailored clothes and a mellow outlook on life. The band was Cannonball, his brother Nat on trumpet, Joe Zawinul on keys, Sam Jones on bass, and flutist Charles Lloyd from West Memphis, with whom we became good friends. The drummer, Louis Hayes, was a great musician. I watched him float those rhythms and realized the idea was *not* to get it down on the floor and stomp the hell out of it. *Don't* be frantic. *Don't* be out of control. We loved Cannonball's band for its restraint; soon after we saw them we changed to what we called the "jazzster" style. Matching shiny suits became a thing of the past as we began to dress with a little more flair. Rick Danko still refers to 1964 as our Cannonball period.

All the Toronto clubs had Saturday matinees for the kids, who could buy chips and gravy, Cokes and lemonade. Since we worked on Saturday nights, we'd go to these afternoon shows if there was someone we'd heard good things about and whose act we wanted to catch.

That's where we met John Hammond, Jr. He was the son of the legendary Columbia Records producer who had discovered Bessie Smith, Count Basie, and a young folksinger named Bob Dylan. John, Jr., was a solid blues singer and player on the college and coffeehouse circuit, keeping the country blues of Robert Johnson and Son House alive, and we really liked what he was doing. Through him we met Mike Bloomfield when we were living at the Chelsea Hotel in New York (R&B singer Jackie Wilson was also in residence at the time). Mike was playing guitar in a young Chicago blues band, and they were said to be very hot. Mike told us to come visit the next time we were passing through.

A little later Robbie and I were driving from Toronto to Tulsa. The big hit song on the black Pontiac's radio was Marvin Gaye's "Baby Don't You Do It." We were all huge Motown fans. I remember that ride because Robbie talked about his childhood. He'd worked at a carnival at one point, and he went on about the mystique of the carny life: the hustlers, the freaks, the ride boys. If we were riding along and he saw a ferris wheel and some colored lights, he'd want to stop and check it out. It was a fascination of his.

We detoured through Chicago, and Mike Bloomfield put us up at his place for a couple of days. He was a wonderful human being! We hung out and met Paul Butterfield, the harmonica virtuoso whose interracial Chicago blues band was on the cutting edge of contemporary music. It was Paul, Mike, Sam Lay on drums, and Jerome Arnold on bass. We loved what they were doing because we were leaning in the same direction: Muddy, Sonny Boy, Slim, "Blue" Bland. The idea became to take this music—electric R&B—and build something new with it.

The best part of this trip was that Butter and Michael took us to these obscure blues clubs on the south side and introduced us to people like Otis Rush and Buddy Guy, who didn't yet have a big audience beyond Chicago. We went to see Howlin' Wolf with Butter's band, a great experience. Wolf ignored the drunks who pestered him and gave his full attention to the young ladies who came up to him with song requests.

April 1964. The Colonel booked us into the Grange Tavern in Hamilton for two weeks at thirteen hundred dollars a week. Bruce Bruno was with us, singing and telling jokes. Then we did three weeks at the Embassy Club on Bellair Street in Toronto, through early May. I think I was renting rooms from Robbie's mom. She was like my own mother, and you could really nest in there. We called her Mama Kosh because we'd come out of Switzer's Deli off Bathurst Street with those big sandwiches, and everything was kosher.

We never rested. Three weeks at the Brass Rail in London, a couple of gigs at the Circle M Ranch in Dundas, and two weeks at the Concord Tavern in Toronto got us into June. Then we worked two weeks at Cafe De L'Est in Montreal. Our Ontario license plates occasionally turned us into closing-time targets when we played in Quebec. A couple of times we had to fight off the locals on our way out of the parking lot.

On June 15 Levon and the Hawks began a two-week engagement at the famous Peppermint Lounge, 128 West Forty-fifth Street in New York. We worked from 9:00 P.M. to 3:00 A.M. for $1,250 a week. The Peppermint had spawned the Twist craze four years earlier and was still a big nightspot for international tourists. The waitresses were excited because the Beatles had been in a couple of weeks earlier, and their long-haired drummer, Ringo Starr, had danced with some of the regulars while the house band played "Money."

While in New York, we reconnected with our friend John Hammond, Jr., who was recording his third album for Vanguard. He asked if we wanted to help, and naturally we did because it was our first time in a recording studio without Ronnie. John, a scholar of the music we'd grown up on, realized the electric blues was the medium of the moment. When we showed up at the studio we found Charlie Musselwhite ready to play harmonica and Jimmy Lewis on bass. Michael Bloomfield was there with his guitar, but he was too intimidated to play in front of Robbie, who was considered the best in the land. So on John Hammond's *So Many Roads* album the piano credit is listed as Michael Bloomfield. (Jaime R. Robertson is listed on guitar, Eric Hudson [Garth is his middle name] on Hammond organ, and Mark Levon Helm on drums.) We did a new version of "Who Do You Love" and songs by Muddy Waters, Willie Dixon, and Robert Johnson, and logged some needed studio time in the bargain.

John was a good friend, and I think he was one of the first to see the possibilities of having an electric band. He helped us get kicked out early by the Peppermint Lounge when he sat in and played the blues with us on Friday night. Backstage the shady owner grabbed me and yelled, "Forget that *blues* shit. What are you, *nuts*? This is a *twist joint*!" We left that night, and lost our front man, Bruce Bruno, who wanted to stay in New Rochelle and marry his sweetheart, B.J. (They're still together.) The day after the Peppermint Lounge gig ended, we headed back to Canada for two weeks at the Grange. On Sunday nights we played Pop Ivy's ballroom in Port Dover for $250. Someone taped our show one night, and the tape still exists.

We rev up to speed immediately with "Not Fade Away." I'm calling the tunes, and announce that the next one's for the dancers.

This was Richard doing "A Sweeter Girl" with two honking tenor saxes: Jerry and Garth. Then "Lucille"; that's me bawling out the vocal. Then an instrumental, "Peter Gunn," with more horns and a Charles Lloyd–inspired flute solo by Ish.

Next we take Barrett Strong's "Money" at the speed of sound, and Richard does a slow, soulful "You Don't Know Me" that gave customers a chance to rest and find the bar.

Now it's time for our Hawk section. We make a wild racket on "Bo Diddley," with Robbie stretching that guitar five years ahead of its time, then blast off into "Forty Days," an old war-horse that always got 'em on their feet. "This next one," I announce, "is left over from our days with the hootchy-kootchy show. You've heard this kind of music down at the Lux Theater [a Toronto strip joint], and Rick is gonna do his female impersonator bit for you, ladies and gentlemen. And by the way, there's lots of corn left, and it's free. And Pop Ivy's got a few free beers for you if you ask nice. *Haw haw haw . . .* We call it the 'Hootchy John Blues,' with Garth and Jerry on the tenor saxophones."

After that comes a blues section, "dedicated especially to Dave that we call 'Robbie's Blues.' " This showcased several different blues styles and let us show the direction we wanted to head in.

After the break Richard tears up "Kansas City," next I yell out "Memphis," then Richard does his best James Brown imitation on "Please, Please, Please." That's me whistling the intro to "Short Fat Fannie" (still a favorite) and Garth playing the crazed sax solo. More Chuck Berry with "No Particular Place to Go" (Robbie is unbelievable) leads into "You Can't Sit Down" (we all solo on the verses) and "Turn on Your Love Light"—classic, old-fashioned horn-band R&B.

"Ladies and gentlemen," I say, "we'd just like to take a short minute, and we'll be right back . . . OK, we call this one 'Put on Your Red Dress, Baby, Because You and Me Is Gonna Do It Up Tonight,' *heh heh heh heh heh.*" This is followed by "Woman Love and a Man," on which I basically shout my lungs out.

Garth has the next spot, a little blues and Bach number that anticipated the intro to The Band's "Chest Fever" by four years. The evening builds to its climax with "Honky Tonk" and finishes with an explosive "Twist and Shout."

Then the lights go low. Midnight was closing time on Sunday, and

Richard ends the show with a beautiful version of "Georgia on My Mind" that defuses the night's energy and the raw power of the sound we were putting out. Everybody loved Richard's voice, especially on that song.

We finished in Hamilton on July 11. The next day we drove to Quebec City for a week at La Baril D'Huitres (the Oyster Barrel) at fourteen hundred dollars a week. Then back to the Embassy Club for two weeks. The first week of August we played the Grand Hotel in Bridgeport, Ontario; the second week was at the Brass Rail in London; and then an eight-week residency at the Concord Tavern at thirteen hundred dollars a week for the band. We basically worked every night of the year after that, finishing at the Friar's Tavern, 303 Yonge Street. Our contract specified that we played Monday through Friday from 8:00 P.M. to 1:00 A.M. There was a Saturday matinee from three to five, which usually sold out because all the young musicians in Ontario wanted to jam with us, and the evening show ran from eight to eleven-thirty.

I write this to emphasize that our work was our whole life. We were playing music five hours a day and rehearsing new material as well. This made us sharp. I mean, we were *honed!* Also frustrated, because we knew that for all our talent and energy, we were still just one step ahead of "Land of 1000 Dances," the most requested song of the day. (We refused to play it.) It was a scene we wanted out of. "I'm tired of being a rankster," Richard would say. "I wanna move on up out of this rankdom we're in." We were all ready for something to happen by the end of 1964.

Richard met a new girl around this time. Jane Kristianson was a young model, born in Denmark, educated in Toronto. When *Playboy* magazine did a spread called "The Girls of Toronto," Jane was the only girl photographed with all her clothes on. Full page, too. We wondered who she was.

"I was nineteen when I met the Hawks," Jane says. "I'd already had the misfortune to encounter Ronnie Hawkins at parties. He was so gross you wanted to hand him a napkin whenever you saw him. He called me his 'little hors d'oeuvre' and once pinned me under him on a bed before someone else pulled him off.

"Anyway, one night late in 1964 another model called me and said to meet her at Friar's Tavern because a great group was playing and

112

she was interested in one of the boys. We were underage, but we somehow got in. A group was playing, all of them tall and clean-cut. I was talking to my friend when the group stopped playing. All of a sudden I noticed they were sitting around us. Richard Manuel was saying funny things, trying to get our attention. He was always doing little routines, teasing people, and in fact had tried to pick me up the night before at another place.

"Someone said that Muddy Waters was playing up the street, and we all left to see him during the band's next break. But my picture had been in the papers as a teen model, and the doorman recognized me and said, 'No way you're twenty-one.' So I couldn't get in. Everyone else went into the club except Richard. 'C'mon,' he said, 'let's go get a cup of coffee.'

"Well, I went with him, and he was very sweet and gentle. That's what drew me to him. Plus his sense of humor. He told me about his family, about his mom, Gladys, and his father, Ed, who had been quite violent when he was young. Then I got to know the rest of the band. Robbie was aloof, quiet, ambitious. Levon was rambunctious and very country. Rick was very handsome, hyper, and funny. Garth spoke slowly and was more sensitive then the others.

"When I was with Richard awhile, they took me down south to Arkansas and Oklahoma in two big station wagons. We'd go to these clubs late at night, and we'd be the only white people. Junior Parker would be up onstage, and everyone would be carrying on. It was wonderful, just being with them."

I remember another incident from this era: the night Robbie almost had his ass whipped at the Tastee-Freez in Fayetteville. I pulled up to the place one night, just in time to see Robbie being muscled in back of the building by a drunken paratrooper who'd learned that young Robertson had been dating his girl while this guy was away in jump school. Now, Robbie never fought, didn't like to fight, so I jumped out of the Pontiac and grabbed Mr. Airborne, who was about foaming at the mouth.

" 'Scuse me, sir," I said. "But you're making a mistake. You got the wrong people."

"No sir," he rumbled, "this is the son of a bitch, and we're just going right behind here and talk it over."

113

"No you're not," I told him. "In fact, you're going to have to disengage right now, because you're outnumbered, and I'll bite your goddamn nose off if you look at me funny!" My eyes were pinned. That stopped it—thank God.

Robertson was more careful after that.

As the year turned into 1965, we began to get restless. The Hawk had taught us to sweat up a roadhouse with hard-core rock and roll, and we knew the satisfaction of wringing a crowd of Saturday night dancers dry until they were begging for more. We were the undisputed champions of Canadian rock and roll.

Were we happy? Guess the answer. "There's got to be more to it than *this*," Rick grumbled one dark and frigid morning, heading back to Toronto after a long job at some bloodletting type of place.

We'd listen to the radio and laugh because, with the exception of Motown, the groups were all so bad. We studied hit records like anatomy students, trying to figure how they were put together and what worked. The big acts of the day—the Beatles and the Beach Boys— came across to us as a blend of pale, homogenized voices. We'd been working for years on a vocal mix that accentuated three distinct voices: me on the bottom, Rick in the middle, and Richard riding on top. We felt we were better than the Beatles and the Beach Boys. We were jealous and considered them our rivals, even though they'd never heard of us.

We talked to the Colonel all the time about breaking out of Canada. Robbie and I spoke about it incessantly. I'd say we were making an OK living and doing all right, and he'd say, "Yeah, but we're living week to week, and we're not getting anywhere." Rick was hot to go to New York so we could get discovered, but as titular leader I wasn't that sure what we should do. Jerry Penfound had already left us, so Levon and the Hawks settled into the quintet format that sustained us for years to come.

The Colonel told us that our first step was to make some records. We had cut a single in 1964 with Henry Glover as the Canadian Squires, which Henry released on his Ware Records label. "Uh Uh Uh"/"Leave Me Alone" were written by Robbie and recorded in New York. I sang "Leave Me Alone," and the lyrics were about our lives:

"Trouble, fight, almost every night. Bad men, don't come around, or I'm gonna lay your body down." Both were harmonica-driven R&B songs that sounded and felt a little like the Rolling Stones, who were interested in the same kind of blues music that we were (and who were about to release their breakthrough single, "Satisfaction").

"That sounds *awful*," Garth Hudson said the first time we heard our record. Garth frowned with displeasure, as only he can. We were sitting in a diner somewhere. "Uh Uh Uh" came on the jukebox, and it was twice as low as anything else. "Too bottom heavy," Garth said. We'd been concerned about getting that presence we liked around the bass pattern, an important part of our sound, but it just didn't translate onto record.

We were friends with Ronnie Hawkins again; he'd gotten another band together as soon as we left his employ. One day we were chewing the fat, and our record came on. The Hawk said, "Son, you're gonna have to forget this Canadian Squires thing because American record companies won't *touch* a Canadian group. Take my word for it. They know the Canadian market is so small they won't get their money back."

We knew then that things had to change.

We cut again in New York in early 1965 under our own name, Levon and the Hawks. Henry Glover was producing, and an engineer named Phil Ramone was at the board, if I remember correctly. Robbie came up with "The Stones That I Throw" and "He Don't Love You," and Richard sang lead on both. They were released on Atlantic's Atco subsidiary in 1965, but we never heard them on a jukebox anywhere. (We also cut a sped-up version of "Little Liza Jane" that we called "Go Go Liza Jane," but this remained unreleased.)

In April 1965 we were back in Helena, staying at Charlie Halbert's motel. We'd been hired by the Marvell High class of '65 to play the combined junior-senior prom. It was planting time in cotton country, and the air was thick with the familiar scent of spring soil and the humid atmosphere of the delta; a wonderful time to be home. My family had relocated, but we still had a lot of friends and kin in the area, so we stayed on a few days after the prom. I think we might have played the Catholic Club in Helena a couple of nights as well.

We woke up late one day and went out to breakfast. Bill Avis turned on the radio:

Clang! "It's *King Biscuit Time*! Pass the biscuits!"

And we hear Sonny Boy Williamson, Peck Curtis, Pinetop Perkins, and Houston Stackhouse wailing the blues on KFFA at twelve-fifteen in the afternoon.

"Holy shit!" Richard said. "I can't believe these guys are still doing this!"

"That's right, folks," announcer "Sunshine" Sonny Payne is saying, "Sonny Boy has just returned from a tour overseas where he has played for the armed services and nightspots in London, Paris, Rome, Berlin, Copenhagen, and many other cities in Europe. So to get the show on the road, here he is: the man in the spike-toed shoes . . . your favorite radio entertainer . . . the king of the harmonica . . . Sonny Boy Williamson in person playing 'V-8 Ford Blues'!"

But Sonny Boy doesn't go right into it. "Just before we do this number, ladies and gentlemen: Tonight's the big night in Greenwood, Mississippi. Don't forget that—yassir!—in Greenwood, Mississippi, tonight. Don't try to meet me there, *beat* me there! Yah!" And the band crashes into the show's first song.

"Hey, Levon," Garth says. "You know where everything is around here. Let's go look for Sonny Boy. Maybe we could hang with him a little."

What followed was the most magical day of our lives.

We stopped in at Mr. Gist's music store, where we were told that Sonny Boy Williamson had indeed just come back from Europe. "He's hot as a firecracker," Mr. Gist said. "Never sounded better. You can probably find him down at the building he's renting from me." We found Sonny Boy walking down the street. Not that it was possible to miss him, at six feet three inches, with a white goatee and a three-piece suit of alternating gray and charcoal-gray flannel he'd had made in England. Plus a derby hat and a brown attaché case for his harps. There was no one else even remotely like Sonny Boy Williamson walking around Helena that day.

We pulled up slowly, and I got out of the car. Sonny Boy didn't even look that surprised to see a white boy accosting him on the street. I said, "Excuse me, Mr. Williamson, but my name is Lavon Helm from Marvell, and I grew up listening to you, and we have a pretty good band here"—I gestured over to the Mercury, where the boys were waiting—"and we wanted to know if you might be interested in going somewhere and playing a little music with us."

He didn't say anything for a moment; just looked at us. Sonny Boy had an intimidating reputation—it was well known that he carried a big knife and would cut anyone who fucked with him—but we weren't intimidated because we had nothing but respect and good intentions toward him. Finally he said OK and got in the car. He didn't say much at first, but we'd caught him on the right day and managed to get him back to the Rainbow Inn Motel in West Helena. There we had a set of drums and a couple of amps set up for rehearsal. We ended up jamming for the rest of the afternoon. Whatever Sonny Boy wanted to do, we just followed him and made sure he had plenty of ice in his cup.

After a while, Sonny Boy put down his harmonica and spat into a tin can. I assumed he was chewing tobacco. "You boys sure can play," he rasped. "Where you been playin'? You know, I'm seventy years old, and you got one of the best bands I've heard." He spat into the can and coughed. We started to play again, and I noticed he was watching us carefully. He was used to showing off for the young English bands he'd been playing with, but now he knew something was happening. He was looking at Robbie like, *Where the hell did this kid learn that?* Then he'd pass the ball to Garth or over to Richard, and Sonny Boy would get a big smile on his face. We could tell that he liked us, liked our readiness to break the rules. Right then and there we began thinking, *Why can't we be Sonny Boy's band?*

We kept on playing. Sonny Boy worked his harmonica like a damn brass section, backward and inside out. He played it sticking out of his mouth like a cigar! He put the whole harp inside his mouth and played. Then he'd spit in the can before calling another tune. In the end he about wrung us out, before inviting us to a local booze camp he liked to frequent. Before we left, Robbie happened to glance at the can that Sonny Boy had been spitting in. It was full of blood.

The booze camp turned out to be some woman's shack way up a dark lane in a bad part of Helena. She sold homemade whiskey, illegal bootleg stuff. She was cooking something over an open fire, and it smelled delicious. "Here, boys," Sonny Boy said, dipping a teaspoon into a jar full of clear corn liquor. "She calls this stuff 'Blind Tiger.' " The five of us each drank a spoonful, and in five minutes we were somewhere between stone drunk and flying on acid. Sonny Boy bought and guzzled this stuff by the pint, while we bought maybe a half-pint among ourselves. Each of us had no more than a sip and a half, and we could barely stand up! But Sonny Boy would laugh and talk and drink. He was getting more comfortable, and that's what we were after. We just wanted to hang out with him. He told us about some English kids he'd played and recorded with over in London: the Yardbirds (with Eric Clapton), the Animals, Them (with Van Morrison), and many more, including Jimmy Page, then a busy session guitarist. Sonny Boy had gone to a tailor and had a few of these wild two-tone flannel suits made. He mentioned that he liked England but didn't like the food. In fact, he'd almost burned down his hotel in Birmingham when he tried to stew a rabbit in an electric coffee percolator and blew out the building's fuses and wiring.

"Those kids over there," he said with a laugh, "they *loved* me. They'd buy me things and treat me like I was God. Hah! They all wanted to play with me—paid good money, too. They love the blues, man. And some of those cats are serious players. That's right. A few of those English cats surprised me. Damned if they didn't. You might be hearing about some of them sons of bitches, damn straight . . ."

By now it was eight or nine o'clock, and other people were coming in or just lurking in the shadows. Word of five white boys drinking with Sonny Boy spread around the area, and soon people were whispering to us to come outside so they could sell us some corn, or dope, or women. "Anything you want, man." They wouldn't come in because they were too scared of Sonny Boy. One guy did approach Sonny Boy and boasted that he was a harmonica player too. "You can't play anything," Sonny Boy growled. "Don't pull that shit on me. Go to Chicago and make me some damn records if you're so good."

Finally the local hustlers really got after us, and Sonny Boy said, "Fellas, let's be on our way out of here. As you can see, there are some folks around here that don't respect my position in the world of music. Why don't we go over and get some barbecue."

On the way over to this barbecue place, Sonny Boy asked what we were doing, where we were going. We explained that we had some jobs up in New Jersey, but that if he was interested we'd come back down and play with him, be his band. Why shouldn't we team up? With us behind him he could be one of the most powerful acts in the world. So we made some big plans to be Sonny Boy's band and sat down to some good barbecue in a place I'd been eating in all my life in the black part of town. We ordered sandwiches, coleslaw, and some sodas. While we waited, someone asked Sonny Boy whether he'd known Robert Johnson. *"Knew him?"* Sonny Boy asked incredulously. "Boy, Robert Johnson *died in my arms!*"

Just then three police cars roared up to the restaurant with their sirens going and their lights flashing. Just like that. They looked at our new '65 Mercury out front with the Ontario plates, got out, hitched up their pants, and came inside. One of 'em demanded, "Just what the fuck is going on here?" This was during the civil-rights days of freedom riders and voter-registration drives and "troublemakers" and "outside agitators." I whispered to the guys, "Be cool and let me handle this."

I got up to meet the cops, cursing myself because I hadn't been thinking and didn't want the guys to witness this kind of shit. "Good evening, officers," I said. "Is there a problem?"

"Oh, there ain't no problem," one answered. "Not as long as you don't mind sitting here eating with a bunch of niggers, there ain't no problem."

I tried to charm the cop. "Sir, my name is Lavon Helm, from over in Marvell, and my uncle is Deputy Sheriff Alan Cooper over there and—"

"Well, I guess Deputy Cooper'd be real proud of you down here in niggertown eating with a bunch of goddamn niggers."

I looked at Sonny Boy, real embarrassed. But he kept eating and didn't say a word.

"Let me tell you something," I said to the cop. "These boys here are from Canada. They don't know nothin' about the bullshit you're trying to sell us. And anyway, we're not breaking any law. We're just trying to eat. Good barbecue is good barbecue."

"Now, you listen up," the cop says. "Here's what's happening: You all are gonna get in that new car of yours, and you say you're from around here, so you know the quickest fuckin' way out of town. And we don't wanna see you around here no more, because maybe they put up with this shit over in Marvell, but this is Helena, and we don't like strangers coming down and eating with a fuckin' bunch of niggers. Now, are we all agreed on this?"

I lost it then. "Goddammit, do you know who this man is? He's famous the whole world over! This is Sonny Boy Williamson, and it's an honor for us to be in his presence!''

The cop just kept looking around. "See that shiny car of yours? Well, maybe you all better do as you're goddamn well told while it's still shiny; while you still have that car . . .''

It was a bit of a Mexican standoff. The guy that owned the place cussed out the cops and told us, "It's all right, gentlemen. Just set and eat your sandwiches; ain't nothin' gonna happen." But our appetites were gone. We mumbled around and finally got out of there, since the next step was to get the shit beat out of us by a bunch of cops. Three civil-rights workers had been murdered in Mississippi the previous summer.

So they ran us out of town. We went back to the motel, got our stuff, and escaped up to Fayetteville, back into the mountains. I hated for the other fellas to see that kind of prejudice up close. We'd had such a glorious day, playing with Sonny Boy and listening to his stories. We'd had only another half hour to go, and everything would've been perfect. We felt bad about leaving Sonny Boy behind. We said, "Don't worry about us, Mr. Williamson. We'll stay in touch. We wanna be your band and have a great time doing it." He smiled, because he wanted to play with us too. He knew we weren't some little outfit that just wanted to jerk off.

Instead of returning to Canada, we headed for the New Jersey shore and the Wildwood–Atlantic City summer circuit. During May and June we played Tony Mart's Nite Spot in Somers Point, just south of Atlantic City. Bill Avis brought us over because he'd worked the Female Beatles there. Tony's place was said to be the biggest teenage nightclub in the East: three stages, seven bars, and fifteen cash registers. There were stools around the bars, no chairs, and the capacity was supposedly thirteen hundred, but twice that many college kids crammed into the place on weekends. It was elbow to elbow. Tony would rotate three groups. As soon as one band finished, the next was supposed to pick up immediately on another stage. Tony didn't want any time to go by between numbers, and if you could make the other band's last note your first, well, Tony liked that. He also had go-go dancers Gail and Christine (advertised in the Atlantic City *Press* as "torrid television personalities'' because they'd appeared on a dance show in Philadel-phia once), as well as our favorite, Charlotte Kersten, or ''Twistin' Miss Germany,'' as she was better known. We played there with some of the best groups in the country: the Skyliners from Pittsburgh (''Since I Don't Have You''), the Fendermen (''Mule Skinner Blues''), Herb Lance and the Classics (''Blue Moon''), and countless others. We tried to top all of these, but then Tony would bring in Conway Twitty, and we'd have to button down our collars and try a little harder.

We kept talking about Sonny Boy Williamson. How could we work with him? We talked to Colonel Kudlets back in Hamilton. What did he think? ''It's gonna be hard,'' he said. ''Where are you going to play? Not in the South. Not up here. Not in most places. It's a great idea, but it's before its time. No one's done anything like it yet.''

Late in May a letter reached us in New Jersey telling us that Sonny Boy Williamson had died at home in Helena. We felt terrible about it, and for me it marked the end of the era I'd grown up in.

Back in Toronto we decided to record some demo tapes and send them around to some names we knew in New York that might help us get into the record business. We recorded something in a little studio in Toronto and sent off three, maybe four copies. In about a week we got a telegram from a well-known music bizzer we'll call Eric Schuster.

HAVE RECEIVED TAPE—CONTACT ME IN NY IMMEDI-ATELY.

Oh, God, I thought. *This is it!*

I called them up and spoke to Eric's right-hand man, who'd sent the telegram. He gushed, ''I can't *believe* how *excited* Eric is about your tape. He's in a complete *state* about it! How soon can you boys get here so we can meet you?''

An hour later Robbie, Bill Avis, and I were on our way to New York. Richard and Rick took turns holding the phone in Toronto. We got to New York, checked into the Hotel Forrest on Forty-ninth Street off Broadway, cabbed over to Eric's office near Columbus Circle, and met the guy I'd talked to on the phone. ''I'm 'The Ear' around here,'' he told us breathlessly. ''Thank God you're safely here! I've never seen Eric so *psyched up* about a group in my life! And the thing is, groups are supposed to be very 'out' right now.''

We walk into the office. Eric Schuster is there with musician Al Kooper—who'd cowritten Gary Lewis and the Playboys' recent No.

1, "This Diamond Ring"—and a couple of guys with that Greenwich Village Musician look: long, curly hair, pinched jackets, shades, tight pants, Cuban-heeled boots. They all give us the eye; to them we're a bunch of greasers from Toronto in leather jackets. Eric is sitting behind this giant semicircular desk, smoking a cigar. We light up as well.

He looks over at me and gasps in Brooklynese, "So how many ya got inna band?"

"Well, sir, we got us a bass player, guitar player, drum—"

Phone rings. "OH, YEAH? *FUCK YOU TOO!* I GOT GENE PIT-NEY MORE FUCKIN' PUBLISHING MONEY THAN YOU REC-ORD GUYS EVER GOT HIM!" *Wham!* He hangs up and looks back over to me.

"So whatta youse wanna do? Make a record or what?"

"Well, sir, I'll tell you want we want to do. We want to get in those old Atlantic Studios where Ray Charles cut 'Hallelujah (I Love Her So),' and we want to make some hit records too. That's all."

Eric gets excited. "That's right, goddammit, some hit records! And be on the *Sullivan* show. You wanna be on *Sullivan*? They owe me a favor over there. Hey! I made Gene Pitney a millionaire," he shouts. "If you wanna be a millionaire too, just keep your mouth shut and listen. Are you all here in New York? Whaddaya mean they're in Canada?! Get 'em down here right now, have 'em in my office tomorrow. We'll sign the contract and be in the studio tomorrow night. I'm gonna make you the biggest act ever to get out of Canada."

Al Kooper and the others smiled at this. We were smiling too. It looked like our dreams were coming true. I called Rick, Richard, and Garth and told them to come on down. I even called a couple of buddies in Arkansas and told them to load up and head to New York to help us celebrate at Atlantic Studios the next night.

Back at the hotel we started talking to Doc Pomus, the famous songwriter. He liked to hang around the Forrest because it was a musicians hotel, and he was always selling songs to people. He kind of had a little office at the end of the registration desk, and he'd be there on his crutches (he'd recently suffered a serious fall) with some coffee and sacks of donuts, working the telephone and conferring with people. I told him about our meeting, and he let me know that the gentleman we were dealing with wasn't exactly burdened by a great reputation within the music industry. "Watch out, boys," growled Doc.

This made me remember back to 1959, when Ronnie Hawkins came back to Canada with his first Roulette recording contract. The Hawk hadn't look as thrilled as he might have, and I'd asked, "How bad is it?"

"Life, with an option," he'd murmured. (Later, when he was pissed off at Morris Levy, Hawk would fulminate, "I'd give an inch of my peter to get out of that contract, and I ain't got an inch to spare.")

Next day, everyone else came in. It was the five of us and Bill. At noon I went into Eric's office. He wasn't around, but The Ear was. I said, "I'm here to pick up the contract so we can have our attorney check it out. The rest of the band is asleep at the hotel so they can be fresh tonight when we sign." I took the contract over to Henry Glover's office in midtown. Henry was doing independent production work, and as a favor he said he'd look over the deal that Eric was offering.

My heart sank as I watched Henry's face while he went over the figures. Finally he threw the contract on the desk and said, "I told you boys, there's these two words: 'retail' and 'wholesale.' Now, look at this right here, and right here, and again right here. This is an even worse deal than the one Morris Levy gave Ronnie, and that was pretty bad. You boys will have to pay each other because nobody else is going to be paying you! You're going to end up paying Eric Schuster every cent you make."

It was life with *no* option.

Henry gave us the hardest advice we could stand. The contract was a complete rip-off. I didn't want to hear it, but I knew he was right. We all talked about it back at the hotel. We were so anxious—chainsmoking, pacing—because by that point we were ready to do anything for a chance to record.

At four o'clock we all went to Eric's office. The Ear is trotting about in excitement. Eric is behind his desk.

"You boys have a chance to look over the contract?"

"Well, actually, sir—"

Phone rings. "TELL DICK CLARK I'M TOO BUSY. CALL BACK IN AN HOUR!" We noticed that Eric had these buttons at his feet. He'd ask you something, you'd be about to answer, he'd step on a button, and the phone would go off! Meanwhile, we're trying to hold out some hope. Back at the hotel Richard had plaintively suggested, "Maybe he only wants *half* of it."

Big Eric is talking again. "Where were we?"

I hear myself saying, "Look, Mr. Schuster, we can't sign these contracts the way they're written. Would it be possible—"

"I don't believe this!" he shouts. "Fuck this shit! You can fucking take it or you can fucking leave it! I don't need this shit!"

"Look, Eric," I try, "we didn't come all this way to Manhattan to be losers. We want to sign with you, but this contract would—"

He gets up. "I ain't got no fuckin' time to argue with youse guys! You either wanna do something for your careers or you don't!" And he walks out, slamming the door behind him.

The Ear looks over sympathetically. "C'mon, guys," he clucks. "Do you *really* want to blow this? Go back to Canada and play those silly clubs? Shouldn't you be *doing* something for yourselves?"

I tell him, "There's five of us, and Bill here, but the papers say Eric gets everything while we get to go along for the ride. No, thank you, sir."

And we walk out.

We slunk back to the Forrest. Doc Pomus was by the desk as we dragged ourselves through the lobby. He took one look at my face—I couldn't say anything—and said, "Sorry, guys. Sorry." Just then our Arkansas friends pulled in. They thought we were going into Atlantic Studios that night. We were all up in my room, talking it over, when the phone rang. Richard picked it up. It was Eric. Richard handed off to me.

"You little punk!" Eric screamed. "You'll never amount to *spit* in the music business! Got it? I see better groups than you assholes come and go every fucking day. There are hundreds like you, only better!"

"You big load of bullshit," I told him. "You told me you had big ideas for us, but you didn't have no idea except to horse-fuck us."

"You fucking little punk. You'll never get a better deal in this town! You ain't gonna be *spit*!"

I lost my head. "Hey, fuck yourself, you cheap son of a bitch! Got no feelings about running right over people's dreams and hopes and prayers. You oughta hop in a cab and get off at the Forrest Hotel and let me *warp your goddamn ass to the sidewalk a couple of times*!"

Maybe that was too much, I thought. Eric wasn't any water lily. He was a big guy from the Morris Levy school, this was his home turf, and now he was really screaming in my ear. "Ah, fuck you, ya little punk, I'm gonna—"

I hung up on him. We were pretty shaken up by then.

After the call we pulled out a couple of pacifiers that someone had laid on us, and we had a smoke to try to calm ourselves down. We were at a loss. Morris Levy was the only other name we knew in New York, and he had passed on our demo tape. A friend from Toronto, Mary Martin, worked for a guy named Albert Grossman, who managed some folk singers we were aware of, but we didn't think our music was really his style. "Looks like it's back to the bars for a while," I told the others. "But we'll get us another shot. I'll call Henry Glover right now."

Our Arkansas friends, meanwhile, weren't used to marijuana, weren't used to New York, and had stumbled into a real downer. They froze at a hard knock on my door. It was John Hammond, Jr., in his fringed buckskin jacket. He had a guy with him—might have been John Sebastian of the Lovin' Spoonful—with real long hair, boots, and a leather bandolier for his harmonicas. These boys helped us commiserate. We were all having a good time when a couple of police cars pulled up to the hotel, flashing red lights and all. It didn't having anything to do with us, but it was the last straw for my buddy Charlie from Arkansas, who was stoned and paranoid and figured this was a big-city pot bust. He took off out the door, down the hall, and through the fire exit, setting off the alarm, and headed down the stairwell. I chased after him, yelling, "Stop, Charlie! Ain't nothin' wrong, buddy!" but he was *gone.*

Richard Manuel asked, "What's he gonna do when he hits bottom?" I didn't know, so I got in the elevator, and by the time I reached Charlie he was in a doorway in an alley behind the hotel, with two uniformed New York cops asking why he was breathing so heavy. I stepped in to do the talking. "Look, officer, everything's A-OK. The bills are paid, no problem with the hotel; you can check the front desk. They know us here. This friend of mine just drove up from Arkansas and got some really disturbing news from home, and he just ain't himself . . ."

One cop said, "Well, you better get him back upstairs or back to

Arkansas, but get him the hell out of here." There's the spirit of 1965 for you. So we put those boys back on the road to Arkansas, headed north to Canada, and hoped Eric Schuster was going to hell.

Bill Avis had left our other station wagon at the Toronto airport, so that's where we drove after we crossed the border at Buffalo. There was a seventy-mile-per-hour speed limit on the Queen E, and I was doing at least ninety, smoking my old briar pipe as we cruised along. At the airport, as I pulled up to the parking garage, someone suddenly yanked open my door. An arm reached across me and turned the key off, then people were grabbing me. Someone pulled the pipe out of my mouth and barked, "Metropolitan police! Outside!"

Yes sir!

We were surrounded by Toronto cops and Mounties. Dozens of 'em, with guns drawn and pointed at us. Robbie looked at me in total disbelief. Garth was in shock. Rick was yelling at the cops, wanting to know what was going on. They told us to shut up and marched us down to a basement room you never want to go in, believe me. They brought in our luggage and searched it. They might've found an old pack of papers and a couple of seeds. Then they took the two cars apart. *Dismantled* 'em. Found maybe half an ounce of pot stuffed between the backseat cushions. So they arrested the six of us for marijuana smuggling.

The cops were real proud of themselves. They told us how they had picked us up at the border and followed us all the way into Toronto. They had eight cars on our tail. "You drove so fast we even lost you a couple times," one of 'em told me. But they were ahead of us too and found us again on the highway that cuts between the lake shore and Route 401. Damn!

We had Bill Avis call the Colonel and tell him what happened. The Colonel called Jack Fischer, God love him, who owned the Commodore Hotel, where we played a lot. Bail was set at ten grand apiece. Jack and the Colonel put up the sixty grand and bailed us out. This was on a Friday, and it hit the *Toronto Star* that weekend: TORONTO POP GROUP SEIZED!!

Our families were devastated. Rick's picture was on the front page of the *Simcoe Recorder*. Garth's parents . . . Mama Kosh . . . Ed and Gladys Manuel. Thank God Diamond and Nell didn't find out right away. Funny thing was, next week in Toronto we had the biggest crowds we'd seen in years. They were lined up around the block to hear us.

After we got out of jail, and after we could all calm down and get settled enough to talk, we figured out what had happened. It looked as though Rick's girlfriend Christine, the same one that the Hawk had caught him with, had this boyfriend, or at least some guy, who was jealous.

"We got set up," Rick agrees in retrospect. "This guy was trying to impress my girlfriend. None of us would have known him, but he knew what time we were coming through the border that day, and he told the Royal Canadian Mounted Police that we were bringing in a trunkful of pot. Major pot dealers, right? And in those days you could go to jail for five years for smoking three joints from a nickel bag. So at the airport this one tough fucker hauls me out of the car with one hand, my feet off the ground, while frisking me with the other hand, saying, 'What have we got here?'

"The high point was that this one RCMP found an ounce of Panama Red in the topcoat I was wearing. He says, 'Mr. Danko, I'm going to see that you go to jail for thirty years for importing narcotics.' The Mountie always gets his man, right? So then he asked where I got the stuff.

"I said, 'Well, sir, this black guy named King gave it to me outside of Birdland. I never even tried it. You know the way God works, this arrest may have been for the best because I haven't even had a chance to try any of this marijuana yet. Maybe there's a lesson to be learned here.' "

We had to go to court, off and on, for what seemed like years. The Colonel found us an attorney who postponed everything. Then we started to see the cops who arrested us coming to the Le Coq D'Or or Friar's Tavern, but now they were cheering us. A couple of them brought along their wives. We even made friends with a few. Soon the story started to die down, but there was this one tough cop who just wanted to see us all in jail.

Rick: "So Levon spoke to this chick he was dating. Her name was Kathy, and she was the most beautiful girl in Toronto. Richard used to say that Kathy made Brooke Shields look like a dog. We knew her through our friend 'No Knees Joyce,' a telephone operator who liked us and let us make our long-distance calls for free. Kathy was sixteen years old when we met her, and she was a gorgeous, gorgeous lady. She looked beautiful, and no one could resist her. Anyway, Levon explained the situation to her, and she kindly gave this cop who was trying to crucify us a blow job. Then she told him she was fourteen years old. He was the chief witness against us, but this was some *weird shit* for him, and he disappeared, and we never saw him again. In the end everyone else got off, and I received a year's suspended sentence on probation.''

In August 1965 we were back in Somers Point on the Jersey Shore, playing Tony Mart's Nite Spot. The marquee read:
THREE GREAT BANDS THREE—OVER 110,000 HAVE PROCLAIMED THEM CANADA'S GREATEST—LEVON AND THE HAWKS—PLUS—DIRECT FROM ENGLAND—THE FUNATICS—GO-GO, COMEDY AND SHOW— PLUS—THE PAWNS, AND THE GO-GO GIRLS—GAIL AND CHRISTINE.

This was the middle of summer, and we were hearing this long record on the radio. "How does it feel . . . to be on your own . . . like a rolling stone."

Robbie Robertson said, "That's a long record. It's gotta be six, seven minutes long."

"Sure has got a lotta words in it," Richard remarked. Garth liked the organ part.

We knew who it was.

Halfway through August someone handed me the phone backstage at Tony Mart's.

"This is Bob Dylan calling," said a voice on the other end.

"Yes sir," I said. "What can I do for you?"

Long pause. "Well, um . . . uh, howja like to play the Hollywood Bowl?"

I think I swallowed before asking, "Who else is on the bill?"

"Just us," said Bob.

Chapter Five

DYLAN GOES ELECTRIC

Lo and behold!

Bob needed a group. We needed a break.

The two needs coincided.

If my memory serves me well, Bob also mentioned that we'd be playing a show at Forest Hills, Queens, late in August, before the Hollywood Bowl date in early September. The shows would be half acoustic and half electric, with the band coming in on the second part of the show. I asked how he'd heard about us, and I think he mentioned some people who'd told him about us when they heard he was looking for a rock and roll band; people like Mary Martin and John Hammond, whose father, John Hammond, Sr., had discovered and signed Bob in the first place. Truth was, the Hawks were *the* band to know about back then. It was an "underground" thing, if you know what I mean. We were like a state secret among hip musical people because nobody else was as tight as we were.

The phone call ended up with me telling Bob that we were real interested in his proposal, that I'd talk to the other boys and get back to him the next day. Then I called the Colonel to see if Bob Dylan could actually sell out these places he was talking about. We'd heard him on the radio, but we didn't have his records, so we had no idea

129

how big Bob Dylan was. Colonel Kudlets assured us that Bob Dylan was indeed big time.

"Mary Martin would fly home on weekends and come down to our matinees," Rick Danko recalls. "She was a good friend of a local group called the Dirty Shames. They did jug-band music and comedy, like the Smothers Brothers, really good. We got to know Mary, and she turned us on to some of the people in Albert Grossman's stable: Gordon Lightfoot, Richie Havens, Peter, Paul, and Mary, and this guy called Bob Dylan. We were going through our jazz period: handmade suits in different styles, very cool. One day she and her girlfriend came to our hotel to wake me up for our matinee, and she brought me Bob Dylan's album *Highway 61 Revisited*. It was about to come out. It was the first time any of us had ever heard him. Next thing I knew, Mary was calling me up to tell me that Bob was looking for a group, and she was telling him about the band."

There was initial skepticism among the band when I told them about the call, because Bob was looking only for a guitar player and a drummer for these shows. He wanted Robbie and me, and I think I was actually his second call after the first guy couldn't make it. And Bob Dylan was unknown to us. I knew he was a folksinger and song-writer whose hero was Woody Guthrie. And that's it. I'd not heard him, aside from *Highway 61 Revisited*. I was into Muddy, B. B. King, and I thought Ray Charles had the best band. I had a Newcombe portable turntable that folded onto its own speaker—monaural, of course—that I'd bought at Manny's music store during that Peppermint Lounge job in 1964. It had three gears and a little dial so you could vary the turntable speed. That way, if you wanted to study the drum lick on "Sticks and Stones" by Ray Charles you could switch it to 33 rpm and then gear down and really listen to how he did it. I was into dance music, something that I could sit around and really dig: Junior Parker, with everybody cracking, everything laying in the pocket—then I'm home. I'd carry this thing on the road so we'd be able to have a party if we needed to. Junior Parker, Sonny Boy, especially Jimmy Reed—you had to have his songs.

To me Bob Dylan was a songwriter, a troubadour kind of guy; just him and a guitar. "He's a *strummer*," Richard said derisively when he heard about the deal. That was a word we had for folksters back then, when we were snobby. We knew he was involved with Joan

Baez and the civil-rights movement, and that Bob had written "Blowin' in the Wind." Some of his records sounded like country music to me, but the songs were just a little bit longer. But that was all right by me. Bob had said this would be an experiment, and we were foolish enough to take him up on it.

We heard from Mary Martin that Bob had sent some of his people down to see us at Tony Mart's. Then Robbie went up to New York to see Bob. They met in a studio somewhere, and Bob was looking at a bunch of electric guitars, trying to figure out which ones to buy. This was Robbie's thing. Back in Toronto he'd get a new guitar, use it a couple of weeks, then sell it to some kid who'd tell all his friends that he was playing Robbie Robertson's guitar. There were hundreds of these floating around, so I'm told. Anyway, Robbie could tell Bob about electric guitars: "Get this one, get that one, this one's a joke." Then they sat on a couch in a room with a couple of guitars. It was the first time Robbie had heard Bob, and he was playing a little rough, and Dylan seemed to want it that way.

Because Bob was going electric. That spring he had done an acoustic tour of Britain, immortalized in the D. A. Pennebaker documentary *Don't Look Back,* and after hanging with some of the Beatles and seeing what the Rolling Stones were doing, I guess he felt he had to change clothes and get himself a band. Mary Martin let us know that a month earlier, in July, Bob had played the Newport Folk Festival with Al Kooper and members of Paul Butterfield's band, including our friend Mike Bloomfield. When Bob brought out the band halfway through the show, the audience booed. The folksters hated the band. There was almost a riot, and they made him stop. Bob was forced to come back with an acoustic guitar and sing "Mr. Tambourine Man." It had shaken him up. Now Bob *had* to go electric, *had* to get this loud, passionate, explosive sound into his music. Thinking back on it, after they'd booed him at Newport, Bob Dylan probably didn't have any choice.

I met Bob for the first time in a New York rehearsal studio. Robbie and I had driven up from New Jersey, where we were in the third month of our stand at Tony Mart's. Robbie hadn't been impressed with the drummer Bob was using and suggested he hire me instead, so I had come to sit in on a rehearsal. Bob was wearing some mod-style clothes he'd bought in England: a red and blue op-art shirt, a narrow-waisted jacket, black pegged pants, pointy black Beatle boots.

I stuck out my hand when Robbie introduced me. "Nice to see you," Bob Dylan said. "Thanks for coming up."

We talked while Al Kooper and bassist Harvey Brooks set up to play. Robbie said we'd heard about the problems at Newport. "That's right," Bob said. "I got booed. You heard about that? I went on as usual, did a few songs, and they seemed to like it. Then Butterfield's band came out, and we were gonna do five numbers from the new album, and people seemed to like it until we started having sound problems. The people down front tried to tell us about it, because we couldn't hear ourselves, and the people behind them thought that the ones up front were booing, and they started to boo. They were yelling, 'Get rid of the band and that electric guitar!' We had to leave the stage. It was bullshit. You shoulda heard it, man. Pretty soon they were all booing."

"Well," Robbie observed, "they're the folk scene. They want their folk music and nothing else."

Bob laughed. "Yeah . . . but I don't know about that. We're gonna change all that now anyway."

Then Bob's manager, Albert Grossman, came in. We shook hands. He was a big guy with long gray hair and rumpled clothes. He reminded you of Benjamin Franklin, but gruff and unfriendly. He'd been a nightclub owner in Greenwich Village and now managed Dylan, Peter, Paul, and Mary, and many others. Albert explained that they were going to tour for a year, all over the world: America that fall, Australia and Europe in the spring of 1966, and back through the United States the following summer. The show was split in half, acoustic and electric, and they were looking for a regular group to support the second half of the show. So the boys strapped on their guitars, and I got behind the drums—a black-pearl set like jazz great Elvin Jones had—and we began, ragged at first. Real ragged. We worked out parts for eight or nine songs, from "Tombstone Blues" to "Like a Rolling Stone," and I couldn't believe how many words this guy had in his music, or how he managed to remember them all. Afterward Bob said to me, "You play as well as this other guy, maybe a little better." And so we kind of made a deal to work together.

We had only a couple rehearsals by the time we played Bob's famous show at the Forest Hills Tennis Stadium on August 28, 1965.

Everyone who showed up for the soundcheck that late-summer afternoon knew that this was going to be one of those historic, make-or-break gigs. The times they were a-changin', and the prophet of that change was transforming himself under the highly critical gaze of what Bob sarcastically called "the hootenanny crowd." There'd been an interview with Bob in *The New York Times* that morning, headlined POP SINGERS AND SONG WRITERS RACING DOWN BOB DYLAN'S ROAD. Bob was quoted as saying, "If anyone has any imagination, he'll know what I'm doing. If they don't understand my songs, they're missing something."

We did the soundcheck in front of fifteen thousand empty seats. It was Robbie on guitar, me on drums, Al Kooper on organ, and Harvey Brooks, whose bass really rocked the big, empty bowl. Bob stood alone at the mike, his hair ruffled by the breeze. He seemed very thin and fragile, and didn't say much to people he didn't know that well, but I knew this guy was like a volcano. He was hot. The press was starting to call his music folk rock, although that really applied more to people who were covering his songs on the radio, like the Byrds and Sonny and Cher. I had the idea that soon the whole scheme of American music was going to change. Songs were going to be about ideas beyond the simple solace of the blues or the old let's-ball-tonight attitude of rock and roll.

Forest Hills Tennis Stadium was packed that night. The whole band had come up from New Jersey. I wanted everyone to feel part of the show because I had an inkling of the way things would work out. In the dressing room Albert Grossman told us that only Frank Sinatra and Barbra Streisand had sold out the place that summer. The atmosphere outside was like a big, reverent party. A stiff wind blew low clouds through the darkness overhead. There was an inhuman roar when Bob went out. This was before big concerts were common, and I'd only heard a sound like that—fifteen thousand fans—at a football game. I was sitting backstage with Rick, Garth, and Richard when Bob strapped on his harmonica and guitar and went out. Meanwhile Albert Grossman was going nuts because deejay Murray the K had taken the stage and was chanting, "*It ain't rock . . . and it ain't folk . . . It's a new thing called Dylan, and its what's happening, baybeeeee!!!*"

"Who the fuck let Murray the K out there?" Albert roared. "Get that asshole out of here!" Albert was threatening to sue as Bob acknowledged the standing ovation.

The crowd had been noisy, but when Bob started to sing, "She's got everything she needs, she's an artist, she don't look back," they got quiet enough. Bob did "She Belongs to Me," "To Romana," and "Gates of Eden" before giving the audience three new songs: "Love Minus Zero/No Limit," "Desolation Row," and "It's All Over Now, Baby Blue." He finished the acoustic part of the show with "Mr. Tambourine Man."

Before we went on, Bob gathered the four of us into a huddle. He said, "We don't know what's gonna happen. It may be a real freak show out there. I want you guys to know this up front. Just keep playing, *no matter how weird it gets.*"

The booing began during the intermission when people saw me and Bill Avis setting up the drums. There was some rhythmic clapping while they waited for Bob, and some conspicuous groaning when Robbie walked onstage in wraparound shades and strapped on the electric guitar. But when Bob came out we blasted into "Tombstone Blues," and I swear to God they didn't know what hit 'em. Robbie fired off a solo like tracer bullets into the crowd, and it was a whole new world. Suddenly Bob was bending and writhing and howling away, and it was real, real, real gone.

The booing started when we finished the number.

"*Boooooooooooooooooooo!*"

"Traitor!"

But some people were clapping, and so we played "I Don't Believe You" and "From a Buick 6."

People booed and yelled between songs. "Yay yay! Shake it up, baby!" "Rock and roll sucks!" "Where's Ringo?!" "Play folk music!" "Where's Dylan?!" Then we did "Just Like Tom Thumb's Blues" and "Maggie's Farm," which sure sounded *incredible* from where I was sitting, but sure enough, after the song someone yelled out, "Scumbag!" and all hell broke loose. We started the intro to "Ballad of a Thin Man," better known as "Mister Jones," and Bob said, "Aw, man, come on, now," as a fight broke out between some mods and rockers. People were being thrown out. People were cursing, but not at Bob. They were mad at us, the band. People were throwing fruit at us! Then some clown crawled up onstage and knocked Al Kooper off his stool. I mean, it was looking ugly.

Bob turned around and looked at me. He laughed and said something to Robbie. To me he yelled, "Looks like the attack of the beatniks around here!" So, storming the bastions of folkster purity, we kept playing "Thin Man" until things cooled down. By the time we rolled into "Like a Rolling Stone" the crowd was singing along. This was, after all, a hit single. I looked out and saw the younger kids—not the old folksters—knew all the words and were singing along. After ninety minutes we left the stage, somewhat shaken, wondering if some of the message had broken through.

Bob huddled with his manager in the wings. We were supposed to go out and play some rock and roll for the encore, but Albert told us there would be none. Bob was pissed off. "Damn beatniks," he muttered.

Six days later we flew out to Los Angeles and played pretty much the same show at the Hollywood Bowl. Afterwards I told Bob I was glad the audience had been more friendly.

"I wish they *had* booed," he said, lighting a cigarette. "It's good publicity. Sells tickets. Let 'em boo all they want."

The band had a long talk on the way back to New Jersey to wind up our residency at Tony Mart's. Robbie and I had an offer to go on the road with Bob, but we didn't want to break up the band. I even had reservations about going with Bob. Ever since we'd left Ronnie, we'd pledged to one another that we were gonna do it by ourselves. Between us we could command seventeen different instruments, and we had Richard, so we never felt we needed a singer to stand up in front. That was always our idea: We were gonna be a band!

"They played Forest Hills and the Hollywood Bowl," Rick Danko remembers, "and Bob wanted Robbie and Levon to join him. And I'm sure Robbie said, 'We've got this band that we play with, and we've been playing together pretty good for some years now, and we'd like to continue to play.' And Bob said, 'When can I hear the band?'

"After that we had a week off, our first in five or six years. We went back to Toronto, played a few nights at Friar's Tavern, and kept a court date resulting from our big bust. That's where I met Bob for the first time.''

Bill Avis adds: "Back in New Jersey we all had a meeting about what was going to happen. Robbie was quiet. Levon was insisting that *no one* was going to get left behind on this one. There was a pact among these men, who'd already been through so much together. The end result was that Levon and I drove into Manhattan after they'd played the Hollywood Bowl. We parked in front of 75 East Fifty-fifth Street and went in to see Albert Grossman. And Levon told Albert, and this is a quote:

" 'Take us all, or don't take anybody.'

"To our surprise—we weren't exactly used to having things go our way—they bought the package, including me as road manager. The Colonel even kept taking his ten percent, like always. Other than that, everything changed. Things got a hell of a lot better.''

We said good-bye and thank you to Tony Mart just before Labor Day 1965. We'd been there since the Fourth of July, and they were sad to see us go, but we were headed back to Toronto. Bob Dylan showed up a few days later to hear the band for the first time. We played at the Friar's Tavern. Our voices were blown from two months in New Jersey and a few days off, so we were mostly playing instrumentals by then, jamming on "Honky Tonk" and "Work Song" (we were still in our Cannonball Adderly period), letting Garth do what he did best. Like everyone else who encounters Garth for the first time, Bob was blown away. He loved the group.

We rehearsed with Bob after they had locked up the place for the night. I have to give him all the credit, because he worked hard with us. He was turning around from being a solo performer and teaching himself how to lead a band. We went through his songs once, trying to strobe those guitars together, and Bob gave us some tapes to listen to.

Bob stayed with us for maybe a week, just hanging out, working on music. He told me he'd wanted to have his own band since he'd left Minnesota in 1961, so this wasn't a big revelation. He was approaching it as an experiment, and I just remember that the atmosphere was real friendly and exciting.

Rick: "We went to court while we were in Toronto and fessed up.

Bob gave a very strong deposition saying we were indispensable to his artistic well-being and couldn't be replaced. Then the witnesses didn't show up, and the judge told us we didn't have to go to jail, so we had to spend a couple of days celebrating and partying. While this was going on, Bob had his mother come up to visit him. I thought that was a nice thing. Mrs. Zimmerman wanted to know where we had our suits tailored, and eventually we took Bob over to see Lou Myles, who made him that brown houndstooth check suit with the pegged waist that he wore all over the world and sang 'One Too Many Mornings' in. It was photographed a lot.''

A couple of weeks later, on September 23, they sent a plane to Toronto to pick us up, and we met Bob at the Municipal Auditorium in Austin, Texas. We had one more rehearsal during the afternoon soundcheck and just started in playing that night.

I was damn sure that no southern audience would possibly boo what Bob was doing, and I was right. The Texas crowd loved Dylan's stuff, and so our first show as Bob Dylan with Levon and the Hawks was a smash. Weeks later, after a lot of booing had gone down elsewhere, Bob told me the Texas audience was the only one who'd understood what we were doing.

The next night we were in Dallas, and they didn't boo us there either. After that we sort of moved to New York, living in hotels. Bob had a place in New York and another hideaway near Albert Grossman's country house in a little upstate New York town called Woodstock.

On October 1 we played Carnegie Hall. The bill read BOB DYLAN W/ LEVON & THE HAWKS. There was some noise when the band came out, but Bob won them over in the end—a pattern that would be repeated for the rest of my time on that tour. The last number of the show was always "Rolling Stone," and at Carnegie Hall a couple of hundred people rushed the stage at the end, shouting for more. I could see Bob standing at the microphone. He was exhausted, spaced out, but really beaming. "Thank you," he mumbled. "I didn't think you'd feel that way."

After Carnegie Hall we went into Columbia Studios in Manhattan and cut our first sides with Bob. "Can You Please Crawl out Your Window" was released as a single in December. We also did another song called "I Wanna Be Your Lover," which was supposed to be a takeoff on "I Wanna Be Your Man," the only song ever recorded by both the Beatles and the Rolling Stones, but it wasn't released contemporaneously.

For the next month we played east of the Mississippi, becoming Bob Dylan's band. We were booed everywhere; by then it had become a ritual. People had heard they were "supposed" to boo when those electric guitars came out. But at the same time we found a *way* of performing with Bob. It was a hell of a challenge, because he was still learning about a band. He would suddenly stop and break the beat, and we'd get confused and not know where we were. We'd look at one another and try to figure out if we were playing great music or total bullshit. The audiences kept booing. We made tapes of the shows and listened to them afterward in the hotel, because we couldn't believe it was that bad that people felt they had to protest, but the tapes sounded good to us. It was just new. Meanwhile, people out front were yelling, "Get rid of the band!" and backstage, people were coming up to Bob and saying—right in front of us sometimes—"Look, Bobby, these bums are *killing* you. They're destroying your career. You're gettin' *murdered* out there. Why do you wanna pollute the purity of your thing with this *dirty, vulgar* rock and roll?"

The more Bob heard this stuff, the more he wanted to drill these songs into the audience. I mean, he was on fire. We didn't mean to play that loud, but Bob told the sound people to turn it up full force. We were the first rock band that played in some of these old arenas and coliseums, and Robbie's guitar used to reverberate around the big concrete buildings like a giant steel bullwhip. It was intense. Bob was hot-wired into it. He usually started as soon as we played a note, really howling at the moon. He'd bend and grind, stage front, miming Robbie's solos while Robbie stood stock-still next to me, out of the spotlight, concentrating on these fireball licks. We could tell a lot of the kids out front thought Bob was soloing, but we didn't care. Sometimes Rick would go out front and dance and sing with Bob a little, but mostly we were in the shadows, trying to be as inconspicuous as possible.

I began to think it was a ridiculous way to make a living: flying to concerts in Bob's thirteen-seat Lodestar, jumping in and out of limousines, and then getting booed. At the same time, we'd have a few days off between shows. We could actually get a breath, a new experience for us. It was getting real strange. We'd never been booed in our lives. As soon as they saw the drums set up during the intermission, it was like, "Light the kerosene!" Sometimes the booing would get to me, especially when they'd throw tomatoes or whatever, and my drums would get stuff on them. A couple of times, when I thought Bob wasn't looking, I'd give 'em the finger. I kept waiting for Bob or Albert Grossman to take us aside and say, "Now, boys, we *told* you it was only an experiment. Sorry it didn't work out." Because I couldn't have taken what Bob endured. We seemed to be the only ones who believed in what we were doing. But the guy absolutely refused to cave in. It was amazing, but Bob insisted on keeping this thing together.

We were seriously booed during a two-night stand at the Back Bay Theater in Boston. That's when it started to get to me. I'd been raised to believe that music was supposed to make people smile and want to party. And here was all this hostility coming back at us. One night Richard said, "How are we going to take this thing to England next year?"

I said, "Richard, it seems a long way around—England—to get where I wanna go. I can take getting booed here; this is my country. But I can't see taking it to Europe and hearing this shit. And anyway, I don't really wanna be anybody's band anymore."

He looked at me and said, "You're gonna leave."

"How did you know?"

"I can just tell," he said. "There isn't a lot for a drummer to do in this music."

I still wanted to see us make some records. I wanted to hear Richard Manuel sing. I wanted to hear Garth Hudson set up those chords. We had an ensemble, and we needed to go in and record.

During November 1965 we went to Minnesota, Ohio, and western New York. Then we did two nights at Massey Hall in Toronto. It was a homecoming for us, but not what the locals were used to, and as usual the response was a mixture of cheers and boos. We were not too thrilled when a local music journalist wrote that Torontonians were surprised to see that a great like Bob Dylan had teamed up with a "third-rate Yonge Street band" like the Hawks. Bob got married on November 25, and the next day we flew out to play two nights in Chicago. More booing.

Our last show that month was in Washington, DC. There'd been a lot of booing and a couple of fights. The vibes were pretty weird. After the show we were coming through the tunnel to the dressing room. A girl reached down from her seat and lunged at Bob's head with a pair of scissors, trying either to get a lock of hair or kill him. In the dressing room, Bob had a scared look in his eyes after that one.

We flew back to New York. We were living in the Irving Hotel, down near Gramercy Park, where Albert Grossman lived. Very late that night, I knocked on Robbie Robertson's door and told him I was pulling out. I said, "You know I've always had the same ambition: *to be our own band*. You had that same ambition too; that was the plan."

He said, "I know that, but Bobby's opening a lot doors for us, man. We're meeting important people, learning how to travel, making contacts that we'd never make otherwise. We're playing three nights a week against six. Jesus, all these years, and we've never had time to think before. Some good's gotta come from this."

I said, "Well, I'm not sure that we're gonna maintain that same policy and ambition for ourselves."

"Yeah, OK," Robbie said, "but what about the *music*? Some of this stuff is incredible. Sometimes I think it's gonna explode."

"Well, I can't always hear it," I told him. "Sometimes I'm afraid of it. Do you remember when we left Tony Mart's?" People had hugged and kissed us and were crying to see us go. My own eyes got a little moist there. "To go from that to being point band for this style of music that Bob can hear, and the rest of us hear as much as we know how, and I myself can't even really hear yet—I want to draw a line for myself. To me, music's always been some good chords and a tight rhythm section. This stuff is too damn powerful for me."

"Lee," he said intently, "we're gonna *find* this music. We're gonna find a way to make it work so that we can get something out of it."

"Not with me, Bubba," I said. "It just ain't my ambition to be anybody's drummer. I've decided to just let this show go on without me for now. Tell the boys that I wish 'em well, and I'll see 'em when it's time to put the thing back together again."

Robbie asked where I was going, and I told him I didn't exactly know, but that they could always find me by calling J.D., my dad down in Springdale, Arkansas.

And that was it.

* * *

Boy, I had mixed feelings as I headed south that morning. On one hand, I'd been proud that I was one of the first drummers that made it easier for Bob to hear himself. I actually enjoyed our times in the studio, rehearsals, the soundchecks. It was great to help him when he had a certain feel that went a certain way. It was great to help him find that common pulse. It was great to meet people like John Lee Hooker, Marlon Brando, beatnik poets from San Francisco, all coming to greet Bob when he came to town.

On the other hand, I wasn't made to be booed. I could look at it and find it kind of funny, at least the part that was directed at me as the drummer. I mean, the Grand Ole Opry used to be the same way; they didn't want any drummers either. But the whole booing thing became heartbreaking, considering the effort Bob was putting out and how easy it would have been for him to play it safe. I was starting to get real pissed off. It was better for me not to be part of that.

Bill Avis recalls: "That was the way it happened. Levon didn't say nothing to no one except Robbie. We got up in the morning, and Levon was gone. Rick said, 'Where's Levon?' and Richard Manuel said, 'He done called it a day.' It shook us up for a minute, but it was also understood. No one liked the booing. No one liked having stuff thrown at them.

"If you ask me, Levon left because of Albert Grossman. Albert was as abrasive as Levon was polite, and so it was just a total personality clash between the two of them. Levon also probably remembered that the Hawks had been his band, and he just didn't feel comfortable not being the leader anymore."

At the time, it wasn't hard to imagine that my days with the band were over. I knew that everyone wanted that recording contract of our own, but maybe it wouldn't work out that way for me.

In my heart, though, I felt this was going to be a temporary thing. In the meantime I'd play with some other people. I intended to go back to Arkansas and play some dances and return to my standard policy, which was to whistle while I worked. When I left Bob's tour, it felt like an immense weight had been lifted from my shoulders. But I also missed my brothers in the Hawks terribly, and the way things worked out, it would be many moons before I saw any of them again.

First I went to Mexico and lived on the beach until I'd spent all my money. Then I met up with Kirby Pennick, a musician friend from Arkansas, and together we discovered that Florida was a bad place to be broke. We were just bumming around. We got the paper, and there was a drive-away Lincoln going from Florida to New Orleans. We just said, "Let's go."

So while the band went off to Australia and Europe, I found myself in New Orleans, a much friendlier town. Canal Street. St. Louis Hotel, between the levee and Jackson Square Park. French Quarter clubs, where Kirby and I played a couple of amateur nights for the prize money. Lots of rounders, comers and go-ers, musicians, gamblers, dealers, Dixie Mafia. Some of those people probably killed Jack Kennedy. There were a lot of characters, and we were always running into people who'd created missions for themselves: *Spy vs. Spy.* I fooled around there for a while until we were so broke we actually needed to work. I was a busboy in a restaurant until they fired me for eating the entrées. The newspaper was advertising high-paying jobs out in the Gulf. That's when we signed on as deckhands with the Aquatic Engineering and Construction Company in Houma, Louisiana:

"Where ya from?"

"Arkansas."

"Sign here."

"Hey, hand! Come on he'p me widdem leads heah. We gonna put a ring around this sucka. Hold this."

Three of us deckhands had to hump this heavy pipe. The master welder would step up, tip his visor so as not to be blinded by the arc light, and zap those leads shut like a surgeon. *Zzzt. Zzzt. Zzzzzzzt.* He'd step back again, cool as the other side of the pillow. We'd be sweating like hogs.

We were on a lay barge, which sat next to an oil rig out in the Gulf of Mexico. It had sleeping quarters, a galley, and a big damn spool with a mile and a half of six-inch pipe coiled around it. We were laying pipe. They had a machine that dug a trench, the pipe would go in, and divers would go down and weld the pipe together. These guys mostly sat around and drank coffee, but when they had to go down one hundred fifty, two hundred feet, they'd get all pumped up preparing for the mission. We laid a quarter mile of pipe while I was on board. I think

I went out twice, because they were pretty good to us. I had a couple of harmonicas, and Kirby was a good guitar player, so we played music for 'em, and they'd let us hide. Some of the guys on that crew: *heavy.* There were people who were hiding out. The foreman was a tough and funny fifty-year-old called Hobo. He'd been in the carnival business, working for some abusive drunk. One night in Texas he'd had enough, and drove the truck with the ferris wheel into Mexico and sold it to a scrap dealer. After that he got into the oil-rig business.

At night we played cards and listened to the radio. "Rainy Day Women #12 & 35" was a big hit, with Bob Dylan singing, "Everybody must get stoned!" It was real funny to hear it and wonder who was playing the drums and how was everyone getting along.

We went to town one time, and I kinda appointed myself foreman. I was the official driver. We went to a Supremes concert, then down to the French Quarter and got *seriously* drunk. I think we ended up at the St. Louis Hotel for two or three days. Then we were broke again and back on the rig.

It was a dangerous job. You could easily get killed out there. One time the night crew hadn't tied down the boom of the crane, and the morning crane operator got up and said, "Hand! Get me a cup of coffee and some cake."

"Sir!" I was in the kitchen, getting three pieces of cake, and I turned around and saw the hook of the crane swing around—the sea was rough that day—and catch that poor son of a bitch in the cab, without a safety helmet. It was awful. Then I started noticing the body bags hanging up on the wall. A helicopter came in and took him away. Someone said they'd have to put a steel plate in his head. I don't know whether he made it or not.

One afternoon, maybe it was in September, the sea started to really pitch. Foreman said, "Helm! Pennick! Get in the crewboat and go out to Number Three"—he pointed to a distant oil rig you could barely see on the horizon—"and bring back them come-alongs and chains and all the bullshit they left out there." We were not too thrilled about this, since it was a long-ass way, and it was starting to blow pretty good, with only about three hours to darkness.

Dolphins are just like dogs. They were in the water and on the water and having the best time of their lives swimming along with us. Over in the west the sky was black, and it was hurricane season; Kirby and

143

I were exchanging nervous glances and smoking lots of Winstons. We got put on that rig, scambled around for those short pieces of chain and some adjustable wrenches, and it started to rain. The sea was raging. We saw the boat coming back, and we threw whatever tools we had on the deck and jumped in after it. "Is that it?" the crew chief yelled. *"That's it!"*

Then we were in the thick of it. The sea was so bad we couldn't reboard our barge. The pilot wanted us to jump between two heaving decks, and we passed on the opportunity. Instead we rode into the shipyard. That's when I took my paycheck, a *good* paycheck, and decided that the Cotton Carnival was coming up, and if I left now and got home in time, the Cavette sisters might allow me to escort them to the festivities.

First I went up to Springdale to touch base and see my folks. I checked in with good friends like Paul Berry in Fayetteville, who told me that Bob Dylan had called a couple of times, trying to find out where I was. I borrowed some money from Paul—whom I'd known for years and whom all of us in the Hawks knew we could count on any time—and hopped another drive-away car to California and hung out with saxophonist Bobby Keyes for a while. I knew Leon Russell out there, and Johnnie Cale, Roger Tillotson, Jesse Ed Davis, and Jimmy Markham—all musicians from the Tulsa area.

Back in Arkansas I played some dances with the Cate Brothers, Earl and Ernie (identical twins) on guitar and keyboard. They had a good little band and were like family, we were so close. In fact, my sister Modena's son, Terry Cagle, became their drummer after I went back to Memphis in the spring of 1967.

I'd heard vague stories that Bob Dylan's world tour had been canceled because of a serious motorcycle accident the previous summer. The boys were in New York, trying to get something going. That was about all I knew. So I borrowed a room from Mary Cavette in Memphis, and studied the Memphis style—Booker T. and the MGs—and watched television for six months while I waited for Lady Luck to deal out her next hand of cards.

In my absence, the collaboration between Bob and Robbie Robertson got more intense. Dylan loved Robbie's playing. "I call it the mathe-

144

matical sound,'' he told a journalist around that time. To another: "Robbie Robertson is the only mathematical guitar genius I've ever run into who does not offend my intestinal nervousness with his rearguard sound.''

They hired Bobby Gregg, the New York studio drummer who played on *Highway 61 Revisited*, to take my place and took it back on the road. They played California for most of December 1965, and everyone came to see them. In San Francisco the city's poets turned out in force: Allen Ginsberg, Lawrence Ferlinghetti (in a Moroccan djellaba) Michael McClure. The music got pretty wild. Bob was running across the stage, playing toe-to-toe, nose-to-nose with Robbie, acting out those lyrics. As much as Robbie played, Garth's organ added that orchestral atmosphere that took it to another level. Rick's craftsmanship and dancing was a counterfoil to Bob on the other side of the stage. ("Rick Danko on bass looked like he could swing Coit Tower," wrote Ralph J. Gleason in the *San Francisco Chronicle* the next day.) They were playing really loud, really on the edge. Garth has tapes from that era that make your hair stand up.

The band was put on retainer around then. In January 1966 they recorded three tracks with Bob in Nashville. The drummer was Sandy Konikoff, whom we knew from Stan Szelest's band the Ravens. (The tracks included a version of "Visions of Johanna" and "She's Your Lover Now.") Three days later in New York they cut again without Garth. These were the early sessions for Bob's new album, *Blonde on Blonde*. The band went on the road in February and March 1966 with Konikoff on drums. Audience reaction remained mixed. They were a hit in Memphis (the Arkansawyers who'd come up for the show knew damn well who was playing the guitar) and got booed in Philadelphia.

Bob and Robbie recorded further in Nashville that March. In April Albert Grossman took the whole thing to Australia with new drummer Mickey Jones, from a New York band called the First Edition. More booing. When they landed in Sydney on April 12, there was a riot at the airport, as hundreds of fans turned out to welcome Bob.

Robbie was very close to Bob in those days, and when he wasn't with Bob he hung out with Albert Grossman. People noticed that Robbie began to change. Bill Avis remembers: "One night in Australia I saw Robbie looking at me funny. He said to me, 'You never liked me as much as you liked Levon.' I didn't know what to say, because

I always did like Robbie. It hurt me, him saying that, and I left the group after that tour was over in May. It looked like things were changing in a way I couldn't get next to.''

After a twenty-seven-hour flight to Sweden, the tour picked up a film crew run by Don Pennebaker, who would film the European part of the tour for ABC television. At the end of April they played Stockholm, where they visited Hamlet's castle and Richard Manuel tried to trade his leather jacket to a Swedish kid in exchange for his beautiful blond girlfriend.

The famous British leg of the tour began in Sheffield on April 30. Bob's acoustic set now consisted of ''She Belongs to Me,'' ''4th Time Around,'' ''Visions of Johanna,'' ''It's All Over Now, Baby Blue,'' ''Desolation Row,'' ''Just Like a Woman,'' and ''Mr. Tambourine Man.'' Standing ovations. Adulation. After an intermission, the curtain parted to reveal the band set up and waiting in front of a giant American flag, which Bob was carrying as a backdrop. This was also a provocation, because the Vietnam War was really heating up, and Bob's Euro audiences expected the Prince of Protest to comment. Instead Bob played in front of the biggest American flag he could find.

The catcalls and booing began before the band roared into ''Tell Me, Momma.'' The set kept building: ''I Don't Believe You,'' ''Baby, Let Me Follow You Down,'' ''Just Like Tom Thumb's Blues,'' the new ''Leopard-Skin Pillbox Hat,'' ''One Too Many Mornings,'' ''Ballad of a Thin Man,'' and ''Like a Rolling Stone.'' The audience would erupt after each song, some shouting approval, others yelling ''Traitor!'' and ''Bloody disgrace!'' This could go on for minutes, during which Bob and Robbie would tune their guitars while waiting for the din to die down so they could play. (In Paris on May 24 Bob tuned for ninety minutes between songs trying to get his guitar and harmonica to sound right together before the band was allowed to resume the show.)

There were surreal press conferences in the major cities—Bob had pretty well joined our accelerated way of living by then—and newspapers in Glasgow, Manchester, and Liverpool splashed pictures of Bob all over their front pages before the shows. Afterward the reviews wrote, ''A pop group could produce better rubbish than that'' and ''He should have left the group in America.'' In Edinburgh one disgruntled customer told the film crew that ''Dylan wants shootin'.'' In Leicester some hoodlums stormed the stage, attacked Bob, and pinned him down before the show could be stopped.

But there were also people who loved the mathematical sound. Local musicians turned out in force to greet the boys backstage. The Spencer Davis Group came by in Birmingham. The Beatles were in the audience during the final show of the tour, at London's Royal Albert Hall on May 27, 1966. This was the show—taped by Columbia Records for a live album, never released, subsequently bootlegged—in which the audience frequently erupts in jeers and rhythmic clapping to show its displeasure with the band, the volume, and the electric Dylan in general. While Bob tuned up for the last song, some idiot in the top balcony yelled *"Judas!"* at the top of his lungs. Bob kept tuning. "I don't *believe* you," he said into the mike, as some people cheered. Robbie turned to the band to start the song. "You're a *liar*," Bob sneered. And as Garth raised the roof with that organ, Bob said, "You're a *fuckin'* liar," to his tormentor as they blasted into "Like a Rolling Stone." According to Rick, hundreds of people walked out.

The Beatles came backstage after the show to commiserate with the boys. John Lennon had been hanging out with Bob at the hotel, and George Harrison was earnestly telling Richard Manuel about meditation. The Beatles were upset by the walkouts and booing, and assured the boys they had been telling people to shut up during the raucous parts of the show. The Hawks were impressed by the contrast between themselves—street kids from the wrong side of the tracks—and the polished Beatles, who wore jackets and ties. Richard told me later that everyone appreciated the respect they received from being Bob's band. It just took everyone to a different level.

Later that night, Bob told Keith Richards of the Rolling Stones that the Hawks were the greatest band in the world. What about us? Keith wanted to know. Bob told him that the Stones were the best philosophers, but that the Hawks were the best band.

Rick Danko explains what happened next:

"We came back from that English tour with Bob pretty fried, man. We were living in New York City, where we'd moved to after playing with Bob. Right after the tour Robbie and I split a two-bedroom suite at the Gramercy Arms Hotel. Then I met this chick named Robin, who was going to summer school, and we shared an apartment in a rent-controlled building on Gramercy Park. We had a great setup.

147

"The original plan was to rest for a couple of months and spend the rest of the year on the road. Then late in July Albert Grossman's office called and said that Bobby had a motorcycle accident in Woodstock and hurt his neck, so the tour was canceled. So there we were. We didn't know what to do. Bob broke some bones in his neck and was in total recuperation mode. We didn't know where Levon was. We were road musicians without a road to go on. We still wanted to record, so we started looking for a place to rehearse some music.

"While I was still living in New York, I started working on a film being produced by Peter Yarrow [of Peter, Paul, and Mary] called *You Are What You Eat*. Bob was in Woodstock and let us know that one of his first projects when he recovered would be to resume filming the movie we'd been shooting in Europe. But that's not how I got to Woodstock. I came up the first time with Richard Manuel as part of Tiny Tim's band for Peter Yarrow's film. It was February 1967. I remember we left the city at about three in the morning so we could film at sunrise. It's about a hundred miles north of Manhattan, so it took us a couple of hours. We were outdoors filming from seven in the morning until three in the afternoon, playing songs in different locations around Woodstock. Richard and I had never been to the Catskills before, and we couldn't believe how beautiful it was, but we were frozen. We went over to Albert Grossman's house and sat in front of a roaring fireplace with his wife, Sally. That day was my introduction to Woodstock. As things happened, Sally Grossman would play a key role in our career, and Woodstock would become our home."

When the early English colonists arrived in New York in 1628, they found the Dutch already there, in New Amsterdam. So they sailed up the North River, as they called the Hudson (the Delaware was the South River), and built a stockade and called it Kingston. The resident Dutch settlers retreated up the valley of Esopus Creek and began to farm the Woodstock valley and the Bearsville flats. According to legend, the Esopus Indians didn't camp in the area but used it for burying their chiefs, and even today the land has a charmed feel about it, protected by great Overlook Mountain and a long chain of only slightly less majestic hills: Indian Head, Ohayo, Mount Guardian, Tobias, Plattekill.

I've heard our local historians suggest that Woodstock's tolerance of artists and show people dates at least to the 1870s, when theater and circus folk began to visit in the summer. Several important artists' colonies were established after 1900 by wealthy New Yorkers seeking a rural alternative to the organized bohemianism of Greenwich Village. The rustic cabins of the Byrdcliffe Colony came first, built over seven old farmsteads under Mead's Mountain and rented out to socially acceptable artists, followed by the Art Students League Summer School in 1906, which moved into the old livery stable. I'm told the young students, with their flowing hair, French berets, and prehippie lifestyle, really shook up the old Dutch Reformed town fathers back then. Painters, sculptors, writers, and composers bought old farmhouses and built cabins on Ohayo Mountain, in Bearsville and Wittenburg, in Hurley and Glenford. Mill Hill Road and Tinker Street in Woodstock sprouted art galleries and academies, which led to a group of artists known as the Woodstock School. By the twenties and thirties, theater people were coming for the summer and putting on plays, and Woodstock had become a full-blown summertime arts colony with a reputation for welcoming talented people who needed a quiet place to work or rest.

Peter Yarrow had spent summers in Woodstock since he was a boy. His mother had some land with a cabin on it, and Peter started bringing up his friends in the early sixties. He was and is a very generous guy. He took Bob Dylan up to Woodstock as early as 1962, and Bobby spent a lot of time up there in that house with his girlfriend, writing songs and playing chess down at the Woodstock Bakery. Milton Glaser, an artist and art director, took Albert Grossman to Woodstock, and Albert fell in love with the place. He bought an old stone house in Bearsville and gave Bob Dylan a private room in back with its own entrance. Immediately, Albert and Sally's became the headquarters of an ever-expanding scene. Albert built a studio complex and a little empire that lasts to this day. This is where Bob met his wife Sara. They got married and moved to an old house in Byrdcliffe in 1965. Their neighbors included composer Aaron Copland and Mason Hoffenberg, best known as the coauthor of the comic-porn novel *Candy*.

After Dylan's motorcycle accident, he teamed up with two filmmakers, Jones and Howard Alk, and began to edit the movie they'd shot in England. Albert Grossman suggested to the band that since they were on retainer, they might as well move up to the country to be closer to Bob, who was getting ready to cut another album. That's how they came to rent the house off Pine Lane in West Saugerties known as . . . Big Pink. "Before we left New York," says Rick Danko, "we went into the studio with John Court, who was Albert Grossman's business partner. The company was called Groscourt Productions. They had this singer, Carly Simon, who they wanted to make into the female Bob Dylan. We cut a couple of things with Carly, like 'Baby, Let Me Follow You Down,' but nothing came of it.

"Next thing you know, we trickle up to the country and land at the Woodstock Motel right in the middle of this quiet little rural town. The owner, Bill, was a great guy. He and Garth became friends, and he went out and found Garth a pipe organ. Garth was interested in Scriabin around then, music and color and all that. Soon people around town started to get to know us. If I was trying to cash a check in the Colonial Pharmacy, someone there might vouch for me by saying, 'Yeah, he's with *the band.*' Meaning Bob Dylan's band. Everyone knew everyone else back then.

"Then we got tired of the motel, and I went house hunting and found Big Pink. It was a pink suburban-looking split-level with three bedrooms and a long view of Overlook Mountain. It came with a hundred acres of woods and fields and had a pond. So Richard, Garth, and I moved in. Robbie rented a house on the Glasco Turnpike in Woodstock with his beautiful French girlfriend, Dominique. She was a journalist whom Robbie had met during Bob's tour. I think they got married right after that.

"Big Pink was our clubhouse. Richard did all the cooking, Garth washed all the dishes (he didn't trust anyone else to do them because he wanted them clean), and I took the garbage to the dump, personally, and kept the fireplace going with split logs. That's how we settled in. We were paid a weekly retainer by Bob, and it was the first time in our lives where we had a chance to relax. We'd been on the road nonstop for six years at that point, and for the first time we didn't have to play joints to stay alive anymore. Then I got Hamlet the dog from Bob Dylan. Hamlet was as big as a bear—a big dog. Albert and Bob had paid about a grand apiece for these pedigreed German dogs that had come from the most illustrious bloodlines in the world, but something went wrong. Hamlet was more like a standard poodle mixed with a German shepherd and a giant shorthaired terrier.

"Bob was having a hard time with the dog one day when I was over at his house. The dog was bigger than Bob, and Bob already had a Saint Bernard pulling him around. I stayed out of that one, but Hamlet and Bob were having some trouble. Bob said, 'Please, Rick, take this dog back to the house with you. No, man, I *insist* . . .' I didn't want anything bad to happen, and Bob had kicked Hamlet out of the house, so he was living outside. So I took him back to Big Pink. We went to the vet—he didn't care—and I had him groomed. He looked so great that the next time Sara Dylan saw Hamlet, she wanted him back! But he was *our* dog by then. He slept on the carpet by the stove through most of the basement tapes music and most of the *Big Pink* rehearsals as well. That dog heard a lot of music.

"When we'd gotten comfortable, we cleaned out the basement of Big Pink, and Garth put together a couple of microphones and connected them to a little two-track reel-to-reel tape recorder, and that was our studio. For ten months, from March to December 1967, we all met down in the basement and played for two or three hours a day, six days a week. That was it, man. We wrote a lot of songs in that basement. It was incredible!"

While the boys were recording, Rick was busy expending the kind of restless energy it took to convince Albert Grossman that it was time for us to go out on our own. It helped a lot that Sally Grossman loved the band and was really on our side. Toward the end of 1967, when Bob Dylan made it clear to Albert that he wouldn't be touring anytime soon, Albert took it upon himself to get the boys a record deal. They cut a demo, which I've never even heard. Robbie said it was terrible anyway. Warner Bros. was interested: Label chief Mo Ostin had sold a lot of records with Peter, Paul, and Mary, and now Albert was telling him we were going to be even bigger. But Capitol Records jumped at the deal while Mo was out of town or something, and Albert said OK. That's when Rick called me at Mary Cavette's in Memphis, where I was still watching TV and waiting.

Rick remembers: "I call Levon and tell him we signed the deal with Capitol. 'They wanna give us a couple hundred thou, Lee. Better come and get your share!'

"He says, 'What's the deal?' So I tell him it's for ten albums over so many years.

"Levon says, 'I think it's a dirty goddamn deal. I don't like it, but I'll be there anyway on the next plane. Maybe we can fix it.'

" 'Do you need an airplane ticket?'

"He says, 'No, but I'll call and let you know what time my plane lands. Tell the boys I'm coming up.'

"And that's how Levon came back into the fold."

Chapter Six

SOMETHING TO FEEL

It's a wicked life
But what the hell
Everybody's got to eat.

—"Goin' to Acapulco,"
from The Basement Tapes

"Levon and his friend Kirby had come to Memphis and lived with me," Mary Cavette remembers. "We were like *Three's Company*, but I was the only one with a job. At the time—this was 1967—I was trying to straighten Levon out, because he'd been a musician for eight years and didn't even live in the daytime world the rest of us inhabited. So I wanted to find him a real job—like an eight-to-five?—but he wasn't about to do that. Then I sent him out for a haircut, 'cause his hair was so long that he was unemployable, and he came back scalped. We all had a good laugh over that until his hair grew out again.

"Levon was biding his time and resting. I could see what he was doing. He slept all day and watched TV in between. I said to him, 'You better watch out, Lavon; they'll send you to Vietnam.' And he said, 'Forget it, I'm not going. I've watched the six o'clock news every night for six months, and I haven't seen one Pepsi machine in Vietnam. No way am I going over there.' "

Then Rick called and said to come to Woodstock. They were all in the room, and I spoke to everyone. I couldn't believe that my band was going to get back together. Everyone sounded a little older and wiser. Garth told me they had a dog, and the woods were right outside the front door. It felt great when I heard him say, "See ya soon, Levon."

I took the Cavette sisters to the Mid-South Fair and then flew up to New York, where the boys picked me up in Richard's black, four-door, slick-as-hell '47 Olds—the one with the long back. We drove north on the New York State Thruway for a couple of hours. During the ride, Rick told me the whole story: six months on the road with Bob, meeting people, Bob's motorcycle accident, Peter Yarrow's movie, moving to the country, working on songs in the basement. And I had to tell 'em about the adventures Kirby and I had been through, from Louisiana to California and back again.

We got off at an exit marked Saugerties. Then west on Route 212 until we turned right onto Pine Lane. It was late on an autumn afternoon, the maples and oaks were glowing orange and red, and I couldn't take my eyes off Overlook Mountain and the rolling terrain. We'd driven by the Catskills a few times on the way to the Peppermint Lounge, but this was my first time in the Woodstock area. From that first day, the Catskills reminded me of the Ozarks and the Arkansas hill country. I had a shock of recognition. Going to Woodstock felt like going home.

We got to the house. The boys were renting it for $125 a month. It was furnished, with a knickknack shelf in the living room and lots of pictures on the wall, plus a neon beer sign Richard had liberated from some tavern. Garth had set up a music room downstairs in the cinder-block basement, with an upright piano, a stand-up bass, a drum kit, amplifiers, and some microphones connected to a Revox tape recorder through an Altec Lansing mixer, so they could record in stereo. Garth had positioned one of the microphones on top of the hot-water heater. I think there was also an oil furnace in the room.

Well, I found a place to bunk, and we went out to dinner at Deanie's, a wood-burnin' Woodstock institution "Known From Coast to Coast," as the sign said. The place was full of musicians, artists, writers—it was *the* local watering hole. There was a line of people waiting to eat, but when we walked in the boys were greeted like old friends, and we got a good table right away. By the way we were welcomed at Deanie's, you could tell that music was more in favor in Woodstock than in other places.

Woodstock proper was a picturesque town with a white steepled church, a village green, and a flagpole. At night the only sign of life was the red neon sign that flashed DRUGS in the window of the Colonial Pharmacy. We thought that was pretty funny, that sign.

At some point they broke the news to me that Richard had become the band's drummer during my absence. And the thing about it was, Richard was an *incredible* drummer. He played loosey-goosey, a little behind the beat, and it really swung. (Later, when we were playing shows, Richard would hit the high-hat so hard the cymbal would break.)

Knowing Richard, I shouldn't have been surprised at this, but I was amazed how good he'd become. Without any training, he'd do these hard left-handed moves and piano-wise licks, priceless shit—very unusual. So I was coming back into a situation where I heard what Richard was accomplishing and had to say, "Hell, Richard plays drums better than me on this one. We better leave it that way." That's how we got to have two drummers in the band. I just realized that my mandolin playing was going to have to improve if I was to have anything to do onstage while Richard played drums.

It's late 1967. The boys told me that they'd been working with Bob on songs and demos since March. He started coming over as soon as he'd recovered from his injury, usually at the same time every afternoon, and they'd all go downstairs and play. "Like going to work," Richard said. In the morning they'd go to Bob's house because he was churning 'em out—ten songs a week for months—writing for his next album. Bob had taken up painting, and all over his house there were canvases of musicians playing guitars. In the afternoons and evenings they'd go back to Big Pink and play for fun in the basement, writing songs for other musicians to cover. Garth's Revox was used to record these demos, which were sent to Bob's music publisher in New York.

Some of the songs already cut had been cowritten by Bob, Richard, and Rick. They had a typewriter set up in Big Pink's kitchen, and Bob might sit down and type a few lines. Then he'd wander off, and Richard would sit down and finish the verse. Dylan and Rick Danko wrote "This Wheel's on Fire." Richard Manuel and Bob cowrote "Tears of Rage." They played me some of these tapes, and I could barely believe the level of work they'd been putting out. The demos they cut with

Bob included "You Ain't Goin' Nowhere," "Nothing Was Delivered," and "The Mighty Quinn (Quinn the Eskimo)." There were a bunch of little songs that Bob had written that were kind of funny, like "Tiny Montgomery," "Please Mrs. Henry," and "Open the Door, Homer," which became "Open the Door, Richard" when they got around to recording it. I could tell that hanging out with the boys had helped Bob to find a connection with things we were interested in: blues, rockabilly, R&B. They had rubbed off on him a little. There was a great rock and roll song called "Odds and Ends," and "Crash on the Levee (Down in the Flood)" had Bob duetting with Garth's organ. Garth even sang on a couple of songs called "Even If She Looks Like a Pig, Pts. 1 & 2."

The boys had also discovered how to write songs. Bob Dylan had opened it up for 'em. When I reported for duty in the basement the day after I arrived in Woodstock, they were working on "Yazoo Street Scandal." Richard was playing drums. It was the first time I'd heard him, and I was just in awe. It was like a *force*, and he immediately became my favorite drummer. I played some mandolin and sang the vocal. That's how I started to work my way back in. I was uptight about playing, because I'd been away from it for so long, but soon they had me working so hard, there wasn't anything else to do.

Richard was writing and singing up a storm. We cut his "Orange Juice Blues" (also called "Blues for Breakfast"), with Garth playing some honky-tonk tenor sax. Richard sang and cowrote (with Robbie) "Katie's Been Gone," and Garth overlayed some organ. Rick and Robbie did a great song called "Bessie Smith."

Around this time we started to work on our vocals. One of the things we'd always loved about soul music was the way groups like the Staple Singers and the Impressions would stack those individual voices on top of one another, each voice coming in at a different time until you got this blend that was just *magic*. So when we cut a song called "Ain't No More Cane" in our basement, we tried to do it like that, with different voices. I'd heard this song all my life: My daddy taught it to me, and the legendary bluesman Leadbelly had also recorded a version of it called "Go Down, Hannah." Our version started with me singing the first verse. Then Richard did the second, Robbie sang the third, and Rick brought it home. We all sang harmony on the chorus, and Garth layered his accordion over everything. Richard played the drums, so I played mandolin. That recording of "Ain't No More Cane" was a breakthrough. With those multiple voices and jumbled instruments we discovered our sound.

That Thanksgiving a few of us were invited to the Traums' house for holiday dinner. Happy and Artie Traum were keystones of the Woodstock music family and warm, hospitable people. I'll never forget my first Thanksgiving in Woodstock, one of the best dinners I've had in my life.

There was contract fever in the air. Bob had recently signed a new five-year deal with his label, and now it was going to be our turn. Bob had left town in October to record his next album in Nashville. When he came back after Thanksgiving we cut "Nothing Was Delivered" and "Long Distance Operator," which Richard sang. I sang "Don't Ya Tell Henry," and we all worked on an unfinished song by Richard and Robbie called "Ruben Remus."

So we had this body of work, music from Bob's house and music from our house. The music from Bob's house had been cut in Nashville with session players there. It was supposed to be overdubbed by Robbie and Garth back in Woodstock when he came home, but when they heard the tapes they declined the opportunity to enhance the already perfect tracks. The music from our house . . . well, maybe you know the story. Bob's demo tapes leaked out from his publishers and the musicians they sent them to, and began to be widely bootlegged, initially under the title *Great White Wonder*. It had been eighteen months since Dylan's last album, and his fans were happy to hear what their idol had been doing during his rural exile. Garth Hudson's funky two-track tapes became the "basement tapes" of legend and renown. (No one I know except Garth knows exactly how many songs were recorded, but Rick believes the best of the material hasn't even begun to surface.)

There was another recording session in our basement around this time. The Bauls of Bengal were a family of itinerant street troubadours that Albert Grossman had met on a visit to India. These Bauls and their late father had played for him all night in Calcutta, so Albert invited them to Bearsville. They were put up in an apartment he reserved for guests in a converted barn down the road from Albert's house. They were real gypsies and real players, happy to get high and sing all night about rivers and goddesses and play their tablas, harmonium, and fiddles. They eventually made an album and even opened for Paul Butterfield—by then living in Woodstock and a client of Albert's—at Town Hall in New York City. I remember Butterfield laughing about that show, because these crazy Bauls sat down and played for *three hours,* and Paul said that Albert was *very* upset.

Anyway, we invited 'em to Big Pink one night. The Bauls had long black hair braided to the waist and were wearing cowboy hats they'd picked up on the drive east from California, where they'd arrived direct from Bengal. (Before heading east in a beat-up old van, they'd played the Fillmore West on a bill with the Byrds.) They loved the bubbling beer sign over our fireplace, and I played checkers with some of 'em, and we were laughing pretty hard. I was smoking a chillum with Luxman Das, and I said, "Man, that's some good weed."

He smiled and said, "Very good, but nothing like my father used to smoke—little hashish, little tobacco, little head of snake."

I said, "Wait a minute. Did you say 'snake head'?"

And Luxman laughed. "Yes, by golly! Chop off head of snake, chop into tiny pieces, put in chillum with little hash, little tobacco. Oh, boy! Very good—first-class high!"

"Snake?" I pressed him. "Are you *sure* you mean snake?"

Now they're all laughing. "Yes! Very good! Head of snake!"

Charles Lloyd was visiting—I think his 1966 album *Forest Flower* had just passed the million mark in sales—and he came over with his saxophone. The Bauls wanted to jam, Garth wanted to record, and Rick and I were maybe gonna sit in. So we moved the cushions from the living-room sofa downstairs, and the Bauls sat in a circle so they could hear one another and began to play their Indian soul thing. A minute later, they were already wailing in their own language; in their own *world,* Bubba. Charles and Rick and I looked at one another and thought, *No way.* So we got up and let the Bauls play. Hours later, Garth's tape machine was still rolling. These tapes were released, years later, as *Bengali Bauls at Big Pink.*

Everybody around Woodstock in those days loved the Bauls. They were close to the bone of what music should be all about: ecstatic, unrelenting. They told us they loved Woodstock too because there was all this forest and no tigers to eat the children and goats. Their presence can best be felt if you look at the photo of two of them—the brothers Luxman and Purna Das—posing with Bob Dylan on the cover of

158

his new album, which came out the following month: *John Wesley Harding*.

In early 1968 Rick Danko—our best businessman—was really pushing Albert to get us a record contract. It was do or die for us. We'd finished our work on Bob's movie *Eat the Document*, which was then rejected by ABC-TV. We were retired as a road band and were focused about what we wanted to do with our time. We signed a management contract with Albert, and a lot of paperwork happened. I had an attorney in Arkansas who negotiated for us, but Albert had a lot of power, and we didn't really have much leeway. Not all of it went the way I'd wanted it to, but it was so great the band was getting back together.

On January 20, 1968, we drove down to Manhattan and played behind Bob at a memorial tribute to Woody Guthrie at Carnegie Hall. We're crashing through the back doors of the hall with our gear, and an old man guarding backstage says, "Hey, what group is this?"

"The Crackers," I told him off the top of my head.

Then we noticed that Bob and Albert weren't speaking to each other.

There were two shows, matinee and evening, and the crowd gasped when we all walked onstage. Bob's hair was cut short and combed, and we were all dressed in gray western-cut suits and cowboy boots. This time there wasn't any booing. It was Bob's first public appearance in two years, and during this time his image had grown to legendary proportions. We'd rehearsed three Woody Guthrie songs at Bob's house the day before—"Dear Mrs. Roosevelt," "The Grand Coulee Dam," and "I Ain't Got No Home in This World Anymore"—and we performed all three after Pete Seeger, Odetta, and Judy Collins had played and actor Robert Ryan had read from Woody's autobiography. It was the first time I'd ever played a dramatic show like that. People were performing in sections with one another, then we stretched out around Bob and helped him do his songs. I don't think Pete Seeger was too thrilled to see us at first, but the audience was warm, and our evening show brought down the house. Bob tore it up!

Playing Carnegie Hall proved to be good for our impending record deal. Things speeded up after that. I recall one meeting at Big Pink where we actually had to come up with a name for the band.

Rick said, "Let's have some real pretentious bullshit name."

"How about the Chocolate Subway?" Richard suggested. "Or the Marshmallow Overcoat."

Laughter. I said, "Tell it like it is. Tell 'em who we are: the Honkies!" I always was the provocative type.

I had suggested we could modify it to the Crackers. Crackers were poor southern white folks, and as far as I was concerned, that was the music we were doing. I voted to call it the Crackers and never regretted it. That's how Capitol signed the band, in any case.

Our names aren't on Capitol Records Contract No. 4325, dated at Los Angeles on February 1, 1968. This contract was actually between Capitol and Groscourt Productions, Inc. Instead we're listed on an "Artists Declaration" as "Group performing as the Crackers." Albert was furnishing our services to the record company. The deal called for twenty-four master recordings a year for two years; roughly two albums a year. In addition we granted Capitol three one-year options to renew the deal at the same rate. It was basically a ten-album deal, and we took it. We had to.

"Life, with an option."

At our insistence, we retained our exclusive rights as Bob Dylan's band. Paragraph six of the contract stated: "Artists shall have the right to perform and record . . . as joint artists with Bob Dylan for any recording company, television program, motion picture, or legitimate stage production for which Bob Dylan is then rendering services. Such activities shall be deemed exclusive from the agreement."

But the irony was that Bob Dylan split from Albert Grossman around this time. "Dear landlord," Bob had sung on his new album, "don't put a price on my soul." The litigation from that parting of the ways back in 1968 is still in the courts as we write this.

So just as Bob was leaving Albert's stable, we were arriving. I guess the joke was on us.

This is where John Simon comes in.

Now that we'd committed ourselves to making an album, we needed someone who actually knew how to go about it. None of us had any idea how to work a recording console or a four-track tape machine. We'd hardly been in a studio in three years. And here was John: young, clean, up-and-coming, ready to roll. He joined forces with us, produced our first album, and became a lifelong friend.

160

Let me introduce you . . .

John Simon was born in Norwalk, Connecticut, in 1941. His father, Louis Simon, was a country doctor and musician who founded the Norwalk Symphony. "I had piano lessons," John says, "and became a jazz fan at fourteen or fifteen. I had a little group in high school, and we got to play various strip joints and lesbian clubs. I was playing baritone horn and brass instruments in the high-school band, then went off to Princeton, where I joined the Triangle Club. We did the usual drag musicals and took them on the usual tour of Christmas balls and debutante parties. In my senior year I wrote a big-band concerto that was favorably reviewed by Martin Williams in *downbeat*—my first good review.

"I got out of college in the early sixties. I dug progressive jazz, hated rock and roll, liked R&B, especially Louis Jordan. I landed a job with the classical-music division of Columbia Records before switching to the company's pop and jazz departments. There was a senior producer named George Avakian, with whom I worked on a lot of projects. In 1965 George and I coproduced an album called *Of Course Of Course* by a young jazz musician: Charles Lloyd. He'd been in Cannonball Adderly's band and was making a name for himself. He was working in the studio with a quartet, including [drummer] Tony Williams, [bassist] Ron Carter, and Gabor Szabo on guitar. One day Charles says to me, 'You gotta meet this far-out guy. He's coming tonight to sit in with us.'

"The far-out guy was Robbie Robertson. I guess he'd met Robbie in Toronto, and here in New York they had the same connection, a guy who lived on the third floor of Charles's building. So Robbie came to the studio, and we cut this track called "Third Floor Richard" in honor of this dealer. That's how I met Robbie.

"Later that year I get a call from Nat Weiss, then the self-described American representative of Brian Epstein, the Beatles' manager. Nat says he has a group that could be the American Beatles, and sends me a tape of three Lafayette University alumni who call themselves the Cyrkle. They were OK, so we cut a single called "Red Rubber Ball," which immediately went to No. 2. It was the cleanest record—which meant it suffered the fewest returns—the company had that year. So at Christmas they gave me an eleven-thousand-dollar bonus and an office with windows and some plants.

"Now the rock era hit. It's the mid-sixties pop explosion. Recording technology became incredibly important because most of the bands we signed were without discernible evidence of any talent. They had great hair and looked right in the clothes, but they had no talent. Producing this kind of record is a nightmare. I didn't want to do it, so they gave me quality musicians like Leonard Cohen and Blood, Sweat, and Tears with Al Kooper, and Mike Bloomfield. Al Kooper saw I was frustrated and urged me to go free-lance, so I did.

"Around this time I met Albert Grossman on the street. I saw him in midtown and went up and introduced myself, because he was the most powerful guy in the business. That's how I got to produce Janis Joplin for Columbia, because Janis was Albert's client. But there was another connection to be made first.

"Peter Yarrow hears from Ed Kleiban [who later wrote the lyrics for A Chorus Line] that I was just the guy to supervise the music for his film You Are What You Eat. This started out as a documentary about the Hell's Angels by Barry Feinstein, Mary Travers's ex-husband and a friend of Peter's. Then the summer of '66 happened, and suddenly the Hell's Angels concept vanished, and we had a lot of wild footage—cans and cans of film—of love-ins and drug-ins, without any focus. Meanwhile, I'd just finished a Dada-esque montage album based on Marshall McLuhan's The Medium Is the Message. In June 1967 I was at the Monterey Pop Festival with Janis, when I get a message to meet Peter Yarrow, who'll stop in San Francisco on his way to Japan with Peter, Paul, and Mary. I played him the McLuhan record on a little portable turntable in the airport lounge, and he figured I was perfect for his movie. So we arranged to meet up in Woodstock, where this movie was being worked on.

"By this time I was starting to smoke a little, get high, expand my consciousness, blow my mind. It was good for me at the time. It got me off automatic pilot. I went to Woodstock and met a film editor named Howard Alk. He was one of the original members of Second City, the Chicago comedy troupe that spawned Saturday Night Live years later. He was a funny and clever guy, and he and I holed up in this house in Bearsville with all these cans of film and a couple of moviolas, trying to make a film out of this sucker. Barry Feinstein's contribution was a barrel of marijuana. The soundtrack consisted of

162

Butterfield, Bloomfield, and Tiny Tim, who was in the movie. Tiny had these musicians working with him . . .

"Halloween 1967: Alk and I are beavering away in this house, when I heard this ghastly sound outside. It turned out to be Howard's birthday, and the guys in the band are serenading him, playing badly on crazy instruments: horns, washboards, squeezebox. There were only four of them: Robbie Robertson, Rick Danko, Richard Manuel, and Garth Hudson. They're wearing old-looking clothes and masks; the whole thing was totally surreal in that flashing sixties way.

"We get to talking, and I learn that this is Bob Dylan's band, and Bob is paying them to live there while he's recuperating from the motorcycle accident. Suddenly the connection was made. Howard knows me, he knows the band because of a song called 'Even If She Looks Like a Pig Pt. 2,' on which Garth sings. Howard said to us, 'Here's a marriage made in heaven.' He figured wacky music, wacky producer. He promoted the whole concept.

"Want to know what that first serenade I heard from the band sounded like? Check the bridge of 'Chest Fever' sometime.

"Anyway, I loved them from the word go. Musically, I was locked into their thing the second I heard it. I went back to New York—I was living on Perry Street in the Village—when I got a call to come back to Woodstock and talk to Robbie about working with them. We talked for a *long* time at the house he shared with his lady, Dominique, on Rick's Road, and he played me a lot of records and discussed the record deal they were going to do with Capitol. Robbie talked and talked, and I kept thinking, *Put your music where your mouth is,* because all we did was talk.

"Finally he says, 'Well, Levon's here now. He's our drummer, and he left but now he's back. Let's go on over to Big Pink, where most of the boys are living.'

"So we drive over there, and the first thing we see is Levon walking out of the woods with his friend Kirby. He was just off an oil rig in Louisiana. We shook hands and looked each other in the eye, and Levon said, 'C'mon, ah wanna show y'all somthin'.' We hiked a half mile into the woods until we came to a cleared patch and a foot-high marijuana plant that Levon showed off like a 4-H ribbon winner.

"So I saw my first rehearsal in the basement of Big Pink, the first time I got a real impression of the boys. Robbie functioned as the point man, the leader. Garth was into horns and equipment and could play rings around everyone. Rick was hyper, funny, business-oriented, with a lot of girlfriends. Levon was an extremely unusual and gifted drummer with a funny, syncopated bass drum and an independent right-foot thing. Very much his own man in every respect.

"And Richard. A sweet, sweet guy. Very drunk, into pills: Tuinal and Valium. Always pushed the envelope beyond where it would go. Drove one hundred fifty miles an hour in his driveway; faster on the road. The first time I met him, there was a terrible raw scab on his right arm. Really grisly. I said, 'My God, Richard, what happened?'

"He says, 'You know that table lamp in our bathroom with the bare bulb? One afternoon I got up, went to the bathroom, and I leaned on the light bulb to look at my eyes in the mirror, and I started to smell something burning, and it was me!'

"So we started rehearsing together at Big Pink. This was before the record deal. Dylan would come by almost every day. Levon was always trying to get Bob to throw a football with him—kind of a silk purse–sow's ear trip, but it was funny. Big Pink was a wonderful clubhouse, with good meals and beer and pot and laughter and hard, focused work.

"While we were working on songs Albert got us some seed money to go into studio A at A&R Sound: the famous studio at 799 Seventh Avenue that Phil Ramone had bought from CBS. We recorded in the barn-shaped seventh-floor studio that had been built on top of the building, where a lot of the famous party records had been recorded. The acoustics were just the best. We did a reel of the songs we brought down from Big Pink: 'Tears of Rage,' 'We Can Talk,' 'The Weight,' 'Chest Fever,' and maybe 'Lonesome Suzie.' And this is what's so important about The Band: Everybody played something that was meaningful and that meshed. There were hardly any solos, and nothing was gratuitous. The studio had four tracks. We recorded everyone live on two tracks. The horns—Garth on soprano, me on baritone—went on the third track, and the fourth was saved for vocals and tambourine.

"We took this reel over to Albert's office and played the songs for Dylan's friend Bobby Neuwirth. 'These are *really great*,' he said, and that was the first validation we had, because this was a very cynical guy who would not bullshit us. Anyway, Albert took the tapes and sold them to Capitol.

"Now it's winter 1967–68. Capitol loves the tape we made and sends us out to L.A. for a month to record in their eight-track studios there. We move into the Chateau Marmont, a crazy person's paradise. Levon and I discovered sushi together at the Imperial Gardens restaurant across the street and have been raw-fish addicts ever since. At Capitol Studios we worked with an older engineer named Rex Updegraft, who told us our music was 'damn cute.' So we went over to Gold Star—home of Phil Spector's Wall of Sound—and did several things, including Big Bill Broonzy's 'Key to the Highway.'

"All told, it took us a month to finish the album, and by April 1968 we were back in New York mixing the album at A&R."

We wanted *Music From Big Pink* to sound like nothing anyone else was doing. This was our music, honed in isolation from the radio and contemporary trends, liberated from the world of the bars and the climate of the Dylan tours. We'd grown up with Ronnie Hawkins, playing that quicker tempo of tunes. Now we cut our tempo, our pulse, right in half. The sense of teamwork and collaboration was incredible. Robbie was writing stuff that evoked simple pictures of American life. Richard was writing beautiful songs like "In a Station" and "Lonesome Suzie." Garth took a great song like "Chest Fever" and composed an organ prelude. Rick's playing and singing were amazing, and that blend of the three voices—Richard, Rick, and me—sounded really rich after we'd worked with John Simon for a while.

We cut upstairs in that big studio on top of A&R, which had a very live sound. I'd set up in the middle of the room. There was a sound-booth against the wall, which is where Garth placed some of his speakers, so it would be a little muffled, the way he liked it. The piano'd be there, and Rick and Robbie would sit on folding chairs, with their amps beside them. That was the way we did it. There were sound-baffles around the drums, and John would kind of lean over them to discuss different drum ideas and strategies because he took it seriously and wanted a solid, professional record. That was the way it worked.

When I think about that album, I still have to laugh about how close the songs were to our lives. The characters that appear in the lyrics—Luke, Anna Lee, Crazy Chester—were all people we knew. The music was the sum of all the experiences we'd shared for the past ten years, distilled through the quieter vibe of our lives in the country. There was a whole movement toward country values in America in those days, as young people searched for different ways of surviving during the Vietnam era. That's in there too.

The main thing was the spirit. We worked so hard on that music that no matter what the song credits say—who supposedly wrote what—you'd have to call it a full-bore effort by the group to show what we were all about.

"Tears of Rage" opened the album with a slow song, which was just another way of our rebelling against the rebellion. We were deliberately going against the grain. Few artists had ever opened an album with a slow song, so we had to. At the zenith of the psychedelic music era, with its flaming guitars and endless solos and elongated jams, we weren't about to make that kind of album. Bob Dylan helped Richard with this number about a parent's heartbreak, and Richard sang one of the best performances of his life. It had those trademark horns and organ and the moaning tom-tom style of drumming that I've been credited with by some observers, but I know that Ringo Starr was doing something like it at the same time. You make the drum notes bend down in pitch. You hit it, it sounds, and then it hums as the note dies out. If the ensemble is right, you can hear the sustain like a bell, and it's very emotional. It can keep a slow song suspended in an interesting way. (John Simon heard this and started calling me a bayou folk drummer, but not to my face.) As a matter of fact, I found the tuning I used in "Tears of Rage" by tuning to the fluorescent lighting in the studio.

"To Kingdom Come" was Robbie's song, and he sang it—the last time he sang on one of our records for years. Robbie didn't sing, wasn't a singer, didn't like to sing, but he sang on this one.

"In a Station" is Richard's song about Overlook Mountain and the relative peace we were all feeling after those long years living on the road. He used to laugh and call it his George Harrison song, by which he meant it was spiritual.

Once I climbed up the face of a mountain
And ate the wild fruit there
Fell asleep till the moonlight woke me
And I could taste your hair.

I've heard this song described as "visionary," and I agree with that assessment.

Isn't everybody dreaming!
Then the voice I hear is real
Out of all the idle scheming
Can't we have something to
feel.

"Caledonia Mission" was Robbie's, and Richard sang the lyrics that alluded to the little problem we'd had with the law a few years earlier.

"The Weight" closed side one. We had two or three tunes, or pieces of tunes, and "The Weight" was one I would work on. Robbie had that bit about going down to Nazareth—Pennsylvania, where the Martin guitar factory is at. The song was full of our favorite characters. "Luke" was Jimmy Ray Paulman. "Young Anna Lee" was Anna Lee Williams from Turkey Scratch. "Crazy Chester" was a guy we all knew from Fayetteville who came into town on Saturdays wearing a full set of cap guns on his hips and kinda walked around town to help keep the peace, if you follow me. He was like Hopalong Cassidy, and he was a friend of the Hawk's. Ronnie would always check with Crazy Chester to make sure there wasn't any trouble around town. And Chester would reassure him that everything was peaceable and not to worry, because he was on the case. Two big cap guns, he wore, plus a toupee! There were also "Carmen and the Devil," "Miss Moses," and "Fanny," a name that just seemed to fit the picture. (I believe she looked a lot like Caledonia.) We recorded the song maybe four times. We weren't sure it was going to be on the album, but people really liked it. Rick, Richard, and I would switch the verses around among us, and we all sang the chorus: *Put the load right on me!* I read somewhere a few years ago that Robbie said "The Weight" was about the impossibility of sainthood. Well, I've sung that song enough times to agree with him.

Richard's "We Can Talk" opened side two. It's a funny song that really captures the way we spoke to one another; lots of outrageous rhymes and corny puns. Richard just got up one morning—or afternoon—sat down at the piano, and started playing this gospel music that became this song with its famous line, "But I'd rather be burned up in Canada/Than to freeze down in the South."

"Long Black Veil" sounded like an old southern ballad, but it was actually written in 1958 by M. J. Wilkin and Danny Dill. We knew it from Lefty Frizzell's version and liked the story of the young man who goes to the gallows for a murder he didn't commit because his alibi was that he was "in the arms of his best friend's wife." I guess we thought it was funny. Anyway, that's Richard Manuel playing a Wurlitzer electric piano on that track.

"Chest Fever" had improvised lyrics that Robbie put together for the rehearsals and never got around to rewriting. The song came kinda late in the whole process and got recorded before it was finished. Garth put together an introduction from J. S. Bach's Toccata and Fugue in D minor with that Lowrey organ and a good solo in the middle. The bridge has this funny, tuneless Salvation Army band feel: Rick on violin, John Simon on baritone, Garth on tenor.

"Lonesome Suzie" was like a miniature portrait that Richard sang in his squeezed-out falsetto, really expressive, with horns and organ. Years later he described "Suzie" as his attempt to write a hit record. It was a quiet song that told a story and was pretty typical of Richard's general philosophy, which was to be kind to people. Richard was complicated and felt things really deeply, more than most people. Everyone who knew him would tell you that. His attitude, often expressed to me, was that you might as well live *tonight*, because tomorrow you could get run over by a truck.

Rick sings "This Wheel's on Fire." These were lyrics that Bob had, which Rick put to music. Garth got some distinctive sounds on that track by running a telegraph key through a Roxochord toy organ. Garth just hit that key when he wanted the sound. I thought we'd cut a pretty good take on it, but when we got back to New York from California there were problems. "The snare drum wasn't loud enough on our four-track recording," John Simon recalls, "so Levon had to go back into the studio and overdub the snare; an awful chore. When it was over Levon growls at me, 'Don't lemme *ever* have to do that again.' "

"I Shall Be Released," which closed the album, was the third song Bob had written with us. (For that reason, we declined his generous offer to play on the album. We didn't want to appear to be trading on Bob's name any more than we had to. We did, however, ask him to paint the album cover, which he kindly did.) It's a prisoner's lament that Bob had sung on the basement tapes and Richard sings in his falsetto voice. Richard cut another version in his regular voice that was just as good. The drum sound was me playing the snares of an upside-down drum with my fingers. The windlike sound is Garth playing organ with one hand and manipulating the stops with the other.

And that, to the best of my recollection, is the way we made *Music From Big Pink*. The record was meant to describe our take on the crazy times we were living in. The year 1968 was like a civil war, a time of conflict and turmoil in the United States. There was tension in the air, sometimes so thick you could barely wade through it. Here's an example. On our way to California to cut the tracks, Robbie had gone ahead with Albert, who needed to talk big business at the Capitol Tower. Garth, Richard, Rick, and I brought up the rear. Cash was still scarce, so Rick bought us plane tickets with a credit card he'd gotten somehow. During a stop in Chicago the man from the airline came aboard, called our names, and asked us to follow him. He told us the credit card was over its limit, and we owed him money. I called our banker in Arkansas, and Paul Berry helped us straighten things out with the airline. While we were waiting for our new tickets, we ducked into the snack bar, which was occupied by a hundred or so airborne troops on their way home from Vietnam to Fort Campbell, Kentucky. They'd been celebrating and were in a jovial mood, at least until we walked in. They got on our case immediately.

"Shit, man, is *this* what we fought a damn war for, to eat with a bunch of hippies?"

"They need a damn haircut."

I'm thinking these boys are about to kick the hell out of us. They all had these big ugly walking sticks with the words "Khe Sanh" carved on top. It got real quiet in there. I figured that when it started, I'd try to run one of them through the door, land on top of him, and start yelling for the cops. Just as the taunting started again, our flight was called. We got up and left, slow as we dared, and I heard Mama Nell's voice saying, *It's better to be a live coward than a dead hero.*

All this time we were settling deeper into Woodstock. We all had that hometown feeling about the area. The town took in the band and treated us like favorite sons. If someone asked, "Is *the band* in town?" they could be talking only about us. That's how the town actually gave us our name. And, of course, they tolerated us.

Richard Manuel and I enjoyed taking a couple of rent-a-cars out in the big, flat field next to Big Pink. We liked to see what our cars were made of. We'd do figure eights and dance with each other at top speed. Then I'd get at one end of the field, he'd get at the other, and we'd run at each other. We'd get right beside each other, cut the wheel, a little leg on the gas, and both cars would just sashay, break off, and bow to each other. Swing your partner, do-si-do! We'd go around again, then stop in at Deanie's for dinner and a few drinks. Richard might sit down at the piano around midnight, and maybe Paul Butterfield would sit in and play. There were many nights like that.

Richard and I were in Deanie's one night, not too long after my arrival in town. We left around two in the morning, feeling very little pain. We were headed back to Big Pink in separate cars to see what they were made of out in the field there, have a little more fun. Richard was a couple of minutes ahead of me on the road out of Woodstock. I was telling the people in the car with me that my leg was still a little stiff because I'd just gone down to Arkansas for a few days and had fallen off my friend Paul Berry's Triumph 250 motorcycle and scraped my leg, leaving a pretty good scab.

The road heading toward Saugerties out of Woodstock has this curve to the left, and it also drops down. You lose some altitude, and it's a bad spot even when it's dry. That rainy night, Richard took the curve too fast, skidded in some gravel, and caught the last fence post with his rear wheel, which threw him over into the ditch, nose first, ass end up in the air. Richard walked away from it. It was a tendency of his to walk away from car wrecks, which was good because he had of lot of them. He was a hell of a good driver, but real nervy.

The police came next, stopped in their lane with their lights on, and pronounced Richard OK. I was five minutes behind all this and determined to catch him. When I hit that bad corner I was doing it as fast as I thought I could and still keep the car on the road. I hit my flashers and dimmed a couple of times, didn't get an answer, so I was gonna take that curve and keep smokin' over that next big hill and past Zena Road, where you could really go down those flats there at a high rate of speed. But bless my soul, as soon as I cleared the curve, I saw a bunch of people in the middle of the road and the police lights.

"That's Levon," a dazed Richard said to the Woodstock police chief, Billy Waterous, as I barreled down on top of 'em.

"Oh my God!" Billy exclaimed. "He's going to kill us all!"

I went off the gas and hit the brake a little, but then decided to zigzag through the people and cars. It was the only way to avoid a high-speed collision. So I zigged, and that was good. Then I zagged, but missed by three inches. An inch and a half of my right nose caught an inch and a half of the police car's left rear. It was that close.

And so we kissed. I demolished both doors of the police cruiser, spun three times, and ended up stopped in the middle of the road, facing the opposite way as Richard. It was a scary scene. My car was wrecked, the police lights were flashing, people were running. If they hadn't jumped out of the way, I'd have killed them all.

I had a girlfriend and a passenger in the car. As soon as I made sure they weren't cut up by the glass, I jumped out of the car and ran to Richard. We grabbed each other by the arms. "Are you all right, man?" "Yes, brother. Jesus Christ! What a fuckin' mess. Are you OK?"

All of a sudden a cop came out of the ditch, where he had jumped to save his life. We didn't know him. He was a county deputy from another town, and helping Billy because they were shorthanded. He was as scared as we were. I turned to go back to the car and check on my friend Bonnie, and the cop said, "You're not going anywhere." I ignored him, sat down in the car, left the door open, and was making sure she was OK when the cop grabbed my jacket and tore the pocket off trying to get me out of the car. This was a new leather jacket I'd managed to buy myself—good-lookin', cut like a suit jacket with good lapels—and he tore the damn pocket right off! I really liked this jacket, so I decided, *Here, let me help you.* I let him help me out of the car, then reached up and got me a handful of his galluses. That was the move he'd been waiting for, so he went for his blackjack.

And I went for speed. I had him above me and was trying to run him backward with my knees in a bad place for him. He was trying to give ground so he could connect with that blackjack. We were doing a pretty good dance backward when Billy Waterous and Richard saw us coming their way. Billy saw the blackjack waving in the air and was going to intervene, but Richard grabbed him around the neck, and they started dancing in circles! Then we all hit the slippery gravel and went down in one writhing pile. Billy had my jacket now, and the other cop was hitting me across the shoulders with the blackjack. That old boy swung again and hit Billy across the back of his right hand with the blackjack! I thought, *Boy, this is a hell of a good idea! How did we let it get this far?*

This other cop swung one more time and caught that little bone that sits right behind the ear. I thought someone had shot off a firecracker, but it was my head. It made everything rock, like you're playing a show and get that electric squeal in the air that makes you woozy, and you think your drum seat is falling over.

Of course, the fight was over, and I was damn glad of that. I didn't want to get hit like that again. I realized I'd torn up a police car, beat on a deputy, and the police chief was worse off than anyone, because the whole back of his hand was swollen into a goose egg. They put handcuffs on me, which was probably a good thing. I'd certainly been drinking too much, and when your blood gets fired up like that and you've got that alcohol in you, that's when people end up killing themselves.

They took us to the station. Some guy came in and looked at me and yelled at the deputy, "Search his boots! He might have a knife in there!" So I reached down and pulled up my pant leg. The scab from the Arkansas mishap had rubbed off in the gravel during the fight, and my leg looked raw and bloody. I said, "Put *that* in the goddamn report," and the guy looked at the cop who'd arrested me, like, "You didn't have to do *that* to him, did you?" Of course Albert Grossman was right there in a flash and had us cut loose that quick. The next day we showed up before Judge Joseph Forno, Sr., also the town pharmacist. He was stern with us, as he should have been, but we managed to stay out of jail and eventually made a friend of the judge, who has been a mentor to me ever since.

In May 1968 we posed for our album picture at a house I was sharing with Rick Danko in Wittenburg, which is west of Bearsville. We'd left Big Pink by then because we all needed more room. This house of ours had a long view of the hills. The photographer was Elliott Landy, who worked for a New York underground paper called *The Rat*. Albert Grossman had discovered Elliott while he was personally ejecting him from Janis Joplin's Carnegie Hall show a few months earlier. Richard brought along some funny hats from his collection, which all of us wore except for Garth. While the photographer was focusing his camera, the young wife of a friend of Garth's was dancing behind Landy, trying to make us smile. As he snapped the first shot, she tore off her dress and did a naked little grind. So there we were, trying to be cool in the face of this outrageous hippie dance. I think that's the shot we ended up using.

As for the way some of us looked in those days, once, Robbie was driving down to the city a little too fast on the Thruway, and a state cop pulled him over for speeding. The officer checked out Robbie in his beard, wire-rim glasses, and porkpie hat and said, "I'll let you go this time, Rabbi, but try to slow down from now on, OK?"

Then we took Elliott up to Ontario to shoot a picture called "Next of Kin." This was more rebellion against the so-called revolution, when it became fashionable to hate your families and repudiate their values. Hell, we loved our families! We'd gone on the road when we were still boys, and we missed our families and would talk about them all the time. So we gathered everyone on Rick Danko's brother's farm near Simcoe and did a group shot with our people gathered around us. That's Robbie's mom on the far left with Garth and his parents. I'm the guy with the hat and a cig hanging out of his mouth. Then Richard's folks, Richard, Robbie and Dominique, Rick's dad with his finger in his ear, Rick, and his brother Terry. Little Freddie McNulty, our beloved mascot, is between Rick and his granddad, who stands with his wife and a bunch of grandchildren. John Simon stands behind in a floppy hat and blue shirt, with Rick's mother and her brothers. Rick's uncle Rick Smith in that group was a famous chicken judge. People would fly him all over the world to judge birds. He showed me how to hypnotize a chicken while we were on that mission. My mom was feeling ill at the time and couldn't make it to Ontario, so Elliott was good enough to go down to Springdale and take a separate picture of her and Diamond, which we inserted in the upper left corner. We also told Milton Glaser, who designed the album jacket, to include a photo of Big Pink with these lines written by Dominique Robertson:

BIG PINK—A pink house seated in the sun of Overlook Mountain in West Saugerties, New York. Big Pink bore this music and these songs along its way. It's the first witness of this album that's been thought and composed right there inside its walls.

I guess that's how we thought of the place: like it was Mother.

When the album was eventually released on July 1, 1968, we were shocked to find it credited not to the Crackers but to a group called . . .

The Band.

Well, it was us. That's what Woodstock people called us locally: the band. When the people on the other side of the desk at Capitol didn't want to release an album called *Music From Big Pink* by the Crackers, they just went and changed our name!

You know, I thought the Crackers was a funny name, and still do. I was shocked when I first heard about "The Band." Calling it The Band seemed a little on the pretentious, even blowhard, side—burdened by greatness—but we never intended it that way. I voted for the Crackers, though.

John Simon reflects: "*Music From Big Pink* came out that summer and was an underground sensation, if not exactly a commercial smash. I can honestly say that I *loved* the music and was enormously proud to be associated with these men. And that's the point. These guys weren't teenagers. They were seasoned veterans whose debut album sounded more like a band in its prime. The songs were more like buried treasure from American lore than new songs by contemporary artists. The reason for that is they were playing out of what I called their 'Appalachian scale,' a pentatonic, five-note scale like the black keys on the piano. That was the palette from which those melodies came.

"*Big Pink* was like nothing that came before it. Nothing like what *they* were before it. A lot of it was Robbie's writing and the pictures he evoked. A lot of it was Levon and Rick's playing and the blend of the three voices, plus Garth's trip. It was just so *rich*. People wanted to copy it, and did. Look at Elton John.

"Of course, the Dylan connection helped. The funny thing was, when Capitol sent out a blank-label acetate of *Big Pink* to press and radio people, everyone assumed 'The Weight' was *the* Dylan song on the album. The Band fooled everyone except themselves."

Music From Big Pink entered the American charts in early August. Competing against the Doors, Procol Harum, Janis Ian, Cream, and Big Brother and the Holding Company, sales were disappointing, and I think it eventually sold a quarter-million copies that first year or so. At the same time, many people regard that record as one of the defining moments of the decade. People have been telling me ever since that *Big Pink* changed their lives.

A certain amount of mystery surrounded our debut. There was no cover shot of the group on the record, only Bob Dylan's painting of five musicians, a roadie, and an elephant. The group photo inside didn't identify us by name. There was no lyric sheet, so you couldn't tell who was singing, and most people couldn't understand the words. We didn't do any interviews, there wasn't much publicity that summer save for a few reviews, and we had to quash Capitol's promotional campaign that tried to market us like some teenybopper group. They were going to ask fans to name Bob's cover painting. Prizes were pink Yamaha motorbikes, pink pandas, and pink lemonade. So we told Capitol to just leave it alone, and they did.

We didn't tour either. My leg was still in bad shape from the motorcycle accident, and besides, our policy was *not* to tour if we could help it. The policy was to keep making music using the methods and work habits that had kept us productive through the basement tapes and the Big Pink era. We didn't care about being stars. We just wanted to survive with our integrity. Even if we wanted to tour, it would have been hard because Richard also had a little accident that put him out of commission. As Jane Manuel recalls: "We had actually broken up the year before, but Richard and I stayed in touch, because he was my first love. In the spring of 1968 he called me; one of his brothers was getting married, and he asked me to drive him up to Stratford, Ontario, for the ceremony. He couldn't rent a car because they'd taken his license away for speeding. So we went to the wedding, to get me in the mood, because Richard proposed, and we got married the next weekend. He was very pleased about this and used to tease me about this total manipulation.

"We went back to Woodstock and lived with Garth in a house on Spencer Road on Ohayo Mountain. Robbie and Dominique were already married and living on Glasco Turnpike. The band rehearsed in our living room, so there were always people trying to get a party going."

This house had a nice view of the Ashokan Reservoir, and a barbecue grill, which Richard tried to fire up one day by building a gasoline fire in the bottom. But he used so much fuel, it turned into a bomb, and he ended up grilling the top of his foot—third-degree burns. So Richard couldn't work for two months, another reason we didn't tour behind *Big Pink* in the summer of '68. And, boy, we were hot. Albert was turning down offers of twenty thousand dollars a night.

We got pretty good reviews, though. Al Aronowitz, in *Life:* "With *Big Pink* the band dips into the well of tradition and comes up with bucketsful of clear, cool country soul that washes the ears with a sound never heard before. Traditionalists may not like it because it's too original. Pop faddists won't like it because it's too traditional."

"I have chosen *my* album for 1968," Al Kooper wrote in *Rolling Stone.* "*Music From Big Pink* is an event and should be treated as one." He finished his review: "This album was recorded in approximately two weeks. There are people who will work their lives away in vain and not touch it."

According to *Time*, "The band from Big Pink plays the best, bone-clean 'white soul' anywhere. Along with their musicianship, a lack of self-indulgence plays a large part in the beauty of their sound." All reviewers noted that this was not a guitar album, which is what people expected from a so-called rock group. But Robbie had soloed himself to death on the Dylan tours, and we were consciously writing songs without much space for solos. This was something that people who liked us picked up on. This group without a name was an *ensemble.*

Al Aronowitz again, this time in *Rolling Stone:* "What the band plays is country rock, with cadences from F. S. Wolcott's Original Rabbits Foot Minstrel Show and music that tells stories the way Uncle

Remus did, with the taste of Red River Cereal and the consistency of King Biscuit Flour. Robertson himself calls it mountain music, 'because this place where we are—Woodstock—is in the mountains.' . . . the kind of album that will have to open its own door to a new category, accompanied by all the reasons for the burgeoning rush to country pop, by the exodus from the cities and the search for a calmer ethic, by the hunger for earth-grown wisdom and a redefined morality, by the thirst for simple touchstones and the natural law of trees.''

Our local paper in Woodstock, by the way, said the album was OK, but we could have done better.

Writers were always stuck when they tried to find a label for us. On Sunday, August 4, 1968, *The New York Times'* critic declared, ''Fortunately, we needn't wait for the Byrds to understand what the country-rock synthesis is all about. Already, the movement has its first major album, *Music From Big Pink* by The Band. You can tell right away this is country music by its twang and tenacity. But you know it's also rock, because it makes you want to move.''

Country rock was the label that finally stuck. We hated it.

When Albert Grossman's office finally got tired of turning down interview requests, Robbie was deputized to talk to the press. ''One thing I'd like to clear up,'' he told *Eye* magazine that September, ''we have no name for the group. We're not interested in doing record promotion or going on Johnny Carson to plug the LP. . . . The name of the group is just our Christian names. The only reason the LP is by 'The Band' is so they can file it in the record stores. And also, that's the way we're known to our friends and neighbors. Another thing, we're not Bob Dylan's band; he doesn't think of us that way; neither do we.

''See, we don't freak out anymore; that was seven or eight years ago. We wanted the album to be loose and easy. There was a lot of instrumental swapping—everyone took turns. It was a very drunken LP. We had a good time.''

Around this time we got a letter from George Harrison, who complained that EMI released *Music From Big Pink* in England in a single sleeve instead of the double-fold jacket of the American version. They printed the title and name of the group over Bob's painting and threw out the ''Next of Kin'' photo. George was a big advocate for us, being quoted in the British press about how *Music From Big Pink* was *the*

177

new sound to come from America and everybody better pay attention. His friend Eric Clapton was quoted in the British paper *Melody Maker* as saying *Big Pink* had made his group Cream, the contemporary kings of so-called acid rock, obsolete. The power trio announced its disbandment that summer.

George Harrison came to Woodstock that fall. We'd appreciated what both he and Eric Clapton had been saying about us in print. It was encouraging to have the Beatles say they were fans of ours. At one point there was discussion of recording with George and Eric, who came to see us a little later on. We talked about doing a fireside jam, real informal, with American and British players and a lot of beer, but nothing ever came of it. Bob and Albert were fighting pretty good by then, so that might have had something to do with nothing like that happening for us.

"Hi, I'm George. Nice to meet you." That's what he was like. Very quiet. I think he was with us for Thanksgiving at Bob's house, and we jammed a little bit and swapped some songs. George and Bob wrote a couple of things together, and there was much talk of us being in a rock western called *Zachariah* that Apple Films was promoting. We were maybe going to do the music with George, but in the end the script was silly—MTV fifteen years ahead of schedule—and it didn't happen.

A lot of people came to Woodstock to hang out with us that fall. My memory is that everyone wanted to know Richard Manuel and just hang out. Albert's office fielded quite a few movie queries for Richard.

It took a while for word about The Band and *Big Pink* to get around, but by the end of 1968 people like promoter Bill Graham were offering us serious money to get out and play. I was content not to tour and just to make records. We had another album due to Capitol, and the beauty of that autumn in Woodstock was inspiring our writers—Richard and Robbie—to turn out some good songs. We already had a working title for the next record: *Harvest*.

Then Rick broke his neck in a car accident, late at night, and our choice of whether or not to tour was taken away.

"Levon and I were living in a house in Wittenburg," Rick recalls, "and I was heading to this house Garth and Richard had, where Van

Morrison later lived while he was making his album *Tupelo Honey*. I was driving a 1953 Bristol, a beautiful English car with an aluminum body, which belonged to my girlfriend's older brother. I was a little too drunk, a little too high. I'd just climbed a mountain and took the S-curve and felt the car sliding. I put my brakes on and hit a tree. I was knocked out but had a lot of flashbacks until I regained full consciousness three or four days later.

"A few minutes later, I'm out of the car, really bleeding, when Bill Avis and his wife come along on their way to Richard's house. I started screaming and yelling, 'Just get me home—back to the house!' I somehow walked into the house, into the bedroom, lay down on my bed, and that was it. I didn't get up for three or four months after that.

"Flashbacks: Suddenly there's people in my room. There's a state trooper, and he's asking for my driver's license. Levon's standing there, naked, because he's been rudely awakened, and there are now six or seven people in the room, and Levon was telling this trooper, 'Now's no fuckin' time to be asking for his goddamn license! Call an ambulance, for God's sake!' Levon, Richard, and Bill came to the hospital, and when I woke up again I'm on the examining table, feeling a lot of pain, and I hear Richard telling the doctor, 'If I hear him scream one more time, I'm gonna break your neck.'

"It must've been the weekend. He must have had a couple of drinks.

"In the recovery room, I wake up in excruciating pain. I had to scream to wake up the nurse. They got me to my own room, but they didn't know my neck is broken, didn't know my back is broken in four places. I'm asking them, 'Why can't I get up?' Someone gave me a shot.

"When I woke up again, Albert Grossman was in the room, talking with a neurosurgeon. I was in for weeks of traction. I told Albert not to tell the press I'd had an accident, and decided to suppress all my hyper instincts and lie perfectly still for the time it took for my neck to heal. Nobody thought that I could do it, but I managed, and that's how it grew back into place.

"The second time Albert came to see me, he said the group was getting offers of four thousand dollars a night. He was saying, 'Can't I tell the press something? Can't the band go out and play?' I said, 'I don't want you to tell the press nothing about my accident, because I saw what Bob Dylan went through, and it was ugly; people saying he was finished.' I didn't want to go through that. Next time he comes, Albert goes, 'They're offering seven thousand dollars a night, eight thousand dollars a night.'

" 'Tell 'em to go out on the road,' I said. 'I'm not the leader of the band.' "

Well, of course we didn't go out without Rick. How could we? The Band was a team. But it was real quiet in Woodstock that winter, believe me. We might've gotten into some mischief because of it.

Chapter Seven

THE BAND

Here my story intertwines with that of the mother of my daughter.

I'd heard of Libby Titus before I met her because people said she was one of most beautiful girls in Woodstock. She was born Irene Justice in 1946. Her Russian father moved his family to Woodstock to work with his brother-in-law producing *Batman* comic strips for Stan Lee, and Libby was raised on Ohayo Mountain Road.

Cut to the summer of 1964. Libby, just out of high school and on her way to nearby Bard College, lands a waitressing job at the Café Expresso on Tinker Street, owned by Bernard and Mary Lou Paturel. Libby is eighteen years old, with a headful of dark, curly hair. She looks good. Here are a few of Libby's memories of that era. She has her own acerbic point of view, so let the reader be advised to take them with a barrel of salt.

"There was incredible excitement that summer in Woodstock," Libby says, "because Bob Dylan had moved to town, and suddenly Joan Baez was driving around in a low-slung green Jaguar, and the café was full of heavyweight bohemians from the Village and Chicago. Bobby Neuwirth. Sara Dylan—never had I seen anyone so beautiful, like a Brazilian Madonna. One night Victor Maimudes, Dylan's road manager, took me up to Albert Grossman's, which was the center of all this. I met Sally Grossman, so beautiful that her body could have been carved on a frieze. She was like a Byzantine hooker! So much life and passion, sexy clothes, everyone flirting. LSD hadn't hit, so no one was out of their mind. It was so beautiful and innocent, that summer.

"Working in the café, I met and became friends with Mason Hoffenberg, this fantastic junkie who'd written the novel *Candy* with Terry Southern and was like the beatnik king of Woodstock. He was so smart and so funny that he made being a junkie somehow attractive.

"I only lasted a year at Bard, and went to New York and got a job at the Café Figaro on Bleecker Street in Greenwich Village, the very crossroads of the avant-garde in 1965. There I met Barry Titus, the handsome grandson of Helena Rubinstein, who invented makeup. He looked like Jean-Paul Belmondo, and swept me off my feet to his apartment on Fifth Avenue at Seventy-fourth Street. Our son, Ezra Titus, was born in July 1966. In the spring of 1968, having left my husband, my son and I moved into a nice apartment on Gramercy Park. Like everyone else I was trying to figure out what to do with myself.

"On July 4, 1968, Mason Hoffenberg comes by in a big white Cadillac and says, 'Libby, wanna come to Woodstock to meet The Band? They'll love you!' So I left Ezra with his nanny and drove up to Woodstock with Mason. We pull into the driveway of this house on Boggs Hill, where Robbie and Dominique were living. I took one look at this gorgeous, pregnant French girl and bonded with her immediately. Mason went off somewhere because he was kicking heroin and left me there for a long time, so I bonded with both of them.

"Rick Danko came over early that afternoon—nervous, hyper, cheekbones, bedazzling, adorable. Rick must have heard there was a new girl in town, because he came over to display himself. He just had to take me off in his old Pontiac to see some awful creek, and I'm in a white Bendel dress and Brazilian espadrilles, very uncomfortable. The chemistry wasn't there between Rick and me that day, so he brought me back to the house and drove off.

"Late that evening Robbie, Dominique, and I go down to the Café Expresso. As we're going in, there was an argument on the street. Two Woodstock natives are shouting at two guys on the street. One is Andy Yarrow, Peter's younger brother. The other is Levon.

"I see Levon and think, *I've never seen anyone so good-looking*

. . . but how weird that he's smashing the side of that pickup truck. I'll remind myself to stay away from him. But I also thought, *Man, look at that. Look at him!* I couldn't take my eyes off him. He was so handsome, and I still remember every detail: blue jeans, checked shirt, cowboy boots and hat, long golden curls, and a beard under green eyes, with a sinewy body that gave him the appearance of a mountain lion.

"That was Levon. There was a direct look between us that night. I could feel it; he was contacting me through our eyes. I *knew* it. That electricity—maybe you feel it only a few times in your life or never at all.

"I saw someone similar to myself.

"And he had that power of his. He could draw you to him. He looks into your eyes and draws you into his sphere. But there was also this violent and untamed side to his nature. He was wild.

"The summer of '68 went on, hot and sunny all the time. *Big Pink* came out, and The Band was getting famous. They were running around Woodstock in their Pontiacs, their fame and youth had arrived, and they were basking in it. Levon and Rick were living in the Cabbott house, a dusty and sexy little cowboy house off the Wittenburg Road. Levon was sleeping with every girl in Woodstock, one after another, like clay pigeons. I wouldn't be one of these girls, and Levon liked that.

"Over the summer I got to know them a little better, enough to sketch them out a bit.

"Robbie Robertson was tall, quiet, handsome, self-contained, in control. He seemed to be more of a rock and roll carny type than he really was. He was a businessman as well as a musician, a folk artist, a great storyteller. He was good to his wife, his mother, the other guys. He alone of them was organized enough to present this mountain-lion energy they all had. He knew how to call it in and turn it into art that could be put on a record. He suffered later for this quality, but I saw him as a great young man!

"Rick Danko was the young buck in the forest, coming into his own. The wild man, the innocent guy who fell for the girl with the tiny waist: Grace Seldner. Rick was hyper and always telling stories about the horrific accidents that were happening to them because they lived so completely at risk.

"Garth Hudson was authoritative about music, distracted, in his own world. He was very funny in a subtle way and more careful than the rest of them. Garth didn't tend to have bad traffic accidents or burn himself up. He was older and wiser, and everybody looked up to him.

"Richard Manuel: self-deprecating, funny, soulful, sweet, extremely self-destructive, major alcoholic. He had zero information how to live. I was a mess myself, but I looked like Eleanor Roosevelt next to Richard. There were signs of what was gonna happen; anyone could see. He'd build a concrete barbecue, fill it with lighter fluid, leave a hole in the bottom, stand over it with a match with his foot next to the hole—third-degree burns and nobody can work that summer. He was accident-prone but making a joke out of it, as if it was some funny thing that wasn't happening to them. It was 'Richard crashed the damn car, ha-ha-ha.'

"One night Rick and Levon made a bet that whoever got to my place first—I was living with Mason Hoffenberg in an old stone house—was going to be the one to sleep with me. They both raced over, Rick crashed the car, and Levon and I got together. We didn't sleep together, but by now I had a crush on Levon. I was *very* attracted to him. Rick married Grace, the girl whose car he crashed.

"But then, after that summer, things began to change. This wonderful, nymphomaniacal group of young rock stars became surrounded by these extremely charming and attractive vultures: John Brent, Howard Alk, John Court, Larry Hankin. Some of them were brilliant, charismatic junkies, like John Brent, who was so magnetic you wanted to be a junkie ten minutes after you met him and heard his stories of beautiful girls in the Village and shooting up with William Burroughs.

"And that's what happened. As The Band was trying to continue their career, a major heroin scene began to surround the picture. They were very dangerous times for all of us."

We went to California to make *The Band*. We had some songs we'd been working on, and wanted to get away from the long winter and the temptations of Woodstock life and do our work. This was our prime now. We were in our era. Instead of touring, our creative energies went into making this record. It was the way we ordered our lives. *We wanted to chase that music.* We were a self-contained unit who'd reach outside for help once in a while. So we hired John Simon again and rented Sammy Davis, Jr.'s house in the Hollywood Hills for a few months (having borrowed $10,000 from Paul Berry in Arkansas so we could live in style). It had a big pool house, which we converted into a studio, plus I lived there. We taped up the metal chimney, sealed off the fireplace, and had Capitol send over a couple of carpenters to box out the windows. We packed blankets around them and taped them all off. To me, things were as satisfying as they could get. It was February 1969.

Garth always believed in visiting the pawnshops whenever we hit a new town, because he found good old horns and rare music books there. By then I could afford to run the first of several Corvettes and buy a good twelve-string Martin guitar if I wanted. Down at a pawnshop on Santa Monica Boulevard I found this set of drums with wooden rims for $130 and fell in love with them. I bought the whole kit with a set of cymbals; a great crash and a real good ride. These were old-fashioned instruments, but they read well on the microphones when you had a tape machine going. So I ended up using the bass, the snare, and one of the two cymbals in that set on the album, and we'd take 'em out on the road when we toured. I also found an inlaid antique mandolin, circa the 1930s, at that shop.

John Simon recalls: "After *Big Pink* I'd gone on to produce a bunch of other stuff—Big Brother, the Electric Flag, Mama Cass—but I was very happy when The Band asked me back. Around the second album I asked Robbie if I could actually join the band. Because we worked so well together and I just wanted to be one of them. He said, 'Man, you know . . . We already *have* two piano players.'

"A cold dude.

"Before we started in California, I went to Hawaii with Robbie, Dominique, and their baby, Alexandra. We were supposed to be working on songs for *The Band,* but instead we worked on songs for my first album for Warner Bros. Then we went back to L.A. and met the others at this house and pool complex we rented for a couple of months from Sammy Davis, who'd brought it from Wally Cox—Mr. Peepers on 1950s TV. It was right above Sunset Boulevard. The place had a living room, kitchen, immense master bedroom featuring glamorous May Britt's bathroom and closet. Upstairs was like a motel, with four bedrooms off the hall. The pool house in back had a separate suite.

A downstairs suite underneath the kitchen was occupied by Robbie, Dominique (who was very pregnant), their daughter, and Robbie's mom, Mama Kosh, who was helping take care of the baby. We all drew straws for the rest. I got Sammy's suite, and Levon got the pool house, minus the big room to record in. Richard and Jane got the double bedroom upstairs, and Garth and Rick got the rest. We all took turns in the kitchen, alternating the cooking, and after the first month we drew again and changed rooms.

"The plan was for Capitol to supply recording equipment so we could record in the house. We waited for it for a month after we arrived. And then I found I wasn't really there to produce the record. I was supposed to teach the guys in the band—meaning Robbie—what I did, so they could make records by themselves. For months Robbie had been asking me, 'What do you do, John? What do engineers do? Could we do it by ourselves without an engineer?'

"Anyway, we hung out for a month, waiting for the studio gear. Capitol gave us a fleet of VW Beetles to drive around in while Robbie was writing the songs. When we finally got the equipment set up, we decided to test it out to see how the studio sounded. We had the second Dr. John the Night Tripper record, which had a discordant version of 'My Country! 'Tis of Thee' on it, with kids singing and all sorts of sound effects. Garth finally got the speakers wired at three in the morning, and we put on Dr. John. Sounded pretty good too—until ten minutes later Dominique Robertson runs in, barefoot in her nightgown, saying, 'Robbie! Robbie! Ze cops! Ze cops are here!'

"We ran outside, and Dr. John is *everywhere*. It turned out we'd tapped into Sammy's poolside speaker system, and we were broadcasting Dr. John at top volume into the Hollywood Hills. We tried not to laugh as more cop cars pulled up, lights came on in houses up into the hills, and the neighborhood dogs began to howl in answer to this insane Dr. John trip.

"So now we had one month in which to record two months of scheduled work. We had a band meeting in the living room of the house the night after the gear arrived. Richard Manuel says, 'What we want is to get a hold of some of them high-school fat-girl diet pills.'

"I asked what he meant, and Richard said they liked these little pink triangular pills that had a line through 'em. So I called up a college drummer buddy of mine, by then a neurosurgeon in San Francisco but still enough of a hippie to prescribe a whole pile of these amphetamines. And that's how they liked to work. I got into it and started smoking for the first time in my life because the pills made cigarettes taste so good.''

We never had any rules about making records. In those days you lived with a tape recorder, strictly trial and error. Living so communally, like in the days of Big Pink, helped pass the ideas around, and with the studio right there we were always experimenting, without any deadlines or worrying about the engineer's overtime. Richard was drumming up a storm—he played on half the album—and John Simon and I worked for hours just getting those old wooden drums of mine deadened down until they had a good *thump* to them. We'd tape up the bottom of that old snare drum with the wooden rim, and it just sounded better than average to me. We'd adjust the lug nuts to get that weeping tom-tom effect where that note would bend down, and you'd hear it go *eeeeuuuuu*.

An average workday might start at seven in the evening, working on those sounds and getting in tune with one another. A lot went into differentiating the instruments to individual songs so there was very little repetition. At night, after a good meal, we'd rehearse, getting our parts and the lyrics right. We discovered the songs themselves dictated who would sing and who would play the supporting roles. That was the real pleasure we got out of playing as a group. After midnight we'd record. Working this way, we cut nine songs during March and into April. We had hardly any interaction with the L.A. music scene and, indeed, rarely saw anyone at all. When a writer from *Look* magazine showed up near the end of the month, he told us the neighbors were whispering about the grouchy, bearded mountaineers who had taken over Sammy Davis's house. Some kind of cult, maybe.

Richard sang on ''Across the Great Divide'' and came up with all those chord progressions and tempo changes in the song. You can really hear the glory and plain *goodness* of Richard's personality if you listen carefully. We had a film projector in the studio, so we could watch movies as part of this whole process. We'd been offered the sound track for Peter Fonda's movie *Easy Rider*, but we'd turned it down; likewise *Ned Kelly*, Mick Jagger's film debut. While we were recording ''Across the Great Divide,'' the Italian director Michelangelo

187

Antonioni came up to the house to visit. The auteur of *Red Desert* and *Blow-Up* wanted us to consider doing the music for his first movie about America, *Zabriskie Point*. Signor Antonioni didn't speak much English, so it was funny when he heard Richard on the playback singing the beginning of that song—"Standin' by your window in vain, a pistol in your hand"—and Antonioni starts gesturing and shouting *"Pistoli!"* in recognition. (We turned down his movie too.)

"Rag Mama Rag" was a collaboration among the band. At the time, it wasn't anything special; as with many songs, we didn't understand its importance until after we'd recorded it. I'm singing and playing the mandolin, and Richard's playing drums. That's Rick playing the fiddle, Garth playing the funky piano, and John Simon blowing tuba for the first time in his life. (There's no bass on the track.) We were trying to bring to mind the feel of those old acoustic songs like "In the Pines" when we cut that. To me, it came as the height of our collaboration: We were all at our fullest. Everybody had input, especially Garth. This is a point that has to be made. We called Garth "H.B." among ourselves. This stood for "Honey Boy," because at the end of the day, after the other instruments were put away, Garth was still in the studio sweetening the tracks, stacking up those chords, putting on brass, woodwinds, whatever was needed to make that music sing. Garth made us sound like we did.

Robbie and I worked on "The Night They Drove Old Dixie Down" up in Woodstock. I remember taking him to the library so he could research the history and geography of the era for the lyrics and make General Robert E. Lee come out with all due respect. It was another of those "workshop" songs we worked on a long time before we got it down. This was when we started halving the beat on a lot of tunes, which gave us a distinctive thing. Instead of keeping full time rhythmically, we found if we halved the beat we could lay the lyrics in a different place, and the pulse would be easier to move to, more danceable. And it made it easier for us to learn to really sing with one another and behind Richard. My problem was that I had to learn to sing and play this half-time meter at the same time. I'd grown up shouting "Short Fat Fannie" over a barroom din while playing at top speed. Now I learned to sing quieter and play as best I could. I had to record a tune six, eight, ten times before I really got it. Incidentally, the harmonica sound is actually Garth overdubbing a melodica over the accordion stop on his Lowrey organ. He also blows some trumpet at the end of the song.

Richard and Robbie collaborated on "When You Awake" and "Jawbone." "I'm a thief, and I dig it," Richard sings. (We recorded the chorus in my bathroom.) Richard sang "Rockin' Chair," "Look Out Cleveland," and "King Harvest (Has Surely Come)." Rick Danko sang "Unfaithful Servant" with those blowsy Band horns. We spent a lot of time on "King Harvest," another song from the previous autumn in Woodstock that summed up what we were about. Some of the lyrics came out of a discussion we had one night about the times we'd seen and all had in common. It was an expression of feeling that came from five people. The group wanted to do one song that took in everything we could muster about life at that moment in time. It was the last thing we cut in California, and it was that magical feeling of "King Harvest" that pulled us through. It was like, *there,* that's The Band.

It was a complicated record. We wanted to make one that you didn't really get until the second time you played it. Some of the songs, like "Rockin' Chair," sound like folks playing accordion and mandolin on the back porch of some farm. Others—"Look Out Cleveland" and the back end of "King Harvest"—are more rock and roll. Old people talk in the songs, like Ragtime Willie, the grandpa in "When You Awake." There was nothing normal about it. The title we had for the record was *Harvest,* because we were reaping this music from seeds that had been planted many years before we'd even been born. But we could have called it *America* as well, because this music was right out of the air. We were saying, *Listen! You can't ignore this.*

At the same time, John Simon was reminding us, "You aren't finished yet." We had nine good ones, but an album was at least twelve, so we'd have to finish the album in New York. This was no big problem, as we had some pieces of good tunes we'd been working on, like "Whispering Pines" and "Up on Cripple Creek."

But before we could tend to that, we were obliged to move the whole show to San Francisco, where Bill Graham had scheduled three nights of performances. At twenty thousand dollars for the weekend, they were the first paid concerts we'd given in three or four years, and would mark the public concert debut of The Band. We were scared shitless.

Originally the idea was not to tour, just be a recording band. I mean, we'd already been everywhere, so the idea of touring didn't have much attraction for us. But Bill Graham, master of the Fillmores West and East, had been bothering Albert about us playing for him and wouldn't take no for an answer. Bill believed in pushing you right onstage. Albert couldn't tell Bill that Rick had broken his neck, so he just said to go to Woodstock and talk to the band. Bill came up, talked to Robbie, and scheduled three nights in San Francisco and a weekend in New York a few weeks later.

Ralph J. Gleason announced this in his *San Francisco Chronicle* column in February 1969: "The Band from Big Pink will make its first appearance in public at Winterland in a three-night stand April 17, 18 and 19. An appearance on May 9 and 10 has also been set for Fillmore East [in New York] as well. The Band from Big Pink has been in Hollywood recording for Capitol for the past two weeks. Their first album has been one of the most impressive underground hits of the past year and an album of immense impact within the field of pop music." It was our good fortune that Ralph J., at fifty-two the most influential music journalist of the day, liked what we were doing and sort of took us under his wing.

We had rehearsed for this toward the end of our time in Los Angeles. We worked on "Don't Ya Tell Henry," from the basement tapes, plus "Little Birds," which my daddy had taught me, and Marvin Gaye's "Baby Don't You Do It," among others. But we were still scared, and I recall an incredible amount of tension in the air. I was nervous and worried about playing in public again, and it would be fair to say we were all beside ourselves with concern about bringing out this music for the first time before an audience. And not just any audience: This was San Francisco! This was opening right at the top; no out-of-town preview or club date. It was Bill Graham Presents . . .

Plus Robbie's wife was about to have her second daughter. The California papers were full of predictions that an earthquake—the Big One—was going to happen the weekend we were due in San Francisco. Just our luck.

We pulled into San Francisco, looking about half past dead, on Tuesday, April 15. Robbie hadn't eaten in two days and was airsick on the plane, but whatever was wrong wasn't cured when we landed. By the time we checked into the Seal Rock Motel, he was running a fever of maybe 103 degrees.

When Robbie felt even worse the next day, Bill Graham wanted to cancel the Thursday opening night and play on Sunday instead, but Albert said no. He and Bill got into it a little, two gonzo personalities on a collision course. "We can't cancel," Albert said, "we're on a schedule, we got babies coming any minute, we got plane reservations, and we'll play Thursday night. I'll guarantee it."

John Simon: "I was on this trip to supervise the music and sound. Once again I called my neurosurgeon buddy, who came over and gave Robbie a complete physical. He had a fever and chills, stomach flu, nothing really wrong. Phil suggested a hypnotist to get Robbie through what he diagnosed as nervous exhaustion, and I think Bill Graham's people found one."

Ralph J. Gleason in that morning's *Chronicle:* "The debut of The Band from Big Pink tomorrow night at Winterland is an event of considerable importance, perhaps more so than even the fans of the group expect."

We had a rehearsal and soundcheck without Robbie that night. While I'm restringing my new mandolin, I hear John Simon, up in the balcony, call to Richard, "If you play that figure, play it with the sticks because we can't hear the brushes up here." We had a discussion with the light-show people about what they wanted to project behind us. Hold the psychedelia, we told them. We felt that there were enough pictures in the music anyway and didn't like the idea of competing with a light show. We didn't bother rehearsing much without Robbie, and all I could hear was my bass drum hammering off the concrete walls. We spent hours setting up stage monitors so we could hear ourselves before giving up and repairing to a Japanese place for some sushi.

Thursday at the motel, Robbie's lying in bed, semicomatose. We're all in the room. The tall, silver-haired hypnotist, Pierre Clement, is rubbing Robbie's forehead, photographer Elliott Landy is clicking away, Albert and Bill Graham are pacing around, trying to figure out what to do. The hypnotist's diagnosis is acute stage fright. In the end they decided the show must go on.

Cut to Winterland that night. The Ace of Cups, an all-girl band who'd recently won the Fillmore West's weekly audition, stretched out their set, as did the Sons of Champlin, a veteran Bay Area band who'd just released a double album on Capitol.

Then: nothing for an hour and a half. Five thousand people waited. It was a sellout. They'd driven up from Big Sur and flown in from Montana, Oregon, Washington. Backstage was jammed with press, girls, rounders, poets. *The New York Times* was there, *Time, Look, Rolling Stone.* Robbie was sick as a dog. Bill wanted to cancel, but Albert again refused to play Sunday night. It was like King Kong versus Godzilla. The rest of us were really down. Finally, at eleven Bill Graham went out front and apologized for the delay, explaining that one of us was sick. Someone yelled, *"Fuuuuck yew!"* from the balcony, and five thousand people cheered. So they played Grateful Dead records over the sound system for another ninety minutes until we went onstage at twelve-thirty with this hypnotist sitting in a chair near Robbie, trying to make him forget his problems. While we tuned up in the dark for maybe fifteen minutes, the people were cheering, and we could hear the girls yelling, "Hey Band! We *loooove youuuuu!"* I looked at Garth to see if he was smiling, and he was.

Next, I could hear Bill Graham talking to the crowd, which was ready to explode. He said something about the historic event that was taking place there that night. Then Bill paused and said, "Ladies and gentlemen . . . The Band."

The roar was almost overwhelming. As we started to play, raggedly, the hypnotist began waving his hands at Robbie, which seemed to have some effect, although it sure looked weird. He had on a blue suit, white shirt, and tie. The day before, he'd waved his hands at Robbie and brought down his fever five degrees in an hour. I wouldn't have believed it if I hadn't been there myself.

Robertson leaned against the piano and looked about to collapse. We were ready to catch him if he did. We played seven numbers for thirty-five minutes and followed Robbie when he walked off, unable to continue. As we were sadly waving good-bye, a young blond girl stood up in front of the stage and yelled, "Play the other side!" The vibes in the hall were bad. "Assholes!" "Shitheads!" Some stuff I wouldn't even print. People who'd come hundreds of miles felt ripped off. They booed and whistled and clapped, but the show was really over, and the audience was bummed as they filed out into the cold San Francisco night.

I'll bet they didn't feel as bad as we did.

Robbie, Levon, and Rick onstage at the Woodstock Festival, August 1969 (ELLIOTT LANDY)

The Band in the rain on John Joy Road in Woodstock, summer 1969. This was the group's first choice for the cover of *The Band;* the record company preferred a shot with Levon facing the camera. (ELLIOTT LANDY)

"Hudson on Hudson" or "The Band on the Hudson." The Band lounging around Rick Danko's old Hudson on Zena Road, summer 1969. (ELLIOTT LANDY)

Rick Danko and Hamlet, 1969. Note Levon's old wooden drum kit after the King Harvest scene had been painted on the bass drum. (ELLIOTT LANDY)

Levon and Rick, summer 1969 (ELLIOTT LANDY)

FIFTY CENTS   JANUARY 12, 1970

The New Sound of Country Rock

THE BAND

"The New Sound of Country Rock,"
Time magazine (January 12, 1970)
(COVER PAINTING BY BOB PEAK, REPRODUCED
COURTESY TIME INC.)

Levon backstage at the Fillmore East, 1970 (ELLIOTT LANDY)

Richard's birthday party, New York, 1970 (ELLIOTT LANDY)

Levon, 1970 (ELLIOTT LANDY)

SIDE I	SIDE II
Life Is A Carnival	Shoot Out In Chinatown
When I Paint My Masterpiece	The Moon Struck One
Last Of The Blacksmiths	Thinkin' Out Loud
Where Do We Go From Here?	Smoke Signal
4% Pantomime	Volcano
	The River Hymn

LEVON HELM
RICK DANKO
GARTH HUDSON
RICHARD MANUEL
ROBBIE ROBERTSON

Richard Avedon poses a "sleeping" Band for the back cover of *Cahoots,* 1971.

Levon's house and studio in Woodstock

Henry Glover *(top)* and Muddy Waters during the recording of Muddy
Waters's *The Woodstock Album*, February 1975 (TURKEY SCRATCH ARCHIVES)

The Band at Shangri-La Studio, Malibu, California, 1975, during the recording of *Northern Lights, Southern Cross. From left:* Garth, Levon, Richard, Robbie, and Rick.

The Band on MGM's soundstage during postproduction work on *The Last Waltz,* 1977. This was the last time the five original musicians played on the same stage. *From left:* Richard, Rick, Robbie, Garth, and Levon. (MICHAEL OCHS ARCHIVES)

Levon as Ted Webb in *Coal Miner's Daughter*, 1980

Levon with the Cate Brothers, 1981. Earl Cate plays guitar at left. Levon plays harmonica at right. Levon's nephew Terry Cagle is on drums. (PHOTO BY DAVID NANCE)

Sandy and Levon, 1981 (Photo by David Nance)

Bob Dylan joins Levon, Rick, and harmonica player Shredni Volper onstage in New York, 1983. (ELLIOTT LANDY)

Levon Helm as Major
Ridley in *The Right Stuff,*
1983 (THE LADD COMPANY)

The Band re-formed in the mid-1980s without Robbie Robertson. *From left:* Levon, Rick,
Richard, and Garth. (TURKEY SCRATCH ARCHIVES)

Levon rehearsing for a movie role in his backyard, 1984. (Turkey Scratch Archives)

Bill Clinton, then governor of Arkansas, and Levon at the dedication of the Historic Helena Depot, 1990 (Photo by Gene Taylor. Courtesy of the Department of Arkansas Heritage.)

The Band in its 1990s lineup. *Clockwise from top left:* Rick Danko, Levon Helm, Garth Hudson, Richard Bell, Jim Weider, and Randy Ciarlante. (COURTESY OF THE BAND)

* * *

Things were much better the next night, Friday, with two shows scheduled. Robbie was better, and when the audience saw us, it was in our classic Band configuration. My drums were on a riser, stage right, next to Garth's organ, also on a riser in the middle of the stage. Richard's grand piano was stage left. These were sight lines we'd worked out years before so we could see one another's eyes to know where the music was going. Robbie stood between me and Garth; Rick, between Richard and Garth. It was right and tight.

All that day, bad word of mouth ran around the Bay Area, so the Friday shows didn't sell out. Backstage was empty except for guards keeping the few visitors out of our dressing rooms. When we went on after Ace of Cups, they gave us an ovation, and we all felt better. Robbie had recovered; he was playing guitar and walking around. Garth built some major tension in the room with his long organ intro to "Chest Fever," and the audience burst into a loud cheer when the dazzling improvisation merged into the chords of the song itself. It was only then that we felt we could make this work. Richard was singing well, and we played a lot of *Big Pink,* as well as some other things: "Ain't No More Cane," "Don't Ya Tell Henry," "Little Birds." People actually clapped when Richard and I changed seats at the drums so I could play the mandolin. We did "Slippin' and Slidin' " for the encore after five minutes of very loud encouragement from the audience. From the best seat in the house, I could see the people dancing and leaping around as we took it fast. Everybody had a smile on their face.

It was the first time in four years we hadn't been booed when we played.

It also marked the first time we worked with Bill Graham, a relationship that lasted for many years. He made things as comfortable as possible for musicians. Working with him was always a very special deal and a cut above anything else. Bill was the one who had it figured out.

Ralph J. in the next day's *Chronicle:* "The first thing that flashed into my mind was, 'this is Levon's band!' I had never thought of that. But there he was, bushy beard, swinging shoulders and his Mephistophelian visage pushed up to the mike on one side of him as he drummed.

'He's got a great voice!' I thought next, and then Rick Danko took over the lead, and I thought, 'There's another one!'

"I don't know why, but even the impact of the album had not really sunk into me the real feeling of admiration I got when I saw them do it. They were together, like a team, like a family, like a band. . . . Somehow four Canadians and an Arkansas country boy found it in themselves to express part of where all of us are at now while expressing themselves in language that can ignite explosive trains of thought inside your head. Out of all the idle scheming, they gave us something to feel."

A couple of weeks later we played four sold-out shows at the Fillmore East on Second Avenue in Manhattan. Cat Mother and the All-Night Newsboys opened, and the audience was with us from the minute we stepped onto the stage in what was described in the press as "suits and ties." These were actually dark western-cut clothes, string ties, and black boots, plus assorted hats from Richard's collection. We tuned in the dark for a moment—the light show had been given the night off—the lights came on, and the New York audience began to scream. Standing ovation. Looming over the Lowrey organ, Garth looked like a biblical prophet in his untrimmed black beard. We were very tightly rehearsed, because we wanted the performances to sound like the records. We stayed close to those arrangements and didn't stretch it out. We did music from *Big Pink*—"Tears of Rage," "This Wheel's on Fire," "Caledonia Mission"—and we couldn't believe the wild response. We mixed these up with "Get Up Jake" (from the California sessions), the Four Tops' "Loving You Is Sweeter Than Ever" (Richard sang great on a nod to our Motown fandom), and "Little Birds."

"Levon's dad taught us this one," Robbie announced. "We hope you like country music here in New York." Wild, stomping applause.

Garth got another ovation when he emerged, shoeless, from behind the organ with his accordion for "Rockin' Chair." We watched from the wings as the crowd sat raptly through the show's only solo, Garth's intro to "Chest Fever." When the rest of us ambled onstage I looked out and saw people on their feet, then on their chairs when Garth hit the first familiar notes. The encore, "Slippin' and Slidin,' " was pandemonium. I thought to myself, *Well, if that's the way it's gonna be . . .*

194

Levon Helm

My other recollection of that weekend is from Saturday night. I'd moved from the drums to the mandolin for "Don't Ya Tell Henry," and I touched my lip against the live microphone and saw a flash. I'd been shocked. It nearly blinded me. I went through the song, tears filling my eyes, my whole face on fire. Our equipment was new, remember, and probably hadn't been grounded properly.

In the dressing room after the show, I'm holding some ice to my lip and listening to Richard give the girl from *The Boston Globe* an interview.

"How didja start out in music?" she asks, notebook ready.

"Well, let's see: I started at nine and quit. Then got back to it when I was twelve. Then I became a party star. In fact, *I became a party!*"

All those old houses we lived in in Woodstock had a lot of character. Artists have lived in all of them: painters, sculptors, the Woodstock School. Richard and Jane Manuel lived in painter George Bellows's old house on Bellows Lane, where he painted some of his famous prizefight pictures. The house came with an old piano that had one key really out of tune; Richard used to work out his music on it. So when we were in California, he spent days retuning the studio piano so "Whispering Pines" would sound the way he wanted it. When we went back into the studio to finish our album a bit later that spring of 1969, "Whispering Pines" was one of the songs we took into the Hit Factory, Jerry Ragavoy's studio in New York.

We also cut "Jemima Surrender" there, which I wrote with Robertson. That was another of those songs about wanting the love of a lady of color; Aunt Jemima was as close as we could get for a name. We switched instruments: Richard was on drums, I played guitar, and I think Rick played a six-string bass. (We made sure to tweak Ronnie Hawkins in the lyrics.) We also recorded "Get Up Jake," about a sleepy ferryman on the Mississippi. ("I *loved* 'Get Up Jake,'" John Simon says, "but it didn't make it on the album because we had enough.") And of course there was "Up on Cripple Creek," which became the song by which we were best known.

It took a long time for that song to come around. It's an example of the way we raised some songs: slowly, bit by bit, putting things together gradually. We cut "Cripple Creek" two or three times in California,

195

but nobody really liked it. Finally, late one night in New York, we got hold of it, cut it once, then turned around and doubled a couple of chorus parts with harmonies. That was it; time for the next one. Garth found that Jew's harp sound by running his clavinet through a wahwah pedal. Little Bessie is an echo of Rick's song "Bessie Smith" from the basement tapes. People always wanted to know who she was, and I'd tell 'em she was Caledonia's cousin.

As of the spring of 1969 we still had never given an interview or done any publicity. We were known by some photographs we'd posed for up in the country, and that was it. Around that time *Life* magazine did an article about us that really played up that image: rustic hermits crafting American roots music up in the mountains.

That became our image, and we didn't fight it. We were hermits after a fashion. We spent that whole year recording and playing a few shows, and then it was back to the hills and lie low. That was what we wanted to do, not go back on the road.

As you've heard, heroin came into the scene around then. We got into it because it was there, and it was free. People were always wanting to do us favors, turn us on, and some of the people we liked to hang around with were doing it, so it came our way—no charge.

I'd feel hypocritical about soft-peddling this, because it was part of the scene and part of the era. It was fun when it started, and then it became a problem, like it often does. I think it was another Woodstock resident, the jazz bassist Charles Mingus, who once said that if God made anything better than heroin, He kept it for Himself.

I stayed with it until I got sick of it a few years later, and went home and cleaned up.

While we were finishing *The Band* at the Hit Factory, Libby Titus came into my life.

"By April 1969," she recalls, "I was doing OK. New York was enjoying beautiful spring weather, my son and I had a lovely apartment on Gramercy Park, Albert and Sally Grossman were living right across the square, Todd Rundgren was teaching me to sing and was going to produce my record for Albert's new Bearsville company. I was seeing Emmett Grogan, the poet who had founded the Diggers in San Francisco. I looked good and felt I was on my way to something.

"I heard The Band was at the Hit Factory, and I went over to say hello. Locked eyes with Levon—*major* flirtation. He made a date with me for that night and didn't keep it. Never showed up. I really didn't care and went to sleep. Five-thirty in the morning, phone rings:

" 'Libby? I wanted to call so I didn't ruin your night completely . . . And I was kinda wondering . . . Can I come over *now?*'

"Half hour later my doorbell rang, and this cowboy walks in. Very handsome, very charming, and he looks around—Persian carpets, velvet sofas, yellow tulips, pale lights—and says, 'Libby, I didn't know you were *rich.*'

"I said, 'I'm not rich. My husband is, and I inherited all this.' Levon looked at me and said, 'Yes you are.'

"I fell in love with Levon that morning: April 28. And he fell for me, I know it. Something major happened to both of us.

"I didn't hear from him for ten days after that. Then the phone rang.

" 'Libby?'

"I said, 'Yes?'

" 'I just wanted you to know that I haven't looked at another girl for ten days—and for me that's real unusual.'

"I just held the line. He said, 'Have you looked at anyone else?'

" 'No, Levon. I haven't wanted to. When are you coming back?'

" 'Soon,' he said. But he didn't really. Because The Band had no room for girls and never had. They were all busy living up to the story of The Band and the whole Dylan myth, which was an attitude that said, Don't get uptight, be cool, don't reveal anything. He couldn't bring me to Woodstock because that would be saying too much to me and to the others. So he'd call me at three A.M., and we'd be together. That was the only time I ever saw him.

"Finally, while they were at the Hit Factory, I wanted to break this cycle—and I couldn't stay away anyway—so I dressed up and went to the studio. Levon was there, but their road manager started coming on to me. Suddenly Levon steps between me and this roadie. He says, 'Libby, I'm going to Arkansas tomorrow morning to see my parents. You wanna come?'

"And I go, 'Yes!'

"Levon was wonderful with me: soft, ultraconsiderate, a gentleman in every way. Next morning we flew to Tulsa, Oklahoma, where Levon's brother, Wheeler, met us and took us to Springdale, where his parents lived. I knew I was dressed all wrong as soon as I walked into the house, because Levon's family looked at my curls and mini-dress with total horror. But I made friends with his mother, who was just great: sweet, kind, higher in mind and spirit. Nell just took me in and did everything she could to make sure I felt at home. It really meant a lot to me."

Summer of '69. No interviews, no publicity, really, and we're still a mystery. Plans to play a bunch of the big pop festivals in the summer. They told us about a big festival set for Woodstock, in which Bob Dylan was supposed to headline. It was going to be an Age of Aquarius type of thing, a gathering of people who felt the same way about the Vietnam War and a lot of the changes taking place in the country. We were totally apolitical, but since it was going to be right down the road, we said we'd do it. Then Bob pulled out because he was already disgusted that our adopted town was becoming a mecca for people seeking . . . Bob Dylan. Then Woodstock itself pulled out, citing sanitation and crowd problems in anticipation of a hundred thousand hippies grooving on Tinker Street. We might have pulled out too, but the deal was done, and we promised to show up if the concert went ahead later in August.

That's how we got to be the headliners at the Woodstock Music and Art Fair.

First, on June 22 we played the Toronto Pop Festival with Chuck Berry, Procol Harum, Steppenwolf, and Blood, Sweat, and Tears. We were looking forward to playing Toronto, but our set was a disaster, with horrendous sound problems. Those amps crackled like machine guns. The Toronto press called us "aloof" because we didn't jump around like the Hawks and stuck to our disciplined presentation of our music. They also described us as "too country." We played "Up on Cripple Creek" for the first time in public at that show.

In the meantime, British promoters had offered Bob a lot of money to appear at a festival on the Isle of Wight a couple of weeks after the Woodstock event. He accepted and asked us to play with him. We said OK because it gave us a chance to renew our friendship with Bob and see some of our English friends. We had a sort of live rehearsal with Bob on July 14 at the Mississippi River Rock Festival in Edwardsville, Missouri. We played our usual set for about three thousand people and then left the stage. But instead of the encore, Bob came back out with us, unannounced, in brown shirt, pants, and boots. His hair was cut short, and no one recognized him.

A lot of water had flowed under the bridge since we'd played with him at Carnegie Hall eighteen months earlier. He'd released his country album, *Nashville Skyline,* and appeared as a guest on Johnny Cash's TV show. His voice and style had changed, and not all his fans applauded his new maturity. But we were happy to rehearse with him, since he hadn't played outdoors since that Hollywood Bowl show back in the autumn of '65. So we played new, easy-rolling versions of "Like a Rolling Stone" and "She Belongs to Me" and did a couple of old things like "In the Pines." When we finally came back to do "Slippin' and Slidin'," Bob Dylan sang on the chorus, waved merrily, and split. "See ya next month," he said to me.

Everybody knows what happened at the Woodstock Festival. How none of the towns in the country wanted the thing in its jurisdiction, how it was hounded out of Ulster County and over into Sullivan, where a Bethel dairy farmer named Max Yasgur let it roll on his hillside cow pasture. Four hundred thousand people showed up without tickets, so they declared it free and open. And it rained, turning the site into a mudbath. We knew that Jimi Hendrix was there, Sly Stone, Janis, the Dead. Paul Butterfield came back to Woodstock after playing the first day and told us that half a million naked hippies were waiting in the mud for us to play. We heard that people were dying out there (three did), as well as being born (two were).

It was funny. You kind of felt you were going to a war. I think we drove down to Stewart Airport, and they helicoptered us into the landing zone and then took us into motor homes to wait for the show. I remember walking around and checking out the thirty-foot stage, elevators in back, immense scaffolding, and an army of muddy people out on the hillside. They were set back about half an acre from the stage. It was the final day of the festival, and they'd run out of fresh food and water. There weren't any dressing rooms because they'd been turned into emergency clinics. There was lots of acid around—they were making announcements about it from the stage—and the audience was immensely under the influence of anything you could think of. This was Sunday, and some of them had been out there four nights already. The crowd was real tired and a little unhealthy. We just sat backstage and did our usual thing: go in, shake hands, eat, play the show, and split. We never hung around.

It rained pretty hard after we got there; a hard Catskill summer storm. So they stopped the show and then started it back up. I think we went on between Ten Years After and Johnny Winter: "Ladies and gentlemen," said Chip Monck, the voice of Woodstock, "please welcome with us . . . The Band."

Inhuman roar from the dark hillside. We looked at one another in disbelief. Garth was shaking his head.

He started playing, and so did I. I played my cymbal, and he hit the bend pedal on that Lowrey organ, and we had a little duet until he slid into "Chest Fever." We were off. We played what was, for us, a real slow set: "Chest Fever," "Tears of Rage," "We Can Talk," "Don't Ya Tell Henry," "Don't Do It," "Ain't No More Cane," "Long Black Veil," "This Wheel's on Fire," "I Shall Be Released," and "The Weight." The encore was "Loving You Is Sweeter Than Ever," which Rick sang for half a million soggy folks holding up lighters and matches.

Then we got the hell out of there, believe me. We took off from backstage in a rented station wagon, pulled through the mud by a bulldozer with a short chain. It took off with us, got us through a field, over a couple of ditches, and then finally onto some hard road. It took us a couple of hours to get the fifty miles back to Woodstock.

By the way, The Band doesn't appear in *Woodstock,* the documentary movie, or on the album either. This is because we were offered half our fee for the movie rights to our performance, and Albert naturally said no. They did film us, in low light because we told them not to mess with us onstage. Our set was recorded, and someone at Atlantic Records told us later that our tapes came out better than anyone's. They really wanted to put them out. We felt we didn't play a bad set, but it wasn't totally up to our standard since Robbie's microphone had been inadvertently left on, and he wasn't much as a singer.

Ten days later we flew to England to play the Isle of Wight Festival with Bob. Libby came with me. We rehearsed a number of tunes with Bob and were prepared to play a dozen or so songs with him if things worked out. I remember taking the ferry across the English Channel to the big island off the southern coast of England on a summer afternoon. Two hundred thousand people had been waiting three days to see us, sleeping in an improvised shanty town called Desolation Row. The flower of English rock aristocracy was there to witness Bob's first paid show in more than three years. He was making eighty thousand dollars cash, according to the quarter million words about Bob in that morning's papers. Peter Fonda's movie *Easy Rider* had just opened over there; we'd turned down the chance to do the music, but "The Weight" had been used to cushion a crucial scene in the film and so gave our whole neofrontiersmen image a big boost. (Albert wouldn't even license the song to go on *Easy Rider*'s sound-track album.)

Bob was supposed to go on at 8:00 P.M., but someone decided the press enclosure in front of the stage had to be cleared out, so the show was stopped. The crowd got angry and started to throw things at the journalists; beer bottles, fruit, and clods of earth came flying toward the stage. At ten-thirty we went on by ourselves and played for forty-five minutes, took a ten-minute break, and then Bob ambled out—short hair, white suit—and played for an hour, with maybe a fifteen-minute encore. We were all tired and jet-lagged and never got around to most of what we'd rehearsed, but the show was fun. Three Beatles and three Stones stood at Bob's feet in the press enclosure, and the audience got into it. We mixed up songs from *Nashville Skyline* with new arrangements of older things. Garth's windswept organ dominated "I Pity the Poor Immigrant" and turned "Like a Rolling Stone" into a gospel song. Bob did a few songs by himself, and we finished with "The Mighty Quinn (Quinn the Eskimo)," "Minstrel Boy," and "Rainy Day Women." I can still hear that big audience shouting, *"Everybody must get stoned!"*

Our new album, *The Band,* was shipped a few weeks after that, in September 1969, eventually reaching No. 9 on the charts. Capitol released "Up on Cripple Creek" as a single, and this got to No. 25 late in the year—our only Top Thirty single.

For the rest of the year, the press treated us like gods:

"*The Band* is a masterful record," declared *The New York Times.* "Like a perfectly cut gem, every time you turn it, it shows you something new."

"This is an album to which you rapidly become addicted," Ralph J. Gleason wrote in the *San Francisco Chronicle.* "They use voices unlike any other contemporary group. The lead singer is either echoed by another singer or joined by one or more voices in a repeated verse or phrase throughout their songs. At times the lead voice and the other voices interweave in a way that sets up a rhythmic pattern. Since The Band's rhythm section itself conducts a continual duet between the drums and the bass, a complicated (though superficially simple) pulse is set up.''

Just so. I think Ralph J. came close to our secret in that review.

''. . . so overwhelmingly good, so perfect together, so obviously one of the most important groups on the scene today.''—*Chicago Tribune.*

''. . . consummate virtuosity, an amazing spread of musical styles.''—*Newsweek.*

''. . . musical depth and substance beyond anything in rock except some of the Beatles' best work.''—*Village Voice.*

''. . . the closest thing to a perfect rock group we have.''—*Vogue.*

''The Band is Life.''—*Tampa Times.*

''. . . quiet, gentle, bittersweet strains, rivaled in musical inventiveness and sophistication only by the Beatles.''—*Toronto Globe and Mail.*

For me personally, though, the killer was published in *Rolling Stone:* ''Levon Helm is the only drummer that can make you cry.'' (Today, when I hear Jim Keltner or Steve Jordan play the drums, I'm the one who's doing the crying.)

Despite these accolades, it proved impossible for us to completely escape our sordid past, especially after *Rolling Stone* published an interview with Ronnie Hawkins around that time. The Hawk had successfully remained in the bars of the Arkansas-Ontario circuit with a succession of good bands. By now he was the grand old man of Canadian rock and roll and lived in a mansion—''Mortgage Manor''— outside Toronto and drove a white Rolls. (When John Lennon and new wife Yoko Ono came to town with Eric Clapton to play a rock and roll revival at a nearby stadium that fall, they moved in with Ronnie and his family while they ran their antiwar campaign. ''John was so henpecked,'' the Hawk told me, ''he couldn't take a shit without Yoko saying it was OK.'') Now Ronnie was getting rediscovered in the wake of our success, and he had a new album of his own out on Atlantic to promote. Remembering our wild youth together, he took a highly confabulated stroll down memory lane for Toronto reporter Ritchie

Yorke in *Rolling Stone:* "We had parties that Nero would have been ashamed to attend. In all the time I been on the road, I must have laid a million girls, a few boys, and an odd goat. The goats were all right too, only you had to go around to the other end to kiss 'em.

"We had so many gang bangs and freaky orgies that I lost count. In every town, there was a dozen. Levon was always the best fucker. I remember this place in Arkansas—West Helena, it was called—there was this colored hooker we called Odessa; wrote a song about her, too. Levon and I would give her two bucks for the night. Levon'd go first, and then I'd go in, and Odessa would say, 'Mr. Ronnie, you can go ahead, but I think Mr. Levon has gone and taken it all.

" 'That Mr. Levon has a strip of meat on him like a horse,' she would say. Yes sir, Levon was well hung. He was a big boy, that one. Never knew when to stop, either. He had more meat than the Toronto abattoirs. Odessa was a good gal, and she could cook up a storm.

". . . Anyway, we named Richard 'The Gobbler.' He's a home wrecker, man, the working girl's favorite and the housewives' companion, or whatever that dumb saying is. If you're hip, you'll understand why we called him that.''

Albert Grossman hit the ceiling when this was published, and we weren't all that thrilled either. The Hawk's vivid account of whoring and pill-popping wasn't what we were about anymore, even though it was pretty funny. Albert called the magazine and threatened a million-dollar lawsuit. A few weeks later the Hawk told *Rolling Stone:* "I called Rick [Danko], and he was sure hot about the article. He said all kinds of things about how bad it was for them, how Albert was upset, and how I shouldn't do that to them. Hell, man, if someone said I had the biggest dick in America, I'd be happier than a dog on meat!

"It's fun remembering old times. I only talked about Levon because I know Rick Danko and Robbie Robertson are married now, and it might upset their wives to recall the wild times we had together.

"Rick told me not to mention their names about anything again. They must want to get a Billy Graham image or something, though that will be pretty hard, I figure.

"I thought the only thing they could complain about was my exaggerating the length of Levon's peter . . . but mind you, *I didn't exaggerate too much.*"

*   *   *

Autumn 1969. "Up on Cripple Creek" got played on the radio, and suddenly we had a hit record. That's when we got the call from Ed Sullivan to do his Sunday-evening variety show. We'd already walked out on Glen Campbell's show because they told us we'd have to sit on barrels in the back of a pickup truck and lip-synch, but we said yes to Ed because he let you play it live.

It was a big day in our lives. I couldn't sleep for two, three nights before we played. Then we got there and rehearsed, and of course there were no voice monitors, so we couldn't hear ourselves. This scared us even more.

We were on with Buck Owens, Pearl Bailey, and Rodney Dangerfield. We set up in a T formation around Garth; the guitar and bass were going through the same amp, so they were about as loud as an acoustic guitar. We were bouncing off one another, but we pulled it off, even though we couldn't hear anything.

The whole country watched it.

We finished the number and started to walk offstage. But wait a minute: Ed Sullivan was calling us back to shake hands! "Come on out here, boys," he said, and lined us up like he did the Beatles five years earlier. "I wanna introduce you. This one here is Robbie Robertson, Garth Hudson, Rick Danko's over here, Richard Manuel and—what is that? *Leh*-von or *La*-von?"

"*Lee*-von," Richard told him.

"Levon Helm. Originally came from upstate New York, but cold weather drove them to San Francisco, where they made their first major public appearance. Let's have a wonderful hand, and I want to tell them how delighted we are to have them on our show."

Back in Woodstock, one of the cops snapped a picture of Richard shaking hands with Ed Sullivan, and gave the snapshot to Richard, who carried it in his wallet for the rest of his life. "Best ID you could have," he told me. I know he showed it to every cop who stopped him for speeding, dozens of times. Richard always swore that sometimes the picture got him off with a warning.

We spent much of the rest of 1969 on the road, during a time of great upheaval in our lives. Band babies were on the way and being born: Paula Manuel came along around then. We were all drinking and doping a

204

little more than our share, and dear old Woodstock itself was becoming overcrowded in the wake of that summer's blowout. That's when Bob Dylan cut and ran, moving his own large family back to the city, specifically to one of the busiest intersections in Greenwich Village.

We played all over America to great reviews and further acclaim. *The Band* earned a gold record for sales of half a million units, and it was obvious that a lot of people who thought *Music From Big Pink* too weird liked *The Band* just fine. In Boston, where we'd been so reviled when we were with Bob, we sold out Symphony Hall and had 'em hanging from the balconies. We got ovations when we changed instruments between songs. We had a rabid audience for our shows at the Auditorium Theater in Chicago; they rushed the stage when we hit the encore, "Don't Do It," like an old-fashioned rockabilly show. The *Buffalo Evening News,* reviewing our sold-out nights at Kleinhan's Music Hall, described Garth as "a bearded, broad-browed Thor in the back, forging back-up riffs and hammering out organ solos."

The shows took enormous concentration to make it sound like we wanted it to, like on the record, and I felt under a lot of pressure in those days. I was definitely burning with a short fuse. An example: We had this road manager, Jonathan Taplin. He was OK, but you wouldn't want to send him for the ammunition. Early in this process he came to my motel room and started to exercise his authority to get me out of bed. But I was on him like a mad dog as soon as I heard his tone of voice, which conveyed something less than the respect that I expected from the employees. I picked him up until his legs were off the ground and kicking, walked him backward, and heard myself saying, "Jon, I'm gonna bite your damn nose off. I'll kill you if you ever talk to me like that again. Do you understand me?"

Of course, I didn't mean anything by it, but I noticed he steered clear of me after that.

My favorite moment was when Capitol sent us to Paris to play one night at the Place des Arts on November 16 as a showcase, since *The Band* had just come out in Europe. We checked into the George V Hotel, and I called up room service and just ate and drank as long as I could. No Arkansas boy ever enjoyed himself in that town as much as me.

Meanwhile, Robbie went up to Montreal to produce an album by a young Tennessean who'd fled the Vietnam draft and taken up residence in Canada. His name was Jesse Winchester, and I played some mandolin on his album too.

The year ended for us with two sold-out nights at Madison Square Garden's Felt Forum auditorium, two days after Christmas. We played for twenty thousand people. I loved those shows, because, despite the packed houses and all the anticipation, we still played together like a bunch of friendly neighbors having fun in the back of some hillbilly general store.

The year's last show was in Hollywood, Florida, on December 29. Then I took Libby to New Orleans, where we checked into a fine hotel and spent New Year's Eve—our first vacation together. Unhappily Mississippi beat Arkansas in the Sugar Bowl, 27–22. From there we rented a Cadillac and drove up to Phillips County, Arkansas, so I could show Libby where I came from. Grandpaw Wheeler Wilson and Grandmaw Agnes made us feel welcome, and I had fun showing Libby the sights and sounds of Marvell, Elaine, West Helena, and the Mississippi River, places I'd left more than ten years before to seek fame and fortune.

The following week The Band was on the cover of *Time* magazine.

Chapter Eight

DIVIDE AND CONQUER

I was almost thirty years old when The Band made the cover of *Time* on January 12, 1970. We'd known they were doing a story on us, because the reporter had been hanging out for a while. "You get out of school in May," I'd told him about growing up on a cotton farm, "and that's when you've already started planting cotton. You work right through until September, and the only break in there is the Fourth of July. I found out at about the age of twelve that the way to get off that stinking tractor, out of that 105-degree heat, was to get on that guitar."

We were astounded by the cover: an explosion of color, with caricatures depicting the five of us as bearded and mustachioed mountain men. "The New Sound of Country Rock," was the headline. "For years, practicing together for as much as ten hours a day, they played one-night stands in grubby towns all over the South and Canada. Later they played invisibly behind Bob Dylan at the peak of his fame. . . . The Band has now emerged as the one group whose sheer fascination and musical skill may match the excellence of the Beatles."

The writer had talked to each of us. "We got healthy when we came to Woodstock," Rick told him. "To us, getting healthy was getting up in the morning instead of going to bed in the morning."

And Richard Manuel was quoted as saying: "Well, we were shooting films up here [Woodstock], and then we were shooting vodka, and first thing you know, we took to shooting fresh air. What a habit!" A dark hint of the shape we were in.

We musicians couldn't have cared less about it, but my family and friends back home really liked us being on the cover of *Time*. The *Helena World* headlined: "COUNTY NATIVE PICTURED ON *TIME* COVER, BUT YOU WON'T KNOW HIM." "He is Lavon Helm, a native of the Marvell community, who started out at the age of nine in school talent contests. . . . Some old-time fair-goers will remember Lavon as the youngster who played the 'bones'—a pair of spoons which he beat against his knees while Linda Helm strummed a one-stringed bass made from an inverted washtub." The *West Helena Tribune* ("FORMER MARVELL BOY MAKES MUSICAL BIGTIME") ran interviews with my dad and mom. " 'I think I'd faint if I ever got a letter from him,' Mrs. Helm said. But she has cultivated the motherly habit of keeping in touch with his current girlfriends, who send her bits of news and clippings."

The same issue of *Time* reported that forty thousand American soldiers had been killed to date in Vietnam.

Among ourselves, being on the cover of *Time* was never discussed. I don't remember even hearing it mentioned. We were happy that it would make us a better draw, because we were about to go back on the road, but we were also trying to stay focused while recording our next album under trying circumstances.

Stage Fright was when everything changed for us. It was an immense turning point, something that was obvious to anyone who bought and played the record.

Rick Danko: "Those first royalty checks we got almost killed some of us. 'This Wheel's on Fire' was never really a hit, but it had been recorded by a few people, and all of a sudden I got a couple hundred thousand dollars out of left field! This was half the writer's royalties from one song. We were all shocked at these windfalls we never dreamed existed. Dealing with this wasn't in the fuckin' manual, man!

"If you've never made a million dollars overnight, like we did, you have no concept of what it can do. We saw it ruin people—kill them! Suddenly we had all the money we needed, and people were falling over themselves to make us happy, which meant giving us all the dope we could stand. People wanted to turn us on for free, do us favors, and some of us were happy to be taken care of like that. There wasn't anything real dramatic about it, because it was a fact of life, and probably still is. I'm here to tell you that it's a *crying shame* to see what success can do to some people. I'm sure it wasn't the best thing that could have happened to the band.''

Heroin was around Woodstock, around New York. It was everywhere. Being a musician, you couldn't avoid it. People told me, ''I can get you some of this.'' It was more of a shared thing back then, but of course after you use a little of it, you start to want all you can get. Later I started to mainline heroin, and that experience would last a couple of years. Once I got into it, it took me a little while to get a handle on myself, and eventually I did.

Robbie Robertson has referred to the *Stage Fright* era as ''The Darkness,'' by which he means this period of addiction and dissolution. But I remember that the drugs were just part of the black mood that settled upon us. There were also the issues of artistic control of The Band and the direction we were going in—if any.

When *The Band* came out, we were surprised by some of the songwriting credits. In those days we didn't realize that song publishing— more than touring or selling records—was the secret source of the real money in the music business. We're talking long-term here. We didn't know enough to ask for or demand song credits or anything like that. Back then, we'd get a copy of the album when it came out, and that's when we learned who got credit for which songs. True story.

The first one, *Big Pink,* went right by us. Some of the credits looked a little funny, but hell, I figured I'd just got back to town after being gone for a long time. Think of ''Chest Fever.'' Do you remember the words? Me neither. I remember Garth Hudson playing the organ. Now check the credits: ''J. R. Robertson.''

John Simon says, ''In those days that was how it was done. If there was a group, one guy tended to write the songs and get credit for them. It kept things relatively simple that way.''

But I looked at Richard Manuel as The Band's singer and writer, and Rick had a couple, and I figured that after all the work we did in California and New York, the second album's credits would spread out to include me and Garth; *especially* Garth, the soul and presiding genius of our band.

209

So when the album came out, I discovered that I was credited with writing half of "Jemima Surrender," and that was it. Richard was a cowriter on three songs. Rick and Garth went uncredited. Robbie Robertson was credited on all twelve songs.

Somebody had pencil-whipped us. It was an old tactic: divide and conquer.

After that, the level of the group's collaboration declined, and our creative process was severely disrupted. There was confusion. It's important to recognize Robertson's role as a catalyst and writer, but I blame Albert Grossman for letting him or giving him or making him take too much credit for the band's work.

I even confronted Robbie over this issue during this era. Can't you see what's happening? I asked. It's the same old divide and conquer syndrome that the management boys *always* pull on musicians. They took Elvis away from his band, Bill, Scotty, D.J.; same thing with Buddy Holly and the Crickets, and Roy Orbison and the Teen Kings. It's the old trick: Isolate the "star" and fuck the other guys. And it's always the worst thing that can happen to the music. Maybe it simplifies things for the company, but it interferes with our job, which is to make better records every time out. We shouldn't care about how much more work a true partnership might be for the brownnosers in the front office.

I went on to express my belief in creating music with input from everyone and reminded him that all the hot ideas, from basic song concepts to the mixing and sequencing of our record, were not always exclusively his. I complained that he and Albert had been making important business decisions without consulting the rest of us and that far too much cash was coming down in his and Albert's corner. Our publishing split was far from fair, I told him, and had to be fixed. I told him that he and Albert ought to try to write some music without us, because they couldn't possibly find the songs unless we all were searching together. I cautioned that most so-called business moves had fucked up a lot of great bands and killed off whatever music was left in them. I told Robbie that The Band was supposed to be *partners*. Since we were teenagers we'd banded against everything and anyone that got in our way. Nothing else—pride, friends, even money— mattered to the rest of us as much as the band did. Even our families had taken second place when the need arose.

I said, "Robbie, a band has to stick together, protect each other, support and encourage each other, and *grow* the music the way a farmer grows his crops."

Robbie basically told me not to worry because the rumors were true: Albert was going to build a state-of-the-art recording studio in Bearsville and wanted us to be partners in it with him. So any imbalance in song royalties would work out a hundredfold within the grand scheme of things. We would always be a band of brothers, with our own place. No more nights in some company's sterile studio. I was beginning to see it. Unlimited studio time. No more breaking down after sessions and losing the sound and all the time it took to sweeten the drum kit. Everything would be set and ready to roll. Garth could build a monster keyboard outfit and never have to move it. Rick would have all his bass amps in one spot. Richard's piano would stay in perfect pitch without changes in temperature and humidity. The guitars would stay in tune. Everything would be set and ready to roll, and we could take a shot at making a record as good as Ray Charles did. We could cultivate and grow a song until we got it right. When we wanted a break, friends would rent the studio from us, and it would pay for itself. All we needed to do was to play music and follow our hearts.

Well, it never quite worked out that way. We stayed in the divide and conquer mode, a process that no one ever seems able to stop, to this day. (Look at Bruce Springsteen and the E Street Band for the latest example.)

So that's when that great sense of teamwork stopped. Who wanted to pour out their souls and not get credit? Richard stopped writing completely after a while, and I don't think Garth got much credit at all until some of the final records.

At the same time, of course, we had a long-term record contract that called for us to produce another eight albums. We were also making good money and enjoying our newfound fame to a certain extent. We liked being recognized as the best band in North America and maybe the world, so we soldiered on and continued to record and tour. Those were the conditions under which we cut *Stage Fright*. But I know that after that second album came out, *The Last Waltz* started to create itself.

211

When that first money started to flow, I went out and got myself a couple of those Martin guitars I'd wanted. Garth picked out a black Mercedes-Benz diesel, Richard a Pontiac Grand Prix, Robbie a BMW, Rick an Audi. I'd always wanted a Corvette since the first ones came out in 1955. I was old enough to know better but dumb enough to go ahead and do it. So I bought the first of three Corvette Stingrays that I wore out between Arkansas and New York. I'd put 'em on the road, and they wouldn't hold together for me. I'd go back, turn one in, and they'd give me another. I put a couple of 'em in the shop real bad. Then I hooked onto a little brown one with a small 350 engine in it. A beautiful car. By the time I tried to turn that one in (you couldn't even hear the radio at seventy miles per hour), the relationship between me and General Motors was beginning to sour. But by then I was tired of 'em anyway.

I also bought some land just east of the center of Woodstock. As usual, I was inspired by Garth, who'd bought a mountaintop overlooking Ashokan Reservoir in nearby Glenford and was starting to build his house. So I just followed suit. Garth gave me my first copy of *Architectural Graphic Standards* and helped me put the water in there. He came over one day with a green switch and walked it off north and south. Then he walked it east and west, and said, "Levon, you could try right here."

We brought this old local in to dig. He regarded water dowsing as blasphemous. He was perturbed, this guy. "If that's what your man says, we'll drill it anywhere you want to." He went down to 150 feet . . . 160 . . . 170 and began to get that satisfied look on his face. Real satisfied, as if he was thinking how stupid these longhairs were for believing in that corny crap. When he got down to 214 feet we hit water: sixty gallons a minute. That's almost an artesian well down where we live.

When we first left Arkansas in 1958, Jimmy Ray Paulman was married, and I saw it cause him all kinds of problems. It complicated his life. To me, wives and steady girlfriends were as deadly as drink. I had that pretty well figured out for myself when Libby came into the picture. I'd been footloose and fancy-free, and now . . .

Libby: "In January 1970 Levon went on tour with The Band and

212

didn't call me for four weeks. Then I heard through the grapevine that he was living with some groupie in California, and I was devastated. He had left his dog with me!

"Levon came back from L.A. and came over to my house one morning at four A.M., like nothing had happened, smoking a big cigar. He had presents for me—expensive soap, a beautiful handmade vest— but I wasn't home.

"So I got his number and called him at this little house he was living in, in Wittenburg. I told him I wanted to see him and be with him; at least bring him his dog. And he said, 'Libby, you can come on up.'

"So I left Ezra with the maid and took off for the country in a blizzard. Halfway up the New York Thruway, the limo broke down. I'm dying to see Levon, so I got out and hitchhiked. Eventually I paid some guy fifty dollars to take me to Levon's shack. I went in and gave him his dog and got into bed with him. It was my way of saying, 'Yes, I do still love you.'

"So Ezra and I moved in with Levon. It was the three of us in this house. There were lipstick-red movie-set drapes down to the floor, pork chops in the fridge, a fireplace, one stick of furniture, and us. At first Levon and Ezra hated each other with undisguised glee, but then they formed a bond. One day, late in the winter, Levon went outside to chop some wood. He turned to Ezra and went, 'C'mon, son,' and my little boy went with him. And when they came back Levon says to me, 'You know what? We're *leaving* you.' My blood ran cold. He said, 'Yep, we're goin' to town to get some juice. You want anything? Because you can't come with us.' And Ezra took his hand, and off they went. A great thing happened to Ezra that day.

"I became pregnant in March 1970. I didn't mean to get pregnant, but I was with Levon and wanted to have his child. Friends came by— Albert, Robbie, and Dominique—and said, 'You're crazy! You could have a singing career! You're gonna mate with this guy, who's totally wild?'

"And I know they were saying the same thing to Levon: 'This girl, she doesn't know what she's doing. She's lost. She's *stray*.'

"I was madly, obsessively in love with this man. In Arkansas, and in Woodstock, people thought I got myself pregnant to capture Levon. That wasn't it. I loved him. Love was what we called it and he took wonderful care of me.

213

"That fall we moved into a rented house near Levon's land, and our daughter, Amy Helm, was born in Rhinebeck Hospital on December 3, 1970."

We were on the road during the first three months of 1970. We told Albert we wanted to play relatively small concert halls where we could concentrate. My main memory of this period is a show we did at Massey Hall in Toronto, with Jesse Winchester opening. Garth's parents came to support their son, who'd just had a tooth pulled, plus Mama Kosh, Bill Avis, Freddie McNulty; all our friends from the days when we rocked the Yonge Street strip with Ronnie Hawkins. Garth's mom told Albert Grossman that she'd heard so much about him that she thought of Albert as family. The place erupted when we walked out, and again at the sixth song of the set, "Jemima Surrender," where we switched instruments: Richard to drums, Garth to piano in his stockinged feet, and me to guitar and the microphone. In the dressing room afterward, Mrs. Hudson said, "You know, Garth, we had *heard* that you were doing concerts in your socks . . ."

After a few shows around Ontario, we went to California: Pasadena, L.A., and Berkeley, where we played two Saturday shows at the Berkeley Community Theater. Once again Ralph J. Gleason caught the way we ticked: "Garth Hudson, who looks like a combination of Beethoven and U. S. Grant, contributed beautiful sounds in both concerts, doubling on accordion and soprano saxophone. Levon Helm, who has the best sense of phrasing for delayed five- and seven-stroke rolls since Gus Johnson with Count Basie, is a remarkable singer with a fine voice. Rick Danko's bass playing is deceptively simple, and he looks delightful as he plays. Manuel's singing and piano playing and Robertson's rare solo bits fall together perfectly. . . . They created a hurricane of emotions and sound, one of the most effective musical products I ever heard. Their program included seventeen songs in eighty minutes, and was thoroughly satisfying. The audience stood outside the hall for a long time. Nobody wanted to leave, it was that good."

Our third record, *Stage Fright,* was recorded quickly to save money. The original idea was to record live during a concert at the Woodstock

Playhouse, the little summer-stock theater we had in town. We had some songs, and we were going to rehearse for a week in the theater and then cut this show on the weekend. But then word got out, and suddenly they had three thousand ticket requests from as far away as California for this little place that held about six hundred people. Then the town coughed, and that was the end of that idea. Toilets, parking, small town, etc. There wasn't gonna be any Woodstocks in Woodstock. So we ended up using the playhouse to record by ourselves. It was a nice room with a rounded ceiling. The stage was the studio, and the controls were in the downstairs prop room. Capitol sent up some recording gear in a truck, which we parked around the back. We didn't have to hear from the label about studio budgets and deadlines. When we got bored we played football, and I taught John Simon to ride a motorcycle in the parking lot.

"I didn't produce *Stage Fright*," John recalls, "because by then Robbie was learning the board himself, and they brought in Todd Rundgren, a young engineer who knew all the hip new sounds. So I was around Woodstock when they were recording, and played on the album, for which I was credited with 'special thanks.' I knew I wasn't gonna be on the next one.

"With *Big Pink,* we just went into the studio, did our best, and it was a hit. That made *The Band* much harder to do. In comparison, *Stage Fright* was simpler. The musicians didn't even mix the album. They gave one set of tapes to Todd to mix and sent another to British engineer Glyn Johns in London, to mix down with completely fresh ears. The album that came out was mostly Glyn's mix, with a few of Todd's in there as well."

With just ten songs and running a little over thirty-six minutes, *Stage Fright* reflected the haste to get it to market to capitalize on our post-*Time* notoriety. The first take on "Strawberry Wine" was the one we used, Richard playing drums. Richard and Robbie came up with "Just Another Whistle Stop" and "Sleeping," which included Richard Manuel's classic lyric: "To be called by noon/Is to be called too soon." Rick sang "Stage Fright," and Richard sang on "The Shape I'm In," both of which became staples of our concerts. I shared the vocals with Richard on "W. S. Walcott Medicine Show" (that's Garth on tenor sax). "Miss Brer Foxhole with the diamonds in her teeth" in the song's last verse commemorates "The Lady with the Million Dollar Smile,"

215

who used to sing with F. S. Walcott's traveling show on the dark outskirts of Marvell when I was a boy. We changed the initials so it would move the syllables around and make it sing easier.

It was a dark album, and an accurate reflection of our group's collective psychic weather. "Daniel and the Sacred Harp" was about selling your soul for music. "Stage Fright" was about the terror of performing. "The Shape I'm In" was about desperation. "The Rumor" was about paranoia. Robbie took most of the credits, played a lot of guitar (*Stage Fright* was called The Band's first rock and roll album), and generally tried to assume full control of that part of the whole process. And with Albert in his corner, there was no alternative but to go along with it. But we all realized something was wrong, that things were beginning to slide. We were in our fourth year of this band and had just turned in our third album, and for the first time we hadn't cut it to our standard. It takes a while to polish a record, but by the time of *Stage Fright* the pendulum had swung, and we were forced to put the polishing rag away. The days when we would *live* with the music were over. It wasn't as satisfying for me to leave it in a rougher shape, when you're positive you could have done it better.

Capital released *Stage Fright* in the later summer of 1970, and it was an immediate commercial success, if not exactly a critical one. The critics picked up that it was a record about loss and the sweetness of success gone slightly sour. *Rolling Stone* called me the best drummer in rock and roll and noted that Robbie wrote the best songs. Richard's "Sleeping" was too laid-back for the reviewer, who noted it wouldn't rate very high on "The People's Marxometer." Critic Albert Goldman called us "The Bland" in *The New York Times*. *Time* gave us a rave; they liked the image of the plowboy in "Stage Fright" and just about all of "W. S. Walcott," which sounded like an Uncle Remus story to them.

The single was "Time to Kill"/"The Shape I'm In," and it did OK, but in San Francisco one of the FM stations started playing a bootlegged tape of us doing "Don't Do It" in concert, and people thought it was our new record. I know *Stage Fright* disappointed some who felt it lacked that one killer song that could tie it all together. In San Francisco, someone wrote that "Don't Do It" was that missing link.

Stage Fright was a hit record anyway. I think it was one of our biggest. We went on the road for the next year to support it, and I recall these as being some of the best performances we ever gave. Richard was singing beautifully, while Garth alternated his wild organ solos with sax on "Great Divide" and accordion on "Rockin' Chair." Rick was mastering the fretless bass, which gave the rhythm section a different feel, and "Stage Fright" was a new showpiece for him.

Rick: "Suddenly that summer we found ourselves playing these huge spaces: Wembley Stadium in London, baseball parks where I looked up in the stands while Levon was singing 'Cripple Creek' and saw the whole third tier rocking eight feet in either direction. There were visions of catastrophe, people getting hurt. 'Uh, Robbie, maybe it's time to play a couple of slow ones . . .'

"Another time a beer company gave us fifty thousand dollars to play their summer festival at Harvard Stadium in Cambridge, Massachusetts. We were supposed to play for twelve thousand fans seated in the end zone of this football field, but it only cost a buck to get in, and the entire city of Cambridge came to hear us. I mean, sixty thousand showed up, and we could see there were more people behind us than in front of us. A lot of these people couldn't see and were real mad, while the people in front of us were going wild. Then that big second tier started to rock. I went over to Levon and whispered, 'Let's do a couple of donkey songs and *get the hell out of here!*'

"I think we did 'I Shall Be Released' and made a beeline for the limousines, but then we saw thousands of people running toward us like they were making for the goal line. You could feel this huge crowd just merging toward us. Security melted away. So we got back onstage real quick and played a slow one to take them out of that rage place they were in. Our usual encore that summer was 'Rag Mama Rag,' but it would've been a disaster; if we'd played a couple of loud rock and roll songs, it would've *exploded.* We had to play it cool so people could walk out of there peacefully.

"Another time that summer [July 10, 1970], we had Miles Davis open for us at the Hollywood Bowl. The show was sold out, and they gave us a list of people who could open, and we chose Miles because we all loved *Sketches of Spain,* right? I don't think we'd heard his more recent material.

"Anyway, backstage we had a visit from 'Dr. Feelgood.' All the musicians knew him, because he'd come by, and if you were feeling

217

bad he gave you a vitamin B-twelve shot. Who the fuck knows what was in there? He'd come to my room, give me a shot, I'd be feeling *incredible,* then he'd take out a suitcase full of precious gems and try to sell me diamonds! Perhaps that night he was trying to sell Levon a big ruby or something, because Levon doesn't even remember we ever played with Miles. There was no telling what was the true content of that shot!

"I heard Miles playing, so I went into the audience after a while, and Miles had twenty thousand people *crouched down.* His electric band was pouring fire into the crowd, and these kids were, like, *cowering* under this onslaught. Miles had these big wraparound bug-eyed shades, and he had his back turned to the crowd, and he was playing and scaring the shit out of the audience. But he never took them over the edge, and that's why he was a master, an outrageous artist. He took our crowd to a place they'd never been before. And we had to follow this. So we came out and played one of the worst shows we ever did. I mean, man! I think I bought a few diamonds myself that night. And of course someone taped the show or stole the board tape, and soon we had our own little bootleg problem in the form of a white-label LP stenciled *The Band Live at the Hollywood Bowl.* The damn thing even got a good review in *Rolling Stone.*

"Everybody knew Dr. Feelgood in California. Maybe it was endorphins in there. . . . Eventually I knew I couldn't keep feeling that good and live. It's against the law to feel that good."

My memory of that summer isn't as clear as Rick's, but I remember some highlights, like playing for two hours at Forest Hills, where they'd booed me and Robbie for daring to back up Bob Dylan. There was some satisfaction when we played the encore, "Rag Mama Rag," and the whole crowd got up on its chairs and danced. Then we did a little tour of Canada with Janis Joplin and the Full Tilt Boogie Band, consisting of some former latter-day members of the Hawks (John Till, who'd been in the Rockin' Revols with Richard Manuel, and a great piano player, Rick Bell) whom Albert Grossman had hired away from Ronnie and put on the road with Janis. Oh, Jesus, when Ronnie finally caught up with us, he started laying into Albert: "Goddammit, it wasn't enough that you stole The Band from me, you sumbitch. What the fuck was I supposed to do? I was still in the bars! Now you got Ricky and John. Every time I get a good band together, are you gonna steal 'em?'' Ronnie and Albert didn't come to blows, but it wasn't all that pleasant either.

When we weren't on the road we tried to keep working. Jesse Winchester was doing another record. I played on John and Beverley Martyn's album *Stormbringer,* and most of us played on John Simon's record as well. We went back out on the road that fall, playing mostly in the South. I think that was when we played one of our greatest shows, at Kiel Auditorium in St. Louis.

Mary Cavette recalls: "Levon always kept in touch with his people back home. He was always tearing back to Arkansas in one of his Corvettes, and we'd see each other from time to time. Next thing we knew, of course, he was a big star on the cover of *Time* magazine. We were all so proud of him, and a little shocked as well. Was this our Lavon?

"But everybody in Marvell always knew the brass ring was waiting for Lavon, so no one was too surprised. When The Band played in St. Louis, I flew in from Memphis, and Diamond and the family drove in from Springdale. It was very exciting: hotels, limousines, the bright lights. It was really the first time that people from Arkansas understood how big they'd become. But I remember the concert was great. We all sat down in front, and Robbie dedicated "The Night They Drove Old Dixie Down" to us. Lavon sang, and it was just great. They played that Little Richard song ["Slippin' and Slidin' "] at the end, and it brought the house down, believe me. We all looked up at Lavon as he was leaving the stage and waving, and we all felt so proud we could burst."

Late in April 1971 Albert Grossman's office announced that we would play a European tour that spring. A show at London's Royal Albert Hall sold out in four hours with no advertising, so they added another the next night, and it sold out too. We weren't that eager to go, but the deal was that Capitol picked up some of the expenses. We started in Germany, playing Hamburg, Munich, Vienna, and Frankfurt. Got a pretty good reception too. I rented a black 911 Porsche and drove it to the next date, Paris, with Ed Anderson, one of the guys on our crew. I'm on the autobahn, cruising at 105, wishing my boyhood friend Fireball Carter could see this, when a police Mercedes blew past me doing maybe 130, blue light blinking. We also got a big kick out of listening to "Rag Mama Rag" over Armed Forces Radio. Then we crossed the Rhine and hit the French border at Nancy. The gendarmes took me and Ed for dope smugglers and had us about one door away from the rubber glove room when I heard them discussing their union. So I whipped out my musicians' union card—Memphis Local 71— and that cleared it up. I told them I was a workingman like them, and they sent us on our way with a wave. (The real miracle of that road trip was that we found our hotel in Paris.)

We did a few press conferences, which got a little embarrassing in Sweden because we were apolitical, and the issue of American war resisters who'd fled to Sweden was the hot topic of the day. The Stockholm press is peppering us with questions, and I look at Richard, who's trying not to laugh, and Garth is in agony, and what could we say except that *we hated the war as much as anyone*. Then some reporter would ask another question about the peace negotiations between Mr. Henry Kissinger and Mr. Le Duc Tho, and finally I had to say, "Look, fellas, these other guys in the band are from *Canada*, and they don't know what the *hell* you're talking about. We came over here to play some music, and if any of you wants to buy a ticket, you're welcome at the show. Thank you very much." And that was it. None of us ever thought to write a song about all the shit that was going on back then: war, revolution, civil war, turmoil. Our songs were trying to take you someplace else.

We finished that Euro tour with two sellouts at Royal Albert Hall in Kensington, London. The Hawks had been booed there last time out. Not this time. Take my word for it—pandemonium. They were on their feet and dancing from the first notes of "W. S. Walcott," our opener in those days. That's about when we started making "The Night They Drove Old Dixie Down" segue smoothly into "Across the Great Divide." And I remember Garth playing the solo on "Unfaithful Servant" with his little curved soprano sax, another one of his pawnshop finds.

We cut our next album, *Cahoots*, at Albert's new Bearsville Studios during the summer of 1971. It was the first record to be made there, and they were still getting the bugs worked out of the place. Originally Bearsville was going to be a joint enterprise between Albert and The Band, an umbrella for various musical projects. That was the dream, according to my understanding, but this feeling of sharing and partner-

220

ship never developed. That's when I decided to build a big old barn on my land to house a studio and home base for anything we needed to do. This project became *my* dream, and I was determined to see it come to life.

Bearsville was the first proper studio we'd cut in since *Music From Big Pink,* so we were a little rusty, and the music on *Cahoots* didn't prove that memorable. The exception for me was "Life Is a Carnival," which Rick Danko and I worked out music-wise and Robbie put to words. It was one of the last of those real good Band songs that came out of that workshop setting we liked. Rick and I worked on that song's sprung rhythms for five days. Robbie was singing "Life is a carnival, believe it or not." That was all he had, and we were all stymied until one day Richard came up with "two bits a shot." That made the song. We kept trying different things with it and finally got it to a place where we could cut it.

Back then, we'd listen to *Big Pink* or hear a track from *The Band* on the radio and realize that we'd had the habit of mixing our records from the bottom. They sounded muddy to us on the car radio. So we got the idea to correct this by adding a high-end horn section to the track. That's when we got legendary New Orleans producer Allen Toussaint to write a horn chart for "Life Is a Carnival." Allen had just produced an album for Lee ("Working in a Coal Mine") Dorsey, and we liked the way the different "voices" of his horns sounded. At the time Rick Danko was writing songs with singer Bobby Charles, who was from New Orleans, so I think Bobby made that connection to Mr. Toussaint for us.

I sang on Bob Dylan's "When I Paint My Masterpiece," that song's official debut, since Bob didn't release his own version for a couple of more months. We figured we couldn't go wrong having one of Bob's songs on the record. Bob himself had been virtually secluded since we'd played with him on the Isle of Wight almost two years earlier. I played mandolin and Garth the accordion to give it that "European tourist" flavor. Richard Manuel played the drums and sang with our neighbor Van Morrison on a raucous number cut in one take, "4% Pantomime." This happened when Van came to Bearsville one night and began discussing the merits of scotch whiskey with Richard. (Four percent is the difference in alcohol content between Johnnie Walker Black and Johnnie Walker Red.) They acted out some lyrics Van wrote about management and a poker game, and Richard sang, "Oh, Belfast cowboy, can you call a spade a spade?" It was an extremely liquid session, Van and Richard were into it, and there was horror among the civilians at the studio when the two dead-drunk musicians argued about who would drive the other one home. Richard drove, and I think he made it. Lord knows he wrecked a lot of cars that year.

We tried to get the jazz arranger Gil Evans to work with us on a number called "Moon Struck One," but it didn't happen. Libby came into the studio and sang with me on "River Hymn," the first time anyone had ever heard a woman's voice on a Band record.

It wasn't a good time for us to be working together, or even to be working. Richard simply stopped writing and for all intents retired. Garth didn't get much inspiration from the material Robbie was bringing in. I'd shot my wad with "Life Is a Carnival."

Rick Danko recalls: "*Cahoots* was when I did a lot of work in the studio for the first time; my first real involvement in recording. I multitracked my voice for the first time on a tune called 'Volcano,' so it was a time of experimenting for me: arranging, producing, getting involved that way. Richard seemed to be tired of the whole thing. Levon wasn't that interested either. I can't emphasize how much success had changed everything. We were outrageous in our behavior, and it was impossible to get people in one place at one time. And when we did, it was hard to work because when we looked at one another and saw how wrecked we were, it was hard not to crack up."

Sometime in this period Bobby Charles came up to Woodstock. He was a hellacious musician from Louisiana who'd written "See You Later Alligator" and had a record deal with Warner Bros. He was writing some songs with Rick Danko while The Band was between albums.

One late afternoon I was studying the hooks on some old Ray Charles records when the phone rang. I heard Rick Danko's voice saying, "Levon, I've had an accident." My heart jumped, but Rick went on, "Hey, man, like I'm OK and everything, but can you come quick and"—here his voice went into a James Bond conspiracy mode— "bring your Jeep?"

I jumped in the Jeep and raced over to the scene of the crime. Rick and Bobby Charles pointed out a big dead deer lying at the side of the road, where it had landed after Rick had rammed it. Rick was saying,

222

"Hurry, man, before someone sees us. We're gonna throw this son of a bitch in the back of the Jeep, take it out in your woods, Levon, and dress it." I could hear the meat-cutter fever in Rick's voice.

"Enough good venison here to last the whole year," Bobby said.

So we loaded up the deer and headed for the woods behind my house. Rick and Bobby rode on my tailgate so their out-of-season kill was hidden. Back in the trees we stopped under what seemed like a nice limb, maybe nine feet off the ground, perfect for stringing up the deer and cleaning and quartering it. I got out of the Jeep with some rope and my hatchet. "Let me cut a sprout for you," I told Rick. "You can stick it through the ankle tendons and hoist it up in the tree. I guess about this size ought to do it." For a model I held up an old handle from a windshield squeegee that had fallen apart. It was maybe a quarter inch or so in diameter.

Rick grabbed the handle. "No, man, don't bother. This'll work fine." He took the old handle and the dry rope and started working them through the animal's tendons. Then he wrapped the rope over the tree limb, and he and Bobby Charles hauled the deer up in the air and tied the rope to the tree. Rick took out his hunting knife, ready to operate. "I haven't done this since I left the meat market in Simcoe," he said.

"Lotta good venison here," Bobby Charles confirmed.

I got back in the Jeep, put the high beams on all that fresh meat, and sat by the heater, content with my ringside seat. "I always enjoy watching a professional at work," I told Rick. Bobby steadied the deer while Rick stabbed it and sliced down in a cutting motion. Just then the squeegee handle broke, and the huge deer fell out of the tree. Both boys jumped back, but—*wham!*—the deer's hind hoof caught the side of Rick's head. Rick was holding his head and staggering, Bobby was trying to hold him up, and I was in stitches in the jeep. I hopped out and helped Bobby steady the butcher on his feet. I checked Rick's head. The hoof had hit him on its smooth side, so there was no cut, but Rick was stunned. "I'm all right," he repeated, but his expression betrayed him.

While Bobby guided Rick through his recovery, I cut and trimmed a sprout the right length and size. Then Richard Manuel showed up. I started to howl as I told Richard the story, and soon we were staggering with laughter and holding each other up. "Sounds like a new chapter from the goddamn *Deerslayer,*" Richard said, and the two of us went into spasms. We knew we'd never let Danko live this down. I mean, this was going into the damn *lore.*

"Gimme that stick, Levon," Rick growled. "You guys will probably enjoy this more than most when it's cooked. Meanwhile, give me a hand, Bobby."

Richard and I sat in the Jeep while Rick and Bobby attached the new sprout to the deer and got it back up in the tree. All daylight had faded to darkness, and the autumnal chill was falling fast, but the show was just starting, Richard and I figured we had front-row seats. All we needed was the popcorn.

Now the deer skinning could begin. Richard called out encouragement—"Be careful with that knife, son"—but lost in his self-imposed mission of supplying fresh meat to all the hungry musicians of Woodstock, Rick was ignoring us. As he was pulling off the deerskin, big clumps of fur came off in a drifting cloud. It was quite a scene.

Finally the skin was off. Only thing left to do was to gut the animal and butcher the meat. But Rick was trained as a butcher and had never worked in a slaughterhouse, so he was having trouble getting the deer's insides to fall out because they were still attached at the deer's rectum. Rick was cutting and pulling while Bobby coached and Richard and I cheered them on. Rick cussed out loud and pulled a little harder, and suddenly the deer's ass tore loose with an awful sound and spewed liquid deer shit with the force of a garden hose all over the ground, over the Jeep, over Bobby, and, most of all, over Rick.

This was when I decided that it was all over. Time to terminate this mission before someone got hurt. I was also afraid Richard and I might die from laughing. Rick turned toward us, his chin stuck up in the air, arms outstretched and dripping, encrusted with dead deer shit from his neck to his belt. He was standing very still, in cruciform position, to keep the mess from spreading anymore.

"Levon," he asks, "you got any water?"

"Only in the radiator," I told him.

"Yeah, and we're savin' that to scald down some of this venison meat," Richard said.

"*C'mon, fellas!*" pleaded Rick. So Richard and I drove to the house. Richard filled a five-gallon bucket with fresh water, and I got a clean shirt and jacket for our meat cutter. Then we hurried back for the finale. Rick used the water and towels we'd brought to clean himself up and put on the dry clothes. He was determined to finish butchering the meat. I figured the shock of the impact had spoiled the meat with adrenaline, so I didn't want any.

"Call the mayor and give it to the school lunch program," Richard suggested.

"Hell, call the governor and donate to the jail," I told them. "Tough meat for tough people."

But Rick had decided what to do. "We're gonna take it to Deanie's and get Stubby, the cook, to make up some chili!"

"It'll make a *lot* of chili," Bobby agreed.

"It's got too much hair on it for me," Richard said. "I like my meat clean."

I thought about this. "Some good hairburger won't be any worse than that sweet-and-sour tomcat meat we ate at the Chinese restaurant the other night," I told them.

"No need to waste this deer," Rick concluded. "By tomorrow night there'll be free chili for all of us!"

And that's what they did. They say Stubby made good chili out of that deer. I never tried any because who needs food when you can live on laughter? You boys care for another furburger? No, thanks, I like mine rare.

Cahoots, released in October 1971, got mixed reviews. The *Los Angeles Times* headlined, CAHOOTS VICTIM OF EXPECTANCY GAP. "For anyone other than The Band," wrote critic Robert Hilburn, "*Cahoots* would be hailed as a splendid album. But the expectancy level will keep the enthusiasm level down. That's the price you pay for re ;ording two masterpieces."

A less charitable reviewer (Greil Marcus) said *Cahoots* sc unded like Robbie Robertson had undergone a lobotomy. It was significant that one of the titles of Robbie's songs was "Where Do We Go From Here?"

Significant because nobody knew. The money was coming in, but we had an array of lawyers and accountants, and as I've said, there was unhappiness with Albert because now the publishing deals were going down with different companies set up for each musician instead of one company with equal shares for all, like there should have been. Now the old pencil-whipping started to really come down, and it was felt that Robbie was getting more than The Band. Greed was setting in. The old spirit of one for all and all for one was out the window. But hindsight—twenty-twenty, as usual—reveals that some of us were in denial. None of this was talked about much among the five of us, so resentment just continued to build.

John Simon joined The Band on tuba and electric piano as we did a major U.S. tour in November 1971 to support *Cahoots*. Taj Mahal opened for us, and we used the shows to warm up for a live double album we intended to record back in New York over three days of shows at the end of the year. I remember we even had a mini-riot one night in Washington, DC, when five hundred kids rushed the stage during the intermission, trampling the seats down in front. During the confusion five hundred more kids without tickets broke through the gates. In San Francisco Bill Graham—more relaxed than in his Winterland-Fillmore days—introduced us at the cavernous, sold-out Civic Auditorium. As usual we played our best in the Bay Area, opening with "Life Is a Carnival" and mixing new songs like "Shoot Out in Chinatown" into our set. After a standing ovation—I never got tired of those—we finished with "Don't Do It."

After the shows, I'd go back to our hotel and call Libby. I'd tell her to put the receiver in our daughter's crib, next to her little mouth. Then I'd just sit for an hour or so and listen to Amy breathe while she was sleeping. That was my main anchor in those days.

"It's the end of the goddamn era, isn't it?" Robbie Robertson said, lighting a cigarette.

"Sure feels like it," I agreed.

A few months earlier we'd been sitting with our ladies after a good French dinner at Robbie's house.

"Let's make a live album and close it down for a while," I suggested. "In fact, let's make it a damn *double*, because we're so far behind in the amount of records we've delivered."

"We could get some horns," Robbie said.

"Have Allen Toussaint come up and write some charts."

There was a silence while we thought about this. We might have been on our third bottle of Chateau Margaux.

"Maybe we could get Bob," Robbie suggested. "He was great at that Bangladesh concert. Maybe he'd do a couple of things with us."

Everyone thought a live double album was a great idea. Maybe this could be a way of making the perilous transition between the original Band and the uncertainties of the future. That's how we all looked at it.

I forget who made the call to Allen Toussaint, but this master musician from New Orleans—maybe the greatest arranger-writer-producer the Crescent City ever gave us—agreed to come up to Woodstock in the cold of December to write some charts for shows we were planning to record. Tall, dignified, said to be as reclusive as we were, Allen checked into Albert Grossman's guesthouse and stayed there because it started to snow as soon as he arrived—the first time he'd ever seen the stuff. We asked what we could provide for him. Did he want a piano? He said he needed herbal teas, a tape recorder, some chart paper, and the heat to be turned way up. The horn charts Allen produced during the week he stayed with us were like crowning our music with spiritual gold, like having a great wizard travel from a far-off land to bestow his wisdom on us.

At the same time, as the December days got shorter and the series of shows at the Academy of Music in New York got closer, we all got nervous. The horns were, after all, an experiment for us. What if we walked out with a big brass section, and the purists in the audience got annoyed? We didn't want "Across the Great Divide" to sound like a cocktail-lounge orchestra from hell. We all felt we were trying to cross a pretty thin wire, but the first time we heard those horns in rehearsals we were basically ecstatic. I mean, we were *flying* with sheer pleasure to hear our music with this extra dimension.

As it happened, we needn't have worried. The shows sold out: three thousand seats per show over three nights. John Simon, Doc Pomus, Bobby Charles, and Dr. John—Mac Rebennack from New Orleans—appeared with us or helped pull it all together. We played the first half by ourselves, and after intermission we were joined by some of the best horn players in New York: Joe Farrell and J. D. Parron on saxes, Snooky Young on trumpet, Howard Johnson on tuba, and Earl McIntyre on trombone. Garth Hudson played solos on both tenor and soprano, and it all sounded incredible. We revived "Get Up Jake," our outake from *The Band*. We finally got a cut we liked on "Don't Do It" after having tried and failed in the studio a couple of times. Garth was sailing through long improvisations on the intro to "Chest Fever." He could soar forever if we let him, taking the audience through Bach, gospel, jazz, nickelodeon, Anglican; whatever he came up with. On New Year's Eve we got one of these mediations on tape, and when the record came out Garth titled it "The Genetic Method," after a scholarly paper he'd been reading about classifying tribal music in primitive lands.

The final night we worked was New Year's Eve. We started the show very late because we wanted to be onstage when 1971—a hard, hard year for all of us—faded out. So we played an old samurai movie and went on about eleven. At midnight Garth interrupted "Chest Fever" for a bit of "Auld Lang Syne."

We finished those shows with Chuck Willis's "Hang Up My Rock and Roll Shoes." After the last encore on New Year's Eve, Bob Dylan came back onstage with us. The crowd had already been with us for three hours, but they roared as Bob came on in an old corduroy jacket, and strapped into a solid-body guitar. We ripped through a bunch of unrehearsed tunes that Bob called during group huddles onstage while the crowd shouted out hundreds of requests. We ended up doing "Crash on the Levee (Down in the Flood)," "When I Paint My Masterpiece," "Don't Ya Tell Henry" (Bob had written this song during our "basement" period, but this was the first and maybe last time he ever performed it), and "Like a Rolling Stone," which Bob introduced by saying, "We haven't played this one together in *six years*." Actually, we'd played it in England two years before, but I didn't care either.

The crowd loved it, and feelings were running high. They shouted along on the chorus—"How does it *feel?*"—and even our new horn section came back onstage and sang with Bob on that final number.

After the show I said to Bob, "When are we gonna go on the road together again?"

He looked surprised. "I'm thinking of touring with the Dead," Bob said.

"Well, keep us in mind," I told him. "We're gonna take some time off now, but maybe we could make it work like tonight, you know, but in a much bigger way."

228

"Let's think about it," Bob said.

The road was dark and cold as Richard Manuel and I rode out of Manhattan in the limo that night. We crossed the Hudson over the brightly lit George Washington Bridge and headed up the Palisades Parkway toward the mountains. It was near dawn when I got home, and I took off my boots and tiptoed across the floor so as not to wake Amy. I sat at the kitchen table, lit a cigarette, and thought about the shows we'd just played. Were we gonna get a good live album out of them? I thought about what Bob Dylan had said. Little did I know it would be almost two years before we saw him again. In fact, we were so fried that it would be eighteen months before The Band played its next show. Our next album of original songs was four years down the road.

January 1972.

I knew it was time to get out of Woodstock for a while. People were getting drunker, and drugs were everywhere. A sense of foreboding filled the air. The town was struggling under the post-Festival onslaught of hippies, runaways, and burnouts, and The Band was fighting. Robbie and Dominique had fled to Montreal. Rick and Grace were getting divorced. Richard was retired. Garth was building his house. The winters were long, and I felt like we musicians were just waiting around for the reading of the will.

Every day we'd hear about new and different publishing deals, until it got so that people were having more fun and making more money publishing songs than they were actually writing them or trying to write them. I think that's why there were no more classic Band songs after that, because people weren't willing to put in that time developing the music and not get something from it. The whole story changed from a musical endeavor to something you couldn't quite deal with. Greed reared its ugly head at every turn. I had told off Albert Grossman, and we no longer communicated. I was just biding my time until a better guy came along.

Fortunately I found something to do. I'd always had a complex about my total lack of musical training—beyond several million hours of field work. But I'd talk to other drummers I admired, and some of them had had a lot of schooling. They could write down their ideas. I was still young enough to act on this desire for some formal training, theory, exercises, the bare rudiments of a musical education. My friend Lindsay Holland got me enrolled for a semester at the distinguished Berklee School of Music in Boston under my real name, Mark L. Helm. I shaved off my beard, and nobody knew me. It was perfect, and two hundred miles from Woodstock, where no one would have to worry why Levon couldn't be happy with the way things were.

Libby remembers: "We moved to Cambridge, Massachusetts, renting a flat in a house on Bryant Street owned by the poet and translator Robert Fitzgerald and his wife, Sally. Levon went to Berklee every day. He set up his practice drums in the basement of the house, muffled by layers of Kotex pads so as not to disturb the professor upstairs. It was a cold winter, so we just kind of huddled in the house. Sally Fitzgerald gave me books by Flannery O'Connor, and I passed them along to Levon, who stayed up all night reading. In the morning he'd say, 'Libby, she's so *heavy.*'

"Levon adored his daughter. He completely bonded with Amy and was a very attentive father, especially in Cambridge, with no pressure from the band or the road. He loved to cuddle with her. He talked to her, took her with him, played the drums with her on his lap. He *admired* her. She was an adorable little girl who understood what she was told and said funny things. So that whole period was our most idyllic time together."

No one quite believed that I'd gone back to school to learn to play the drums. I think they sent John Simon up to Boston to check out this rumor.

"I thought it was amazing that Levon was studying," he says. "Remember, this was the guy that *Rolling Stone* had just called the best drummer around. I went to class with him, and he was incognito. The instructors called him Mark. He wanted to refine his technique, and instead of taking some master class, he went back to basics and was learning it all over again. I thought it was extremely interesting."

Rick Danko: "When I was young I either worked too hard or I didn't work enough. Either stayed away from home too long or stayed home too long. As we're getting older, we're coming closer to figuring that out. So now we're talking about our first sabbatical: '72, '73. Since I wasn't recuperating from any accidents, it was a wild kind of time. It was funny to have too much time on your hands.

"Levon had checked into Berklee, and Robbie was in Montreal, where they were thinking of buying a house. I went up and looked at a big estate (it was sixty thousand dollars then; you couldn't touch it for ten million dollars today) but decided the winters in Montreal were too damp. The winters were damp on the peninsula I grew up on in Ontario; it was drier in Woodstock. I thought, *If I'm not here, I'd rather be somewhere warm.* I produced an album for Bobby Charles from New Orleans at Bearsville. I think everyone played on it except Robbie, who was out of town. Then I went to Florida and worked on benefit shows for dolphin research. We had a couple of trailers on some burnt-out land on Key Biscayne, a lagoon with a couple of dolphins, and some deep-freezes stocked with blue mackerel. We ended up letting the dolphins go, but we had some fun and kept the Secret Service guessing, because this was near the house of President Nixon's best friend, Bebe Rebozo, and they used to watch us through the binoculars and try to figure what we were up to.

"This whole period . . . thank God everybody changes. We all had a habit, something we were going through. We learned that success is like an animal. When there's no limit, you do whatever you want, and that not only happened to The Band, it happened to almost everyone we knew who had this kind of success. Some people deal with it, some people don't. Over the years we might not have dealt with it right, but we're still here, still communicating with one another. If there's any long-term example to be set, I hope we get to set a few yet!"

Rock of Ages, the double album recorded in New York the previous year, was released in the fall of 1972. It was the most fun I ever had making a Band record and one of our biggest hits: six months on the *Billboard* charts, *Rolling Stone*'s Album of the Year, and the single, "Don't Do It," even cracked the Top Forty. Normally, we would have toured to support the album, but it was felt that playing the same songs in the same places would have been so much spinning our wheels. No one was up for it, so we just let it lay. "I loved *Rock of Ages,*" says John Simon, "because it really summed up the whole era of The Band. I'd played on the *Cahoots* tour and, like a lot of people who worked with them, hoped the Band would get back to work playing shows. But it didn't happen. I spoke to Robbie about this. He said, 'I don't wanna go on the road, because I just had a long talk with Levon, and

I really don't wanna get busted with a suitcase full of heroin. And have you seen Richard? I don't think Richard could go on the road even if he wanted to.'

"So instead I joined Taj Mahal's band for two years. He's a wonderful musician, and was just getting into his Caribbean heritage and mingling it with the blues. He taught me how you live the blues: viscerally, not intellectually. It was a great experience for me, but it would be a while before I was able to link up with my friends in The Band again."

Richard at this stage of his life was a totally maximum guy. He loved cars, and was known and loved by every cop in the mountains, famous for driving his Ferrari at 140 miles per hour on Route 87 and back roads alike. Part of it was the sheer joy of the chase. Once he tried to outrun a state patrolman in that Ferrari of his. He was about ninety seconds ahead of the cop when he got to his house. Richard drove into the garage, closed the door, ran upstairs, and got in the shower. When the cop knocked on the door, Richard answered in a towel, dripping wet. "Couldn'ta been me, officer," he said in that voice that came from deep within his chest. "I just got up."

The cop didn't believe it and didn't want to back off. Finally Richard closed the session by dismissing him with: "How can I miss you if you don't leave?"

I know Richard blamed himself that The Band wasn't working. He was in very poor condition in 1973. Jane left him for a time, and Mason Hoffenberg was living in his house, supposedly to make sure the drug dealers didn't victimize him too much. Albert was trying to get Richard to record, but it wasn't working. It looked like Richard was going to drink himself to death, but I didn't know what to do. We had an unwritten code, for better or worse, that we didn't interfere in one another's lives. This was before the days of crisis interventions. His own pain was in turn painful to behold, like a person whose skin had been burnt off. He'd say, "Aw, man, I'm too wasted to work. I know I'm holding up The Band, but what am I gonna do?" Bob Dylan went up to talk to him in this period but wouldn't go in the house because there were dog droppings all over the floor. We were all frightened that Richard would kill himself in his car, but when he did have another wreck the car dealers refused to rent him another one.

Maybe the greatness we heard in his voice, that catch in it, came from all that pain. To this day, we don't really know.

By that time I'd been messing with heroin for a while, and it was a good time to stop. A lot of good people were going down. So I made it my business to make a move away from some bad habits. The key was to *move,* to have somewhere to go. So I went home to Arkansas, where I knew I couldn't get any more when I ran out. My mom looked after me, and I basically checked into her house, consulted a couple of doctors, and went to bed for the four or five days it took.

Back in Woodstock I started building my barn on the land I'd bought a few years before, down the lane from the house I was renting for Libby and the kids. Designed and built by my friend Ralph Shultis, the barn had living quarters, a studio, and a place to make films or TV shows. We were living on royalties, so the money came in spurts, and that's how the barn got built. I think the electricity and the heating got turned on during that long, cold winter of 1972–73.

At the same time, I began to feel the pull of California, at least in terms of The Band's immediate future. Let's go out and cut a record, I said to the others. I figured it would help us shake off the Albert Grossman legacy and maybe give us a new lease on life. It was definitely getting to be time to make a move. Besides, you couldn't get sushi back east in those days.

We came out of retirement in July 1973 because some promoters put together a hell of a payday for us to play a supposedly small festival at a racetrack in Watkins Glen, New York, with the Allman Brothers and the Grateful Dead. The promoters guaranteed ticket buyers each group would play for three hours, with a massive jam at the end. A hundred thousand tickets had been sold, but *six hundred thousand* kids showed up, making the whole thing even bigger than Woodstock. In fact, Watkins Glen might have been the biggest single show in history in terms of audience.

I think we rehearsed for the show in Woodstock. Richard didn't like to rehearse, and neither did I, but it had been more than a year since we'd all been together, and Robbie had a new song, "Endless Highway," that he wanted to debut at this show. (We usually rehearsed on the road, where it could take four or five shows before it all came together.)

They flew us into the Watkins Glen site by helicopter, but right until showtime it looked like the show might not happen. The county authorities kept trying to shut it down for the usual reasons—clogged roads, sanitation—but the townspeople wanted the income and wanted the show to happen. In the last days before the festival, the county made the organizers buy tons of crushed gravel, and they laid out a little town on ninety acres, with roads and paths marked off by little flags. Then they made 'em truck in five hundred portable toilets. On the day before the show, the county said it had to have seventy-five grand worth of storm fencing. Every time the town did what it was supposed to, the county would find another five violations, but the organizers were going for it and had enough money to solve their problems.

We got to the site, and I asked about the soundcheck. Bill Graham, who was staging the show, pointed to the steep hillside overlooking the racetrack. There were already tens of thousands of kids out there—healthy, happy, eating their picnics, and throwing Frisbees. Bill said they'd been there since the day before.

I said, "Well, we'd like to tune up, rehearse a couple of our numbers."

"What the fuck do you want me to do?" Bill shouted, gesturing toward a quarter-million kids. "Ask 'em to *move*?"

So we went out and tuned up in front of the crowd, and they loved it. We accomplished in ten minutes what usually took us three times as long. Then the Allmans played for an hour, then the Dead. These were just the soundchecks, but the kids already had enjoyed a nice little show.

It was a pretty good atmosphere. "Hell of a lot better than Woodstock," Richard growled.

The Grateful Dead played the matinee, and we went on about six o'clock on a beautiful summer's evening, just as the earth was cooling after a real hot day. We were somewhat abashed as we faced an audience none of us had even remotely envisioned, more than half a million people, and a funny thing happened. We started playing, a little nervously, but it was starting to build after maybe half an hour. Then I heard Rick Danko yell, "That's it!" and saw him unstrapping his fretless bass. Raindrops splashed on my cymbals, and Robbie and Rick were running for the wings, hands off the instruments, lest they be shocked.

Jack Wingate, a friend of ours from Garth's hometown in Ontario, was standing at the side of the stage and happened to have a fifth of Glenfiddich scotch whiskey, which he encouraged us to taste. Then it began to rain like a cow pissing on a flat rock. We were starting to get bummed out because it looked like Watkins Glen was gonna be another Woodstock-style mudbath. So we're waiting, and Garth has a couple of sociable pulls on this whiskey his homeboy has, and all of a sudden the roadies are shouting and scrambling, and Garth climbs into his organ seat and starts to play by himself. It was extra-classic Hudsonia: hymnody, shape-note singing, gospel, J. S. Bach, Art Tatum, Slim Gaillard. Cool stuff. The immense throng of kids loved this, and then . . . the rain petered out. Just like that. It seemed clear to me that master dowser Garth had stopped the rain. We went back, synched up with Garth, and launched into "Chest Fever." When they heard the drums, half a million kids started to dance. What a sight! When I changed the tempo slightly, I could see a million knees *wobble*. Watkins Glen—burned into my memory.

"Why don't we just do our old nightclub act?"
I forget who said it, but that's how we came up with our next record, *Moondog Matinee*. It had been two years since our last studio album, and we needed to resurface. Contractual obligations had to be met, but some workshop tapes didn't pan out, and nobody had any new songs, so we went into Bearsville Studios that summer and cut some oldies. A lot also got cut at Studio A in the Capitol Tower in Hollywood, a famous room used by Frank Sinatra and Nat King Cole with large orchestras. I remember some consternation when we heard that John Lennon was doing the same thing at the same time with Jesse "Indian Ed" Davis on guitar and Phil Spector producing, but this was an indication of the low level of creative feeling in 1973 and an instinctive need to get back to rock and roll's purer roots.
I sang on Fats Domino's "Saved" and Chuck Berry's "Promised Land," prophetic in light of our subsequent relocation to California. We also pulled together a long arrangement of "Mystery Train," shades of Elvis Presley (credited to Junior Parker and Sam Phillips), with an additional verse written by Robbie Robertson. Richard sang Allen Toussaint's "Holy Cow," Sam Cooke's "Change Is Gonna

235

Come," and a bunch of others. Richard was "in a period," as Rick would say, which meant that he was drinking pretty hard, but once he got started, man: drums, piano, play it all, sing, do the lead in one of them high, hard-assed keys to sing in. Richard just knew how a song was supposed to go. Structure, melody; he understood it.

As I've said, there was very little collaboration among us after *Stage Fright* in terms of creating new songs, but we still worked hard when we had to. We all decided we wanted to try to get an arrangement of "Ain't Got No Home" by Clarence "Frogman" Henry, and we ended up getting a pretty good cut. Garth made me up one of those hoses that you sing through while holding the guitar. He rigged it up, put it in my mouth, and he'd play the thing with me while I sang. That's where we got the "lonely frog" voice the song requires. We brought in a local friend, Billy Mundi, to play the drums while I sang, because I wanted to play that bass line. I ended up playing bass on "Mystery Train," with Billy and Richard playing drums and going backward against each other. And when we needed an extra track, Garth supplied us with an interpretation of "The Third Man Theme" from the movie of the same name.

Moondog Matinee was named in part as a tribute to Alan Freed's rock and roll radio show, but the title also referred to the torrid afternoon shows we used to do in Toronto for the teenage-girl crowd ten years earlier, a much simpler time. The album was released later that year, after it had been mixed in California and wrapped inside a painting depicting the five of us loitering in a cityscape that was half Helena and half Cabbagetown, the old Toronto neighborhood where Robbie had grown up. Capitol released "Ain't Got No Home" as a single, with the original "Get Up Jake" on the flip side, but it only got to No. 73. By then we were off on another vector entirely.

During the summer of 1973 we'd been hearing rumbles that a young record executive named David Geffen was pursuing Bob Dylan. Bob had refused to renew his long-term contract with CBS, and had gone off to the Mexican desert to film *Pat Garrett and Billy the Kid*, leaving things hanging in the air. We heard that Geffen had offered Bob a lot of money and his own label. Instead of returning to New York when the movie was wrapped and the sound track cut, Bob stayed in L.A. and leased a house.

The writing was on the wall.

Around this time, David Geffen came to Woodstock. The word was that he wanted us to sign with his Asylum label, and we would do an album and tour with Bob. David invited me to dinner, but I passed. Then I heard that he had flown off to Paris with Robbie and Joni Mitchell. Next thing we knew, Robbie had put his house on the market and had moved his family to California.

I'd been saying for a year that California was the logical next step. The music business had relocated to sunny Los Angeles, and we needed to be there to survive. So The Band pulled up stakes and left Woodstock in October 1973. I set up Libby and the children in a house near the beach in Malibu, rented a suite at the Miramar Hotel in Santa Monica for myself, and traveled between California and the Catskills, where I was intent on getting my barn up. I still had strong feelings about Woodstock, and I figured we were going to need that barn someday.

It was easier for some of us to leave Albert Grossman than it was for others. He was important to us as a friend and businessman—it couldn't have happened without him—but we were growing in different directions. Albert was cozy in Bearsville, but we were having the sunshine and wealth of Southern California dangled before us. We also realized we were still a few records away from the end of our deal with Capitol. We had more years on us now, and most of us had children to think about. I thought things had seemed a little too cozy between Albert and Robbie, and that helped to get me through the transition out of there.

So we moved to California and set up a new regime. Instead of an old-fashioned manager like Albert, we had a team of bean counters: lawyers, accountants, advisers. We all employed people to keep tabs on things and exercise fiduciary responsibility so we wouldn't have to. No one in The Band really wanted to play that role.

Robbie and Richard sold their Woodstock houses. Garth kept his, and so did I. I stayed at the Miramar Hotel or over in Malibu. Rick was back and forth a lot before deciding to bring his family out to California.

"My original idea," he explains, "was to move to California for about three months. Instead we came out and stayed eight years! I remember I got totally drunk on the plane coming out. Levon and Libby were renting a house belonging to Robert Wagner and Natalie Wood in the Malibu Colony. I had directions to our house farther up the beach, but I had to stop at a pay phone near the Colony and call Levon. 'Help,' I told him, 'I'm lost.' Because I was jet-lagged and hungover. 'Tell me where you are,' he said, and I described the place. Levon said, 'Hold the phone,' and tapped me on the shoulder about a minute later. It was good to see him.

"He said, 'Son, your place is another twelve miles up the road, but whynchoo brings these kids on in, and we'll get 'em fed and bedded down, and you can go to your house when you're feeling a little better.' That's how we arrived in California."

Nobody's done what Bob Dylan's done for us over the years. He helped Rick and Richard write those songs and was part of our workshop. Bob Dylan knew that The Band was not in great shape, and he wanted to help us out of the sense of goodness he felt for us. Bob could've had his pick, but he chose us out of loyalty. I think we all had a big meeting on November 1 in California. Management was giving us our marching orders: We were going to record an album with Bob Dylan for Asylum. Then we were going to tour with him in early 1974 for six weeks, for which we'd each get several hundred thousand dollars plus a share of the recording and publishing money from a double live album, also to be released on David Geffen's label. That, we were told, was the deal.

"Hey," I said. "Uh, wait a minute! What about our contract with Capitol?"

Levon, they said, don't you remember? Your contract specifies that you can do outside work as Bob Dylan's backup band.

"I know that," I told them. "It's just that we have three more albums due Capitol under our deal. Can't one of these records with Bob come out on Capitol, so we can get our obligations over with sooner and get on to the next part of our lives?"

They looked at me like I was crazy and shook their heads. When I was out of earshot, our management boys asked one another, "Why can't Levon be happy?"

I didn't like the setup, but I couldn't fight it. I didn't have the strength to do personal battle with David Geffen and *our own people,* whom I bluntly accused of making things come out in everyone's favor but ours in the long run. You've got to choose your battles in life, and this was one I knew I wasn't equipped to win at that time.

Bob Dylan was nervous about his first tour in eight years. The struggles, bitterness, and disappointment of 1966 seemed worlds away, and then some. Bill Graham had it booked, and the money was astronomical for the time. People were saying it would be the biggest tour ever mounted. We started to prepare for the campaign with marathon rehearsals, thirteen hours at a stretch, and then in early November we took three days out and cut *Planet Waves* at Village Recorder in West Hollywood amid super secrecy. (The studio had been reserved in the name of Judge Magney and the Jury.) It was basically an organ-harmonica-guitar album, one of those speedy deliveries. Bob had a few songs and wrote the rest in the studio. He liked keeping it real simple. We'd run through 'em once, and then Bob wanted to cut. I play mandolin on "Forever Young," one of the few things we recorded twice, and Richard plays some nice drums on "Never Say Goodbye." The record was done quickly, and then the year turned, and suddenly we were back on the road with Bob Dylan again.

It was a much different story this time.

Tickets for the tour went on sale by mail in December 1973. They got five million letters requesting an average of three tickets apiece, and estimated that 4 percent of the American population wanted to see the shows: forty concerts in twenty-five cities during January and February 1974. Bill Graham had been planning rock's most ambitious tour ever for several months and had kept it secret by reserving the biggest halls in the country—Madison Square Garden, Chicago Stadium, the Los Angeles Forum—while refusing to say who would be playing. We were assured privacy, traveling from city to city on *Starship One,* a converted 707 jetliner redecorated as a flying Las Vegas lounge—complete with bar and private compartments. Bill Graham and his staff weren't even allowed to fly on our plane, lest Bill's rambunctious temperament ruffle the atmosphere. The tour publicist was told to stay at a different hotel than the rest of the tour, in order to keep the press away.

Dayton Stratton, our old buddy from Arkansas, was hired to help with security. He was doing pretty well from his clubs in Arkansas and Oklahoma, and I'd just got a chunk of tour money, so we each chipped in and bought a plane of our own, a good-looking Beechcraft six-seater. Dayton was an experienced pilot. It had six-cylinder Lycoming engines, good power, good speed, and that's how we got up to frigid Chicago for the first shows of the tour on January 3, 1974.

The shows were designed to run about two and a half hours. The first hour was Bob and us, then Bob alone, then The Band alone, with a big group finale and encore. We'd rehearsed for two days right after Christmas in the empty L.A. Forum, but felt very unready when we hit Chicago, despite a long soundcheck that morning where we ran through the whole show except for Bob's part alone.

We understood that people were excited by Bob's comeback from a long public absence, but we were astounded anyway when we walked onstage in the darkened hall in Chicago and saw the entire audience stand and hold up their flaring lighters in a roar of tribute to Bob. Imagine nineteen thousand candles in the dark, people calling and whooping. It was a moment, I'll tell you. I could see the normally taciturn Dylan was moved. He walked over to the drums and looked at me, about to say something, but instead he turned back to the microphone and launched into an old song of his called "Hero Blues," which caught everyone off guard, including us.

The stage was a jumble of amps and old furniture—a rolltop desk, carpets, bunk beds, and Tiffany lamps—that looked like some old Klondike prospectors' camp. Bob was in jeans, an old suede jacket, and a white shirt whose tails were hanging out. Then we did "Lay Lady Lay," "On a Night Like This" (from the new, unreleased album), "The Night They Drove Old Dixie Down," and "Stage Fright," which Rick sang playing fretless bass while Robbie tore up the lead guitar and Bob played rhythm guitar, his back to the audience. Then it was "It Ain't Me, Babe," "Leopard-Skin Pillbox-Hat," and "Share Your Love," which Richard Manuel sang in his best whiskey-and-cigarettes voice while Bob played the harmonica. Bob got his third standing ovation of the evening when he started "All Along the Watchtower," and then Richard sang "Endless Highway" as Bob left the stage. He came back in a pair of shades and did the tunes that got us booed at Forest Hills back in '65: "Ballad of a Thin Man" (with Garth playing those same mysterious organ fills for Mister Jones there) and "I Don't Believe You." When he finished, Bob stepped up and said, "Back in fifteen minutes," and we collapsed into the dressing rooms in total exhaustion. The amount of energy that playing for those big audiences required was incredible. I know I felt wrung out like a sponge. I noticed my hands shaking when I lit a cigarette.

I looked at Richard. He'd come out of a dark period, and we all worried about him. His shoulder-length hair was wet, but he smiled and gave me a look that said this was going to work. For the umpteenth time, I thanked the heavens for having Garth Hudson in the band.

Bob went back out and did his set: "The Times They Are A-Changin'," "Song to Woody," "Lonesome Death of Hattie Carroll," and "It's Alright, Ma," which had the line "Sometimes the president of the United States must stand naked." This always drew a big cheer in that year of Watergate, when an American president would resign his office in August.

This was a hard act to follow. We went up on the stage, picked our way through the furniture, and received an ovation that lasted three minutes. I called a huddle around the drums. "Call it," someone said. That's when we decided on the set list, right on stage. We did four songs—"Carnival," "Shape," "When You Awake" and "Rag Mama Rag"—then Bob came back and did "Forever Young," which was a little like blessing the audience. We finished with "Like a Rolling Stone," and came back after the ovations and did "The Weight" for an encore. Then Bob came back, and we finished with five minutes of "Most Likely You Go Your Way (And I'll Go Mine)."

And that was it. With minor variations, we played that show for the next six weeks. We kept from getting bored by finding new ways to play the old songs, but we kept coming back to what we'd once gotten booed for. Bob Dylan had stood his ground, and the world had gone round a couple of times since then. The audiences were closer to our own age—thirty-something—and were attentive and polite. I sometimes had a funny sensation: that we were acting out the roles of Bob Dylan and The Band, and the audience was paying to see what they'd missed many years before. We all felt that way, including Bob. We couldn't help it. The tour was damn good for our pocketbooks, but it just wasn't a very passionate trip for any of us. The one funny thing I recall is the time Richard became dissatisfied with the caliber of the groupies and asked the crew to take Polaroids of the girls who wanted to visit backstage.

We lived and traveled like six kings amid the excesses of all that

241

seventies rock and roll money: the fastest jet, the longest limos, the biggest suites, tons of white powder. We did two nights at Maple Leaf Gardens in Toronto and had a big reunion with families and friends, including the Hawk. I don't even remember much else. You get on one of these big tours, and after a few shows you don't know where you are. The road manager points to the stage, you climb aboard, and then you have to concentrate and go to work.

One show I do remember well was Atlanta. Jimmy Carter was governor of Georgia, and I guess his kids came to the show, because we were invited out to the governor's mansion afterward. Richard and I drove out in a limo, enjoying a smoke and the three-man motorcycle escort. The Carters made a family party out of it, and I got to meet the governor, and he gave us a tour of the mansion. But the part that Richard and I liked best was when Rosalynn made breakfast for us. Bob Dylan sat down and ate, and I think he enjoyed a good southern breakfast with the Carters as much as any of us.

The last night of the tour was February 14 in Los Angeles. Rick and Richard had both lost their singing voices, and mine was ripped to shreds. Ringo Starr was backstage, and we swapped hugs and drummer stories. Warren Beatty, Cher, Neil Young, and a lot of others had come to see us, so we put on the best show of the tour. After "Rolling Stone," Bob made Bill Graham take a bow, and then we played a new arrangement of "Blowin' in the Wind." The audience went nuts, it was a minute after midnight, and we were thrilled because six weeks of touring were over. Bob stepped up to the mike and spoke to the cheering people: "On behalf of The Band, I want to say thank you and good night." That was more than he'd said to any audience during the whole tour, other than "It's great to be back in Seattle, home of Jimi Hendrix." Rick Danko walked over and patted Bob on the back, and it was over. I skipped the parties afterward and went out for sushi with Paul and Mary Berry. Later, as my limousine turned north off the Santa Monica Freeway onto the Pacific Coast Highway, I thought it was strange that none of our shows with Bob had been filmed.

All during that tour I'd had a funny feeling, a foreboding that something bad would happen. Looking back, it was something we all felt.

After it was over, I was supposed to fly back to Arkansas with

Dayton Stratton and take care of some business at home. At the last minute I didn't go because we were moving houses or something, so I stayed in Malibu. Not long after, Dayton was flying home from Texas. We think lightning hit him on the approach to the airport at Fayetteville, and the damn tail came off the plane. Dayton tried to aim for the road but hit at a forty-five-degree angle. He was killed instantly.

Boy, that one shook us up. We knew we'd lost a partner. You never had to worry when Big D was around.

Exhausted and drained, we scattered to our homes. It would be another year before we met again to begin the series of events that led to The Last Waltz.

Chapter Nine

THE LAST WALTZ

The Band took a couple of months off after that big tour with Bob. We leased a seaside ranchette up in Malibu, built a recording studio in the master bedroom, and used it as a clubhouse and studio where we and our friends could record albums and cross-pollinate one another's music. We called it Shangri-La, after the fabled paradise in *Lost Horizon,* because to us Malibu felt like a paradise after years of gray Catskill winters. We all loved Malibu and its spectacular landscape of mountains crashing down to the sea, its fresh foods, fine wines, beautiful girls, and easy living. We were stars in a place that seemed to exist only to cater to stars, and so we tried to live it to the hilt while we could. Richard and I did a *lot* of laughing together, hanging out at Shangri-La with our raucous English buddies like Ringo, Eric Clapton, and Ron Wood.

We went back out in April to do some big shows like the World Series of Rock in Cleveland, where we played in front of eighty-eight thousand fans. For me it was good to be working again, because things weren't working out between me and Libby, and this gave us a chance to make a break that we both needed. She and the kids moved to Brentwood, and I continued to see the kids as much as being a weekend dad allowed.

245

Before the Flood, a double live album from our tour with Bob, was released by Asylum Records in July 1974. Like *Moondog Matinee* and *Planet Waves* (which had come out halfway through the tour earlier in the year), reviews were only lukewarm, as if the press were starting to tire of us after years of slavish reporting and reviews. While the album did well and made us some money, I continued to complain that these deals failed to take our commitments to Capitol into account. We still owed them a bunch of records. I'd talk to our accountant, our lawyer, our manager, but they didn't want to hear anything I said. They figured Robertson was the leader of The Band, and he tended to follow the advice they gave him. So it was frustrating for me, and I just started a process where I backed away from the whole thing as far as I could without actually quitting the group.

Shangri-La, our beachfront clubhouse off the Pacific Coast Highway near Zuma Beach, had a checkered past. It had been an expensive bordello in its previous incarnation, so it came with a Naugahyde bar and a lot of bedrooms with mirrored walls, one of which I commandeered as my HQ when in Malibu. We put in a good pool table, stocked the bar, and built a twenty-four-track recording studio in what had been the master suite. Down toward the beach there was a horse shed, with a couple of stalls and a tack room, which had been Mr. Ed's when TV's talking horse had been a resident. We had Mr. Ed's stable converted to a bungalow, and Richard moved in and basically stayed there for the next year, drinking seven or eight bottles of Grand Marnier orange brandy a day, relying on the sugar in the liqueur to keep his weight up. Robbie, Garth, and Rick were all living in houses near Shangri-La and were becoming involved in various outside projects.

I was in and out of there for most of 1975, as we struggled to make our next album, which took longer than any other we ever made because it became *impossible* to get everyone together at one time. I was also spending more time fighting with The Band's management than I was thinking about making good music. The main issue was our investment policies, which I felt were all wrong. We had a big chunk of money coming to us around then, representing publishing money and royalties from the success of *Rock of Ages,* and money from the tour and albums we'd done with Bob. Suddenly we'd been goosed into a much higher income-tax bracket and had to make executive decisions way beyond our comprehension. Our management wanted to invest in a condominium development in Colorado Springs and some weird tax shelters involving oil and natural-gas exploration—potentially lucrative investments that also happened to be extremely risky. We were told that our management team's other clients—Bob Dylan, Neil Diamond, Peter, Paul, and Mary—were really prospering from these fast-growing investments. Meanwhile, I knew about some prime land in northwest Arkansas that was for sale and *certain* to be developed. Friends of mine were involved, and the investment would be a low-risk, high-yield kind of deal.

Our management wouldn't let us do it. I was outvoted. Our money and some of Bob Dylan's went into these condos and oil wells. I got disgusted and began to disengage. I hated to do it, but things in The Band had passed beyond my control, and I had to get out of there. I decided to keep my base of operations in Woodstock, finish building my barn, and let things happen in California without banging my head against the wall out of sheer frustration. (When they told us, some years later, that we needed to buy seven hundred replacement refrigerators, the condo investment didn't look so hot anymore. When the oil and gas shelters collapsed in the 1980s, a lot of famous people lost a lot of money, and it made the papers as a financial scandal. Meanwhile, the vacant land I'd wanted to buy at home was soon developed into the first drive-in bank in Arkansas. I think there's a Holiday Inn there today.)

I still get angry when I think about it. We needed help and good advice, and we just didn't get it.

Back in Woodstock I hooked up with my old friend and mentor Henry Glover. I'd met Henry when I was eighteen years old and the Hawks came to New York to record. Now I was almost thirty-five years old and once again turning to Henry to help realize my ambitions. He and I talked and talked and decided we should work together as a team. Between my musical contacts and his expertise in the music business, we felt we could do some worthwhile projects. So we formed a company and called it RCO, which stood for "Our Company," and started to realize several dreams we'd both had. The first of these was to bring Muddy Waters from Chicago to record an album in Woodstock. I got a twelve-thousand-dollar advance from the record company in early 1975, which helped to pay the plumbing bill for my barn. Muddy Waters came to Woodstock in February. He brought along Pinetop

Perkins to play piano and Bob Margolin, his regular guitarist. We produced a pretty good album for him in a barn with a mobile truck and artists like Dr. John and Paul Butterfield, who at that time was working with his band Better Days. Most of The Band played on it as well. Muddy was wonderful to work with and extremely generous of spirit, and just to spend some time with him was a great honor for me. That, and the spirit we got out of our version of Louis Jordan's "Caledonia." We had a lot of fun giving Muddy the keys to the town at a reception in the great bluesman's honor on the Woodstock town green on February 14, 1975. I wish you could have seen the look on Muddy's face when he stepped out of that limo and saw two hundred cheering people waiting for him on a bright winter afternoon. (We were all thrilled when *Muddy Waters in Woodstock* won a Grammy Award for best blues recording.)

I spent the rest of that year back and forth between Woodstock and L.A. In March The Band (minus Richard, who didn't make the flight) and Bob Dylan played a big benefit in San Francisco that had been organized by Bill Graham to raise money for high-school athletics. Neil Young played some keyboards and did a couple of numbers with us too. Neil was making a record in L.A., which both Rick Danko and I worked on. I continued to see Libby and the children, and had other girlfriends as well. I helped the Cate Brothers, my buddies from Arkansas, land a record deal with Asylum. Earl and Ernie had developed into one of the best bands in the South, playing the same circuit we used to ply as the Hawks. My original idea had been to produce the album for the Cates, but there were schedule problems, and the record got produced by Steve Cropper, master guitarist with Booker T. and the MGs, so instead I just rooted 'em on and played on their record a little.

In June Columbia released an album called *The Basement Tapes* by Bob Dylan and The Band. The twenty songs had been picked from the demos Garth had recorded in the basement of Big Pink back in 1967, sweetened in some cases by guitar overdubs recorded by Robbie that year at Shangri-La. As usual I expressed my unhappiness at releasing yet another album that didn't count toward our record deal (Capitol told us we were "on suspension" at the time), but I got outvoted once again. Tough luck.

Why, they wanted to know, can't Levon be happy?

Our seventh Band album, *Northern Lights, Southern Cross,* came out at the end of 1975. It was our first recording of original music since *Cahoots* four years earlier. Some of our fans were surprised we even put out a new record at all, since it was assumed we were in semiretirement and had left the field to the Allmans, the Eagles, Steely Dan, and other bands that had come along. We'd worked on this new music for months, on and off, and in the end got eight extended songs, all credited to Robbie Robertson. I sang on half: "Forbidden Fruit" (about the lure of heroin), "Ophelia" (Grand Ole Opry comedienne Minnie Pearl's real name), "Ring Your Bell," and some of Robbie's tribute to the Cajuns, "Acadian Driftwood," which had that old three-voice Band mixture on the verses. Rick Danko did one of his best vocals on "It Makes No Difference," and Richard sang beautifully on "Hobo Jungle" and "Rags and Bones." One number, "Jupiter Hollow," was a showcase for Garth, who really earned his nickname of H.B. (Honey Boy) on that album, because he was the one to put in the studio time that sweetened the record and put it in that state-of-the-studio mode. Shangri-La had twenty-four tracks, and Garth used that leeway to craft as many as half a dozen keyboard tracks on a single song using the ARP, Roland, Mini Moog, and other synthesizers he was working with. A lot of this stuff was tied together with a computer keyboard, which Garth wielded like the wizard he is, giving the music an almost orchestral overlay. Garth also played horns all over the record and dubbed a piccolo and bagpipe onto "Acadian Driftwood," whose fiddle part was added by Byron Berline. We also had an outtake called "Twilight," a little reggae song that we liked enough to use as the B-side to the "Acadian Driftwood" single and to put in the set when we started playing shows again the following year.

Northern Lights, Southern Cross was the best record we'd made since *The Band* in 1969, but it got only middling reviews, and Capitol couldn't break the first single, "Ophelia," on the radio. I don't think we even got a gold record out of it. The press blamed Robbie, since he'd taken all the credit as our principal writer. We were photographed walking the sands of Malibu in our usual beards, shades, and hats, and were castigated in *Rolling Stone* for not having new ideas. And all I heard on the radio as I drove my little BMW 2002 down the coast to go see the children was Fleetwood Mac's new, self-titled album, which had taken America by storm. Soft rock, they called it, and it was supposed to be the coming thing.

Eric Clapton began recording his *No Reason to Cry* album at Shangri-La early in 1976, and the Band played on a track called "All Our Past Times," which related to Eric's friendship with Richard Manuel. Eric liked the atmosphere at Shangri-La, and he and Richard were going through some of the same tribulations regarding life. Also working on Eric's record were Ron Wood from the Stones, the great Billy Preston, and Bob Dylan, who kept trying to get Clapton to record a new song he'd just written, "Seven Days." It turned out that Eric had enough material, but Ron Wood liked the song so much he cut it at Shangri-La a few weeks later for a solo album of his own, with Mick Fleetwood on drums. Those were the glory days of Shangri-La, a relaxed place to cut a record. I had my own room there, and I'd bring the kids up for a few days at the beach. I was also going back to Arkansas with the children as much as time allowed, since my mom could never get enough of having Amy and Ezra around.

The Band went out on tour that summer of the American bicentennial. It was our first national tour in two years. Late in June 1976, we redeployed at Stanford University's Frost Amphitheater in Palo Alto, California. It was a sold-out matinee with the Flying Burrito Brothers opening, and the sun had bleached the half-naked crowd by the time we made our way to the stage aboard a fire engine spraying water on the parched crowd. I got up on the drums, made sure everybody was in his place, saw that Garth was set and ready behind his high-tech panel of keyboards, and started playing the drum lick to "Don't Do It." The kids began to dance and cheer, Rick Danko hit the bass line, Richard came in on piano, then the guitar—and we were flying.

We did ninety-minute shows that summer all over the country, playing our familiar songs and more recent material from *Northern Lights*. "It Makes No Difference" gave Rick a showcase in the middle of the set, and I did "Ophelia" and "Forbidden Fruit." Everyone was watching Richard carefully, and he had good nights and bad. Sometimes he shouted and spat out the lyrics to "Tears of Rage" with biblical fervor; other times he sounded painful to hear, but still drenched in the conviction that Richard brought to a song. Richard could hurt you with that voice of his.

On June 28 we played outdoors in Santa Barbara, our first appearance in Southern California in six years (excluding the Dylan tour). We got one of those rapturous greetings that we all loved, and as the Fourth of July bicentennial neared, Garth began working American anthems into his "Chest Fever" introduction, which made everybody laugh; a nice part of the show. I remember that Richard could barely sing at that show. His voice was so hoarse that he faltered, but he struggled so hard with "In a Station" that once again everybody's heart went out to him. Despite all the self-destructive behavior, you just couldn't be mad at Richard.

Our shows usually started rough but ended smooth. The moment where we faded "The Night They Drove Old Dixie Down" into "Chest Fever" was always magic for me, and Richard sang the thing as if for his very life. "The Band," said the *Los Angeles Times* the next day, "reexerted [sic] its role as America's premier rock band, but it needs to deal more forcefully with the issue of its past vs. its present." A few days later *The New York Times* concluded its review of a Westchester show: "Having performed its magnificent early music during the concert's first half, The Band devoted the last half of its set to more superficial numbers from its more recent albums. The performance was musically impeccable, but it lacked the grand, almost desperate intensity of the first part of the show."

We really hit our groove late that August when we played three sold-out nights at the Greek Theatre in L.A. All our families and friends came, and the shows were some of our best. I loved looking into the wings and seeing all the Band children—beautiful little boys and girls—dancing and wiggling as they proudly watched their daddies play.

Around this time we played a pretty good show at the Carter Barron Amphitheater in Washington, DC, which was broadcast on a widely syndicated rock radio show called *The King Biscuit Flower Hour*— pretty ironic, since I'd grown up listening to *King Biscuit Time* on KFFA back in Helena.

The Band started to unravel maybe two thirds through this tour,

251

which turned out to be our last with the original lineup. Robbie's son was born around then, making it harder for him to get on that plane and go to the show. We had a couple of bumpy rides on that tour, and it didn't take too much air turbulance to make us remember our prayers, especially in the wake of Dayton Stratton's tragic accident.

Around then Rick Danko signed a solo deal with Arista Records. I knew he'd been unhappy with things for a long time, and I think he'd seen the end coming and wanted to get on with his career. As he told me at the time, "For me to sing three or four songs a year, do some background vocals, and then not go on tour . . . Well, it's just not enough to keep me occupied, and I can't afford to go crazy anymore."

Then in September, just as we really started to play with some real fire, we were forced to cancel ten dates—a quarter of the tour—when Richard injured his neck in a boating accident near Austin, Texas. Robbie got superstitious when this happened. It was part of the last straw for him, since he was already wound up about being away from home and the general situation. We weren't really talking too much at the time, me and Robbie, and things deteriorated further when he told me he was thinking of hanging it up.

I didn't say anything, just looked at him.

"I have this, like, premonition," he told me. "I mean, look at it. You can just tell that something's gonna happen, that something's . . . *wrong.* I don't know, Lee. Do we have to spend the rest of our lives on the road? How long before we can't stand each other or end up like Sam and Dave, man, fucking knife fights in the dressing room?" He took a drag of his cigarette and waved it in the air. "Or maybe it'll be like the Ink Spots, the Mills Brothers: One day we'll do a show, and they'll say, 'Shit, we've seen you old guys a million times. Why don't you *go home?*'"

"You're strung pretty tight," I told him.

"I got a bad feeling," Robbie repeated. "The numbers don't add up anymore."

The doctors had prescribed six weeks of traction for Richard's injury, but someone found a team of Tibetan-trained healers at a foundation in Dallas, who came and gave Richard some therapy and told him to go to bed for three days. We resumed the tour at the Palladium in Manhattan. Richard looked ill, and no one was smiling. So we opened with "Ophelia," which led to "The Shape I'm In." Richard took the first verse and growled it so beautifully that we all grinned at one another in relief.

Sometime in September we got word that Robertson and our management wanted to put it away. Robbie had had enough, and they decided to kill The Band and go out with a bang. At first I thought it might be a joke, but Robertson said he'd had a bellyful and was dead serious. In fact, it turned out they had a plan. Robbie wanted us to play a farewell show in San Francisco, where it all started for us, sometime around Thanksgiving. He wanted everyone we'd played with along the way—from Ronnie Hawkins to Bob Dylan—to perform, but without bringing their own musicians. We would be the backup band for our guests. They were already lining up people from all phases of our career: Hawk, Muddy Waters, Paul Butterfield, Van Morrison, Neil Young, Ringo, Eric Clapton, Allen Toussaint, the *Rock of Ages* horn section. It was gonna be the concert of the century, maybe the show to end the whole so-called rock era. That's what they told me, anyway.

The only problem was, I didn't want any part of it. I didn't want to break up The Band. And I told this to Robbie one day in early October 1976 at our lawyer's office. It was one of many acrimonious meetings we had, but even though I always got there on time, I always had the feeling the *real* meeting had started an hour earlier. I was actually too late.

The lids of his eyes drooped as I spoke. I think he'd been up all night working on a Neil Diamond album he was producing, and he looked real tired and burned out. Robbie lit a fresh cigarette with the end of the one he'd just smoked. I'd known him—or thought I'd known him—for seventeen years, since we were both teenagers. Eight years in the bars and eight years on the arena circuit had come down to this.

Now he was saying he was sick of it all. He said he wanted to keep on recording and making music with us, but he didn't want to go on the road anymore. "We're not learning anything, man," he told me. "It's not doing anything for us, and in fact it feels dangerous to me. Look what's happening, Levon. I'm getting superstitious. Look at Dayton Stratton. Every time I get on the plane I'm thinking about this stuff. The whole thing just isn't healthy anymore."

"I'm not in it for my health," I said. "I'm a *musician,* and I wanna live the way I do."

253

He said, "That's what I want to do. I want to *live*. I'm tired of the danger out there. How long before the odds run out? How long before someone dies? I am *through* with the road, man, and that is that. It's a done deal."

There was a silence. He lit another cigarette.

I said, "What if the rest of us want to continue as The Band?"

Robbie thought for a minute, and his face darkened. "We could stop it." By "we" he meant that big business had taken over. I knew he and our management had already approached Warner Bros. about a new record deal, and Warners was real interested in getting The Band. Bill Graham had been contacted about the last concert, and there was even some talk of documenting the whole thing for a feature film. Robertson was saying the rest of us didn't have any choice other than to do what we were told.

This made me enraged. "The *fuck* you could stop it," I said. "I know big business is running this thing now, but if you think you have control over my life and if you want to prove it, I'll meet you back here in the morning with my lawyer, and we'll get the fucking stenographer in here, do the goddamn shorthand, and we'll see who has control. We'll go over the goddamn *contracts* and see who ends up running the show, because I'll fight you tooth and nail just to feel better about it. You may think you're running the damn show, but I'll prove to you at ten o'clock in the morning that you ain't. I'll show you, you son of a bitch!"

"Aw, Levon, come on . . ."

"No, man, *you* come on. I don't completely understand what your motives are to destroy this group, but I do know it's a crying shame to take this band from productivity to retirement because you're superstitious, or for the sake of a final payday. I know you got all our lawyers and accountants and whatever on your side—if you ask me, they could all use a stake driven through their hearts for all the good they did us—but this whole thing is dead wrong."

He didn't say anything, and the meeting was over. I walked out.

I didn't really know what to do about this situation. I thought of fighting it, but then I called Jim Gallman, my lawyer in Arkansas, and told him the story. He thought for a while and told me I was beat. He told me, in short, "You can't fight 'em and win anything, so my advice is, do whatever the contract says, *even if it makes you puke.* Do it, puke, and get out of the way. Then you can cuss 'em out, tell 'em whatever you want.''

So that's what I did. I went back to Woodstock for a while and waited to see what would happen. I talked to the other guys in the group. Some of us figured that The Band could go on as a recording unit, and use that framework as an umbrella to do our own things. Rick told me he'd lost or had to pass up some good opportunities because working under our banner seemed more exclusive than it had to be. He had a record deal of his own to think about anyway.

Once we all agreed to do it, we rationalized that this last big show would give us each a running start to the next phase in our lives. Eventually I got to the point of saying, OK, I'll put my own band together and see what happens. I was the still the least in favor of ''The Last Waltz,'' as Robertson was calling this final show of ours. I was the one who insisted he wasn't tired of traveling and sleeping late in good hotel suites and eating in fine restaurants and playing for people, but I decided I didn't want to put myself in any intractable position. I could even understand wanting to stay home with your family and work on movie music, but I didn't want to be that guy. So around this time I called Henry Glover and told him to start thinking about gearing up RCO for another project, and let's make it a big one.

So The Last Waltz got set up with very limited input from me. I wish we could have put out fifty albums, and played twice as much and reached out to ten times more people than we already had. But I also resolved not to have too many regrets and not to put up with too much horseshit concerning The Last Waltz. I went along with it like a good soldier, but for the record, I didn't get a lot of joy from seeing The Band fold itself up.

Nor, so we heard, did a lot of people when they were approached to play. Bob Dylan said it made him real sad. Neil Young said he wasn't ready to hear this bit of news. Bill Graham was shocked as well but saw the dramatic possibilities. He offered the Winterland Ballroom, site of our first show as The Band, on Thanksgiving night, complete with a full turkey dinner with all the fixin's, dancing to an orchestra, followed by our show. In other words, one of Bill Graham's patented extravaganzas, at twenty-five bucks a ticket. We took the date.

On October 18 details were released to the press. The next day the

255

news was in every daily paper in the country. The *Los Angeles Times:* "After sixteen years on the road, The Band—which has put together the most distinguished and acclaimed body of work of any rock group of the last decade—is apparently calling it quits. At least for touring purposes." *The New York Times* reported: "The Band, perhaps America's most respected rock group, will give a 'Farewell' concert in San Francisco on Thanksgiving Day, according to spokesmen close to The Band and to the many guest artists planning to participate. . . .

"Robbie Robertson, the group's leader, confirmed yesterday from Malibu, California, that the concert would take place, but said that all other aspects were still in the planning stage. Mr. Robertson said The Band would not tour 'ever again' after Thanksgiving, leaving its five members free for individual projects. But he added that the group would continue to make records. 'The Band will never break up,' he said. 'It's too late now.' "

This was also what Robbie and our management boys said when they went in and tried to con Mo Ostin at Warner Bros. Records. They told Mo we weren't retiring, just quitting the road. Gonna continue as a recording unit called The Band, developing new product until the cows come ho.ne. In October Capitol released *The Best of The Band,* a ten-song anthology that was our ninth album for the label. Now we owed them one more under the terms of the contract that Albert Grossman had negotiated for us back in 1967–68, a world away in time. Warners was assured that we would deliver our last album to Capitol by the end of 1976 and be free agents, ready to sign another record deal. The record and movie rights to our Thanksgiving show were also part of the negotiations.

The way it ended up, Warner Bros. put us on retainer instead of under contract. They paid the group two thousand dollars a week each for the next twenty-eight months, and in return got the album and movie rights to what became *The Last Waltz.*

Jimmy Carter had been kind enough to receive us in the Georgia governor's mansion when we passed through Atlanta back on the 1974 Dylan tour, and now he was running for President against incumbent Jerry Ford. We'd been getting calls asking us to help the campaign, so that October we released a single of "Georgia on My Mind" in Mr. Carter's honor. It had been cut at Shangri-La, and Richard sang it with the soul factor turned pretty high. On October 30, 1976, just days before the election, we played "Georgia" on *Saturday Night Live,* and a few days after that Jimmy Carter was elected President of the United States.

When they first told me about making a movie out of The Last Waltz, I was against the idea. I figured that with all the guest artists coming in, we already had to learn more than twenty new songs—chord changes and dynamics—that we'd never played before in our lives, and new artists were being added to the show all the time. In fact, no one we asked turned us down. No one even said, "I'll think about it," or, "I'll get back to you." They just said, "Where and when?" Musicians got their expenses paid, but no fees. Bill Graham was in for a 10 percent administrative fee to take care of his expenses, but he always maintained he went about fifty thousand dollars in the hole for The Last Waltz. Dr. John came in, then Joni Mitchell was added. (We'd known her in Toronto, and Robbie had played on her *Court and Spark* album a couple of years earlier.) When I heard that Neil Diamond was going to play, I asked, "What the hell does Neil Diamond have to do with us?"

Robertson just produced his album, I was told.

"But what does he represent to The Band?" I asked.

Robbie called me up at the Miramar. "Well, Neil is like Tin Pan Alley," he said. "That fifties Brill Building scene, songwriters like Doc Pomus . . ."

"Why don't we just get Doc Pomus?" I suggested.

He said that he and Neil had written a couple of songs together, and maybe they could do one of 'em in the show.

I was glad I insisted on Muddy Waters.

Anyway, that was another one we had to learn. I know this put me under a lot of pressure. I asked Robertson how many chances we'd get on each song.

"We're filming the show live," he answered. "One take each song."

And so the film was more or less shoved down our throats too, and we went along with it. Do it, puke, and get out.

Martin Scorsese was part of the movie crew at the Woodstock Festival and had edited the three-screen movie *Woodstock.* Later he made his mark with *Mean Streets* and *Taxi Driver,* personal, small-scale films that put him at the top of most people's Favorite Director lists. The producer of both of these was Jon Taplin, our former road manager. Robbie thought that nervous, fast-talking Marty was his ticket into Hollywood and asked him to film The Last Waltz.

"Van Morrison?" Scorsese said. "Are you shitting me? I've *got* to do this!" This was in early October, maybe six weeks before the show. Scorsese had just finished shooting *New York, New York,* a big-budget big-band picture with Liza Minnelli and Robert De Niro. Scorsese's crew had just been working with a proscenium stage like the one planned for Winterland, but on a soundstage. Many Hollywood production legends—cinematographer Laszlo Kovacs, famous lighting and set designers—were still available. Almost overnight, Scorsese and Robertson produced a 150-page shooting script so detailed that lighting cues were matched to chord changes in individual songs.

They went to Mo Ostin and asked him to pay for it, and he said that Warners would put up the money if Bob Dylan was going to be in the movie. That was the condition. So Bob was approached about this, and they told us that Bob didn't really want to be in the movie because he was working on his own movie, *Renaldo and Clara,* shot during the previous year's Rolling Thunder Revue tour. So we explained the situation about Warners wanting to finance only if Bob appeared in the film, and I think Bob said he would think about it. It was an ambiguous answer, but they went ahead and told Warners that Bob was in on the whole deal. That's how we got Mo Ostin to loan us $1.5 million for the film, even though we weren't on his label.

Bill Graham, by the way, wasn't into the movie either. He saw The Last Waltz as a historic live event with The Band bonding in farewell with the same audience that had greeted us in our debut seven years before. He was more concerned with the logistics of feeding the fifty-four hundred expected customers and guests, and didn't want big movie cameras and booms blocking their view. There was a lot of reassuring before Bill went for the whole film idea.

John Simon's involvement with The Last Waltz will give you an idea of the atmosphere surrounding the group. "In the old days working with The Band," he says, "there was nothing on paper, no clear-cut deal that said, 'If you perform this work, you get so much.' I was usually so high that I didn't much notice or even care. If you were broke, you called Albert Grossman, and he'd give you money. Over the years, I eventually noticed that I didn't get any royalties for the two Band albums I produced. In early 1976 I asked Albert, and he sent me to Robbie. Robbie referred me to their accountant, who said he would check and get back to me. No royalties were due, he claimed.

"That autumn Robbie called about The Last Waltz. He said, 'The concept is that we're going to be the backup band for our favorite acts. We want you to be the music director. You're the man to do it.'

"I said, 'Sure, I'd love to do it. And while we're at it, would you ask the accountant one more time if you owe me any money?'

"A couple of weeks later, a check arrives for sixty-two thousand dollars. Then Robbie called with some cockamamie story asking if, just for bookkeeping purposes, we could make this the last check for the two albums. Besides, he assured me, The Last Waltz album would be so huge, there wouldn't be any more financial problems after its release. Being the credulous type, I signed away all future royalties from the first two Band albums—and of course never saw a penny from The Last Waltz. I don't think many people have, because Warners eventually charged the cost of the film against the album. A lot of people got conned, and you let yourself be conned because they were so attractive.

"I flew out there, and we had rehearsals at Shangri-La, which was a fun place to hang out. It had a bar-lounge, a good pool table, and the master suite had been turned into a recording studio. No one but Garth read music, so I had to arrange and work with The Band to learn the songs. Everything was complicated. Bob Dylan was expected to show up at any minute to rehearse, but never actually made it. Henry Glover, Allen Toussaint, and Tom Malone worked on the horn charts. Joni Mitchell came to rehearsals and couldn't name the weird tunings her songs were written in, so Garth had to figure out the chords. Ronnie Hawkins was living there, attending the rehearsals and getting to know the big English musicians who liked to hang around the bar at Shangri-La: Eric Clapton and his [future] wife, Paiti [George Harrison's ex, and the inspiration for "Layla"], Ringo, Ron Wood. Hawk was enthusiastic, like a cheerleader. 'All these big-time English guys,' he told me, 'I've never seen this. I'm in Toronto. To me, this is the big time! This is it, baby!' "

259

* * *

I think we got to San Francisco about a week before Thanksgiving and moved into the Miyako Hotel, which had a pretty good sushi bar. Down the street at Winterland, nine big movie cameras were pointed at the stage. Scorsese was so hyper, I couldn't understand what he was saying most of the time. He talked so speedily that it was unintelligible to me. He and Bill Graham—it was incredible! Bill was worried about the customers, Marty about his film, and it got adversarial. People were crying about money all the time. They had long rows of tables ready for the banquet. I said, "Let's get some nice amber lamps on those tables, so it'll look elegant and muted," and they said, "Are you kidding? There's no budget for that!" In fact, they kept saying there was no budget for anything.

Famous set designer Boris Leven raided the storage room of the Opera Company of San Francisco for props from *La Traviata:* columns, chandeliers, crimson wall hangings. That was the "set" of The Last Waltz. Scorsese said it looked like a crazed Luchino Visconti movie. Bill Graham was complaining that the dirty balconies of Winterland wouldn't look good on camera, and we told him the balconies weren't gonna be on camera; the cameras were pointing at the stage. But he insisted on spending thousands of dollars to build a painted wood facade over the dirty balconies. Meanwhile, we were having trouble flying in Muddy Waters's guitar player because he wasn't in the original budget. There were a lot of fights, a lot of screaming. When Bill Graham let go, boy, the old spit would fly. I didn't see too much of this, mind you. Bill Graham going off on someone—it was more like something you heard.

Cocaine was a big, big deal at the time. Bill Graham had painted one of the dressing rooms white, walls and ceiling, and put a thick white rug on the floor. The only thing in the room was a sleek glass table with razor blades artfully strewn about. They had cut the noses out of Groucho Marx masks and pasted them up on the white walls. Hundreds of big pink noses and nostrils. A tape played sniffing noises. This was the "Cocteau Room," and it was often filled with people tapping the razors on the table.

"It was California in the 1970s, and everybody was coked up," John Simon reflects. "Not me. I was the musical director, the honcho.

We had a dress rehearsal at Winterland the night before the show, and it fell to me to call the shots. Someone had to move things along. My favorite rehearsal was with Muddy Waters and Paul Butterfield at the Miyako Hotel. Muddy Waters had the dignity of a king, but he also responded to this great, powerful band, and generally radiated tremendous authority. Muddy Waters and The Band. It was like the confluence of two rivers of music. *That* was the rehearsal I remember.''

Two days before the show, our studio manager tried to talk to me. He was one of the boys on the other side of the desk. I could tell from the awful look on his face that there was some problem, and he'd been *delegated* to deal with me.

"Levon," he said, "we've invited too many people. The show's gonna run for hours! We, uh, we gotta take someone off the show."

I was in a mood. I snarled, "Go tell Robertson to tell Neil Diamond *we don't even know who the fuck he is!*"

Some of the Arkansas contingent who had flown in on my friend Don Tyson's private plane were in the room and laughed at this, but I wasn't laughing. I couldn't believe it, but I knew what was coming.

This flunky said, "Um, we've *all* discussed it, and we're thinking about, ah, maybe, you know, taking Muddy off the show."

I just looked at him.

"Anyway, we were hoping maybe you could talk to Muddy for us."

There was silence for an awful thirty seconds. I was trying to get a grip before I answered, before I lost control. We were all under tremendous pressure because of this movie. The whole damn thing had been hijacked to the *nth* degree.

I had to clear my throat before I could speak.

"Not only will I *talk* to Muddy," I managed, as I began to get worked up, "but I will also take Muddy back to New York, and we will do the goddamn Last Waltz in New York. Him and me. That's right." Now I was getting going. "Yes, I'll talk to Muddy, you no-good, low-grade sumbitch! Now get the hell out of my sight, before I have some of these here Arkansas boys stomp you to death!" And indeed, some of them who'd come up from Springdale and Fayetteville for the party were looking mighty askance at our employee at that point. I began to get up, but he disappeared before I could do any more damage. Muddy stayed in the show.

261

* * *

The Last Waltz looked great on paper, but I worried how it was going to go down until the last minute. Each of our guests had different sound requirements, so our big dress rehearsal went on for twelve hours as stage positions were blocked out for the cameras and the artists ran through their songs while the hall filled up with friends and the press who'd come from all over America and Europe to cover the event. Nine 35-millimeter cameras were positioned and repositioned, and the light guys worked on their cues, but nothing was filmed. Not enough in the budget to film the dress rehearsal, I was told.

A big mistake.

Bob Dylan rehearsed by himself behind locked doors in the Miyako's basement piano lounge, the Osaka Room, preferring to keep his own counsel. We went over and played a few things with him, and not a word was exchanged about the possibility of his being in our film. His people said that Bob was still thinking about it.

The lines circled the block well before Winterland opened its doors around six on Thanksgiving. The marquee read: BILL GRAHAM PRESENTS THE BAND IN THE LAST WALTZ. People had dressed up for the occasion, everyone was on their best behavior, and I don't think there were any hassles out front all night. Bill Graham's Thanksgiving feast had been prepared from 220 turkeys, 500 pounds of cranberry sauce, 90 gallons of brown gravy simmering in crocks, a ton of candied yams, 800 pounds of mincemeat, 6,000 rolls, and 400 gallons of cider. The stuffing was made of 500 pounds each of onions and celery, 70 bunches of parsley, and sixteen quarts of herbs sautéed in 100 pounds of butter. Everyone got a good meal, and I heard you could go back to the buffet table until you were full. If you didn't eat meat, you could sample some of the 400 pounds of fresh salmon from the Alaska fish company owned by Lou Kemp, a Minnesota boyhood friend of Bob Dylan's. He had organized the Rolling Thunder Revue and was looking after Bob during The Last Waltz.

As people finished, they could get up and dance to a thirty-eight–piece orchestra, encouraged by three teams of professional ballroom dancers. A lot of folks danced, and while they were on the floor Graham's staff bused the tables and made them disappear.

A little yellow badge got you backstage. People told us they couldn't believe this was the last time they'd be hearing our songs, so the atmosphere was actually a bit subdued. Muddy Waters waited like an African statue with his piano player, Pinetop Perkins. Van Morrison and Ringo laughed with Richard. Albert Grossman paced around (he managed Butterfield and his band, Better Days), looking more like Benjamin Franklin than ever. The Hawk was hollering that he was so goddamn full of sushi, he felt like a three-hundred-pound thermometer. Joni Mitchell was beautiful in her simple leotard top with a silver thunderbird at her throat. I looked around for a camera: Why wasn't anybody there with a hand-held camera to get this part of it? But all the cameras were pointed at the stage.

The show began around nine, amid a Peruvian backstage midway between exhilaration and terror. We played a full show (with Robertson's microphone turned off to avoid the kind of problem we'd had at Woodstock), beginning with "Up on Cripple Creek" and going through "The Shape I'm In," "It Makes No Difference" (with Garth soloing on that curved soprano), "Life Is a Carnival," "This Wheel's on Fire." At this point the crack horn section, starring Howard Johnson on tuba, stepped up, and we played "W. S. Walcott Medicine Show," "Georgia on My Mind," "Ophelia," "King Harvest (Has Surely Come)," "The Night They Drove Old Dixie Down" (maybe the best live performance of this song we ever gave), "Stage Fright," and finished with "Rag Mama Rag."

When the applause died down, someone yelled out "Freebird!" and everyone laughed.

There was no break. We'd been onstage for almost two hours, and the guest set had to happen right away. So we brought out Ronnie Hawkins first, as a tribute to our original chief and mentor, the man who taught us all we knew, or at least some of it. The Hawk was in a snap-brim straw cowboy hat, a black suit over a "Hawk" T-shirt, cowboy boots that made him seven feet tall, and was totally in charge. He counted off "Who Do You Love" with a line from "Bo Diddley" and prowled and growled his way through the song ("Take it easy, Garth, doncha gimme no lip!"). When Robbie played his original solo from the record of "Who Do You Love" we'd cut with Ronnie back in 1963, the Hawk took off that hat and fanned the guitar. "Down, boy! Cool it down!" The camera loved it.

Next came Dr. John: shades, beret, gold shoes, sequined jacket, the image of a Crescent City hipster, smoking a cigarette. He dedicated "Such a Night" to all the fellas. I loved Mac Rebennack and appreciated the irony of the lyrics to the song he did with us, "Such a Night," because he took up with Libby after The Last Waltz, and the two of them were an item for a long time.

We continued our tribute to Louisiana with Bobby Charles, who did "Down South in New Orleans" with us, because this was the music we all loved the best. Then Paul Butterfield came out for "Mystery Train" and played the harp beautifully under the harsh white spotlight. He and I traded verses, and for me it was a special moment.

Then it was was Muddy's turn. He came out with Pinetop and Bob Margolin, and Butterfield stayed on. We did "Caledonia," and sixty-one-year-old Muddy was a little shaky at first. I think this annoyed him, because he then tore into "Mannish Boy" like an old bull who had something to prove. Butterfield, who'd been studying breathing techniques, held one sheer harp note for five minutes as Muddy gestured and danced. The whole place woke up to the power of Muddy's performance, one of the high points of the show. "I'm a hoochie-koochie man . . . I'm a rolling stone . . ."

I was trying not to be too conscious of the cameras, but I noticed that they didn't seem to be shooting Muddy. Later we realized that because of some fuck-up, all but one camera had been turned off. We almost missed his entire segment. As he was walking offstage, I stood up to applaud, and Muddy grabbed my head in his big hands and kissed my forehead! What a feeling! But the director hadn't bothered to walk Muddy on and offstage, so there was no film of this.

Then Eric Clapton came out and did "All Our Past Times" and "Further on up the Road," which we'd often played in Levon and the Hawks days. Neil Young did "Helpless" and "Four Strong Winds." Joni Mitchell sang three songs from her two most recent albums: "Coyote," "Shadows and Light," and "Furry Sings the Blues." Finally, an extremely nervous Neil Diamond did "Dry Your Eyes," which he'd written with Robbie.

By now it was after midnight, and the crowd was subdued. The momentum of the show had been lost halfway through Joni's set. Richard Manuel turned the piano over to John Simon and began to sing "Tura Lura Lura," the Irish lullaby. Van Morrison (in a maroon suit) made his entrance amid much cheering—this was Van's first appearance onstage in more than two years—and The Last Waltz was suddenly revived with a spectacular version of "Caravan." John Simon conducted The Band and the horns as Van burned through his great song—"Turn it up! Little bit louder! Radio!"—complete with kick-steps across the stage at the end. Van turned the whole thing around, God bless him for being the showman that he is.

By then we were pretty much wrung out, but we did "Acadian Driftwood" as the last tune before intermission, with Joni and Neil Young singing along in a gesture of Canadian solidarity. We'd been on for more than three hours by then, and my hands were bleeding. We were all half past dead, but there was to be very little rest during the much needed half-hour intermission.

It was a madhouse backstage. Jerry Brown, governor of California, wanted to shake hands with us. We had to rehearse a new song called "Evangeline" that Robbie had written only the night before, because we had to perform it during the last part of the show for the sake of film continuity. In fact, the piece was still unfinished, and Robertson and John Simon were huddled in a corner, frantically trying to figure out an arrangement we could play without rehearsal. As this was going on, the San Francisco poets were declaiming their work onstage. They'd been rounded up by our friend Emmett Grogan, who'd founded the primal hippie activist group the Diggers. Emmett got Michael McClure to recite some Chaucer, Lawrence Ferlinghetti to say his beatnik parody of the Lord's Prayer, and Diane Di Prima, Lenore Kandel, and others to recite. The music-saturated audience was grateful for the break and gave each poet loud applause that reverberated into our dressing rooms. Meanwhile, all our management people had vanished, and someone was telling us there weren't enough limos to get Muddy, Pinetop, and Bob Margolin to the airport to make their flight to Chicago. I grabbed the great Don Tyson, explained the situation, and Don put Muddy and company in his own limo so those fuckers that worked for us wouldn't try anything stupid, like telling Muddy Waters he had to wait.

Bob Dylan had come in with his people during the first part of the show and retreated to a dressing room off-limits to everyone else. Halfway through the intermission, about fifteen minutes before we were due back onstage with Bob, he decided he didn't want to be in the film.

I wasn't that surprised. Howard Alk had been saying all week it wasn't going to work because Bob didn't want to compete with himself by having *The Last Waltz* and *Renaldo and Clara* go head to head. But there was never a decision made until the last minute, and this was it, the last minute. Bob's lawyer came out of Bob's dressing room with an awful look on his face. Robbie was totally pale. They said, "Bob doesn't want to be in the movie."

Scorsese went nuts. Without Bob there would be no movie. It was all over. More than a million dollars were probably down the drain. Scorsese was beside himself. He demanded to know why Bob wouldn't be filmed.

Robertson said that Bob just wasn't into it. He just felt there was already too much film of him in his present state. There were ten minutes to go. No one knew what to do. Albert Grossman was there but couldn't influence Bob; Bob didn't want to be influenced. So they asked Bill Graham to intercede. He went in and came out shaking his head. Bob, Bill said, claimed he didn't even know anything about being in our movie. Never heard of it. Bob didn't want to be filmed. In fact, when he went on, Bill was supposed to make sure that all the cameras were pointing *away from the stage*. They sent Bill back in to explain to Bob how dire the situation was. "Don't worry," Bill said over his shoulder. "I'm gonna make it happen." Man, they were all biting their nails. I think Bill really pleaded with Bob for us, for the sake of the history of it all. He got Bob to the point where any film that might be shot would be carefully scrutinized by Bob before being considered for use. He was in there for a couple of minutes, but it seemed like an hour. No one could believe this. With about five minutes left, word came down that the last two songs in Bob's part of the show could be filmed, and only the last two.

Bill Graham saved their asses that night.

Garth started the second half with his stately intro to "Chest Fever," coaxing a whole palette of techno-sounds from his keyboards. Then we managed to play "Evangeline" in a sort of country two-step, reading the lyrics off cue cards held behind the cameras, but the lack of rehearsal really told the story. We finished with "The Weight"—

our song—Garth Hudson shining on piano, and the whole house and the six horn players all singing along.

At that point Bob Dylan walked out in a big white hat that seemed to glow under the spotlight. Black leather jacket, polka-dot shirt. He plugged right in, said hello, and stormed into "Baby, Let Me Follow You Down." I looked out from behind the drums. The cameras were off. Technicians climbed down from the booms, and the soundpeople took off their headphones. I hoped that our boys taping the show in the mobile truck parked outside the hall were rolling, but to tell you the truth, I just didn't care that much. Bob knew what he was doing, and it wasn't much skin off my nose. Dylan's people were stationed at the side of the stage to make sure there was no filming.

Bob's guitar was turned way up, so I just took it fast. Things certainly got lively. Bob shouted out the lyrics, feinted back from the mike like he used to when we played this in 1965, and danced around the stage a little. In the audience: pandemonium. I mean, people were excited to have Bob there.

To cool it down, he cut right into "Hazel," from *Planet Waves.* Then farther back in time with "I Don't Believe You," also from Dylan and the Hawks. Mmm, good performance. Bob was hot and unusually commanding. I looked over at those cameras; they were still cold.

Two more numbers left. The technicians scrambled for their head-sets, the cameras swung around, the lights went on, and it was movie time again. We did "Forever Young," and when Bob finished he swung back into "Baby, Let Me Follow You Down." Surprised, we played along, figuring that Bob realized we were missing something good by not having any of the old rock and roll on film. At the side of the stage Bill Graham shouted down Bob's people, who were trying to get the cameras turned off so the big finale could be filmed with Bob in it. So they had this fight during the reprise, and you could hear Bill yelling, *"Fuck you! Roll the fucking cameras! Roll 'em!!!"* Meanwhile, Bob's smiling and we are too, so we just kept it up and hoped for the best.

Everyone came out for the finale, "I Shall Be Released." Ringo Starr sat down at Richard's drum kit, and Ron Wood plugged in as well. The night was pretty much over for Richard by then, and the damn cameras couldn't even find him during the verses he sang. When he missed a cue, Bob jumped in and sang the verse. All our guests sang backup, and it was a nice moment. Bill Graham tried to get the governor out onstage, but Jerry wanted to stay in the wings with actress/singer Ronee Blakely, so Bill threw my towel at him.

It hadn't really hit me that when the song was over, so was The Band.

The stage cleared of our guests, Ringo Starr and I sat there for a second, looking at each other. The Last Waltz was over. Relieved, I figured it was time to play a little music, so me and Ring started up. Dr. John came out, then Stephen Stills and Carl Radle, Eric Clapton's bassist, then Neil Young, Garth, and Rick Danko. Bill Graham dragged Clapton out and strapped him into his guitar for the jam, and Ronnie Wood came out. We jammed for maybe thirty minutes, judging by the tapes. Finally The Band came back on, and we did our last song, "Don't Do It."

When it was over, we were all spent. "Thank you," Richard told the crowd. "Good night." And then, "Good-bye." I looked at the clock. It was two o'clock in the morning. All the cameramen were slapping one another on the back. Some people were crying at the demise of The Band and placing bouquets on the stage. I got up, stretched, lit a cigarette, shook some hands, and left the stage. In the dressing room was an envelope with a couple of thousand dollars in it. Bill Graham had given a bonus to each member of The Band, just because he was so happy The Last Waltz was over and had gone down well.

It was one of those nights, and no one wanted to let go of it. By 3:00 A.M. our guests were just finishing the turkey dinner we'd laid on at the Miyako Hotel, and the Osaka Room turned into a party. Dr. John and Paul Butterfield were jamming with Steve Stills. I visited with actor Brad Dourif, a neighbor from Woodstock, who'd just had a big success in *One Flew Over the Cuckoo's Nest*. The Arkansawyers were whooping it up while Don Tyson handed out Razorback T-shirts to one and all. Bob Dylan was sitting with some friends from Minnesota, telling reporters that he was already nostalgic for The Band. "After all," Bob said, "I've been with those guys a long time."

John Simon came and sat down, and I asked him how he thought the recording had gone. John mentioned that Bob Dylan's lawyer had gone into the truck immediately after the show and seized the tapes Bob was on, so there would have to be negotiations. I thought that was pretty funny.

I wasn't destined to be part of the fun and games. I left the party around four and went back to the hotel. Amy and Ezra were in San Francisco with me and were sound asleep in my suite. I woke the baby-sitter and told her she could go. As the sun rose over San Francisco, I thought about the whole story of The Band. The original idea, as I recalled it, had been for us to use Bearsville Studios as a sheltered environment for making American music, using all the traditions we'd learned over the years. That dream had died amid the old divide and conquer mentality. My only hope was that it wasn't too late to live that dream and somehow keep the people who loved The Band on our side. Even then Henry Glover was helping me put something together. We were going to try to make my own dream of having my barn replace Bearsville come true.

When the kids woke up, I took them over to F.A.O. Schwarz and said, pick any toy in the place. That's how we celebrated the end of The Last Waltz. A few days later I caught a plane to New York.

The period after The Last Waltz was a time of real scrambling for me. I was determined to get on to the next thing, fearful of being left behind in a competitive business. Henry Glover made a deal with ABC Records and started putting together a good band for an album and a big tour. I told Henry that I'd always had a fantasy of joining Booker T. and the MGs, for my money the best band in the country; legendary studio musicians who'd played on more hit records than you could count. Henry said he'd see what he could do.

Then it was back to Shangri-La to work on *Islands,* our last album for Capitol. It was really more a collection of odd pieces than an album, but it did fulfill those awful contractual obligations. I got to sing on "Ain't That a Lot of Love" (made famous by Sam and Dave) and a couple of others, and Richard did himself proud on "Right as Rain" and "Let the Night Fall." We also stuck "Georgia" on there as well. The title song, written by Garth and Rick, turned out to be an instrumental because Robbie never came up with lyrics for it. When Capitol released *Islands* in March 1977, it got to No. 64 and disappeared, the poorest showing by any of our albums.

At the same time, Rick Danko was working on his solo album, recording partly at Shangri-La, so things were busy at the clubhouse. Rick was writing songs with Bobby Charles and Emmett Grogan, and using the local musicians: Eric Clapton, Ronnie Wood, Blondie Chaplin from the Beach Boys. It was the usual constant atmosphere of work-as-party.

Then there was *The Last Waltz*. Within a few weeks of the show, we heard that English movie mogul Sir Lew Grade had offered three million dollars for our farewell movie, sight unseen. Scorsese issued a statement that if The Band wasn't satisfied with the footage, it would never be released, and would be the most expensive home movie ever made. They'd shot 160,000 feet of film, but problems began to mount as soon as they started to screen this material. The sound track was poorly recorded and had to be overdubbed and remixed for the movie and the album. Then it was decided that the whole thing was too lily-white and missing something crucial, so the Staple Singers were recruited to join us on an MGM soundstage in Culver City to record another version of "The Weight." The San Francisco version had come too late in the show, and my performance was, to say the least, less than magical.

It was great to hear Mavis Staples singing the verses of "The Weight" on that stage. The Staples had been the original inspiration for The Band's vocal blend, so it was more than appropriate to hear Mavis and her father blending their voices with ours. Mavis Staples was so awe-inspiring that after the first take I left the drums and approached her. "Hey, Mavis," I begged, "you've got to lighten up a little. I mean, don't go blowing us off the stage." She laughed. Her voice and presence were as powerful as Aretha's, maybe more so. Later, during a break, Richard Manuel asked Pop Staples if he knew why the French people went to Canada and the black people went to America. Pop said no, he didn't. Richard told him it was because Canada and America had a bet and Canada lost.

We also did another version of "Evangeline" with Emmylou Harris, as dry-ice machines turned the still air of the studio into a gauzy fog to soften the images and conjure up the bayou atmosphere of the song.

She represented our homage to country music, joining the other genres we'd tried to pay tribute to in *The Last Waltz*. Finally The Band was filmed playing "The Last Waltz Suite" by ourselves as a mostly string ensemble: Richard on dobro, me on mandolin, Rick on bass, Garth on accordion, and Robertson playing a harp guitar.

When we finished on the soundstage, that was it. We thanked the Staples and Emmylou, and didn't discuss the fact that this was the last time we would appear on a stage together. That day, it really was over. We done led the horse to the barn and took off the saddle.

Anyone who ever saw *The Last Waltz* understood from my attitude during the postconcert interviews (filmed at Shangri-La) that I was pretty pissed off about the whole situation. The idea was for us to sit around the campfire and shoot the shit about the good old days, maybe pick up some instruments, let the good times roll. The interviews took place over the course of a few days and generally started after midnight. I already had a bad attitude when I realized the cameras had completely ignored the spirit of the event. So Scorsese sits me down at a table, and they turn on the camera, and I know he wants to hear about the Midnight Ramble and the medicine shows and Sonny Boy Williamson on *King Biscuit Time*, but all I'm thinking is what a *sin* it is to take a good group from productivity to oblivion.

"Uh, Levon," Scorsese began, "Is there anything you wanna, like, start off on?"

I glared at him. "*You're* the one that's supposed to be asking this fuckin' shit," I told him. He was taken aback. He shifted his papers very nervously. And I said, "I mean, this shit don't mean nothing to me." I looked right at him. Nothing. I was just coarse and rude, *country* rude, because I was so damn angry. I believed then and I believe now that The Band is bigger than all of us.

Eventually they got enough interviews, and it petered out. Richard later complained that he was so drunk at the time, he couldn't remember being filmed. Garth was filmed at six o'clock in the morning, looking quite exhausted after being woken from a nap, and I know he was disgusted with the way he was depicted in the interview portion (although his remarks on the healing properties of music were actually the most eloquent sequence in the whole film).

They would have these meetings that went on forever about all the business things that were going on. New publishing companies were being set up for *The Last Waltz* and our supposed new music for Warners. Noises were being made about Robbie wanting to buy out his fellow musicians' shares of The Band. They wanted me to spend the rest of the year overdubbing *The Last Waltz,* and I told them to go to hell because I had my own record to do. In one of these big meetings about the fate of The Band, I finally had enough after yet another scheme was referred to by our accountant as a "genius idea."

I got up. " 'Genius,' my ass," I said. "There ain't a genius within walking distance of this self-infatuated crowd." No one said anything. "That's it, boys, it's too late, you've lost it. I'll let you *geniuses* have it." I said some other things too. I took the path of greatest resistance. I had an attitude because I was younger and a lot more willing to scrap. I left without beating the shit out of them, but I made the mistake of cussing 'em out so bad I had to leave town, and I also believe they later put the IRS on my trail. That's what kind of people we're talking about here. There ain't but one answer for any of them sons of bitches—shoeshine or no—that didn't lift a finger to keep The Band together in any kind of way: playing, writing, movie partners, whatever. We were a good team, and it was a shame to destroy it.

So I left California, and postproduction on *The Last Waltz* went on without me. I promised 'em all I would stay out of the picture, give it a good leavin' alone. I'd already contacted MGs bassist Donald "Duck" Dunn and former Hawk Fred Carter, Jr., about recording, and we finished getting up my building in Woodstock so we could record in it.

Richard, Rick, and Garth stayed too long. Someone managed to convince them it would be a good idea to sell their publishing and their shares of The Band to Robbie Robertson. I doubt that the sale was in their best interests, but it was a clean break. They tried to see if I was interested in selling too, but I told my lawyer not to return their calls. So I never received any offer.

Garth Hudson was right when he described music as medicine and musicians as possessing the power to heal. But if the doctor is going to make house calls, he'd better be prepared to play. When I'm a working musician, I feel like I'm successful no matter how big the show. If I'm not working, I feel useless as hell. As a drummer, I need a bassist and a guitar player to even begin thinking about playing music, so the next thing was to get a band that could play in the big leagues.

The RCO All-Stars consisted of musicians who had all grown up along the Mississippi River: Booker T. Jones on keys, Duck Dunn on bass, and Steve Cropper on guitar. Fred Carter, Jr., flew out from Nashville to play some guitar. Paul Butterfield played harp, and Mac Rebennack played his trademark keyboards, guitar, and deep-gumbo percussion. The horns were Howard Johnson, Tom Malone, Lou Marini, and Alan Rubin. This lineup made its public debut on *Saturday Night Live* on March 19, 1977, and recorded the ten songs on *Levon Helm and the RCO All-Stars* that summer on twenty-four tracks at my house and at Shangri-La. We got a good cut on "Milk Cow Boogie" and "Rain Down Tears," my favorite tracks on a pretty fair record. The rest was a cooperative effort. Mac, Fred Carter, and Booker T. all contributed tunes, Duck Dunn and I rearranged a couple of oldies, and we even got Chuck Berry's "Havana Moon" in there as well. When I brought the tapes out to Shangri-La to mix, both Garth and Robbie contributed some accordion and guitar to Earl King's "Sing, Sing, Sing." After the tensions of working with The Band, the RCO All-Stars was just what we had in mind: a friendly, cooperative atmosphere in which to create music that people can have a good time with and maybe even dance to.

We finished the album that fall and had a big party at my Woodstock barn in October to celebrate and play for our friends. The opening act featured six-and-a-half-year-old Amy Helm on vocals, with her eleven-year-old brother, Ezra Titus, on guitar. It was one of those classic golden Catskill autumn afternoons. The cider was cold and fresh, and the fried chicken was crispy. It felt like that dream had been realized. I had a hell of an album, and we'd booked a fifty-date tour through early 1978. Things looked pretty interesting.

Just as the RCO All-Stars record came out, I collapsed. Kidney stones. Prostate gland. I wound up in the hospital. I told the doctors I'd been working on the album and tour, driving cross-country to check in at Shangri-La, then driving back east with stops in Arkansas along the way. I was burning both ends of the candle on both coasts and in the middle. For the first time in my life my wild ways caught up with me, and I was really ill. They told me I was lucky to be alive and insisted the tour be canceled. You can imagine what my heart did when I heard that fifty dates were out the window, how that felt. The doctors did promise that if I was real good, we could go play Japan later that year like we'd planned. We managed to salvage a couple of American dates: New Year's Eve at the Palladium in New York and a single show before 37,500 at the Superdome in New Orleans during the 1978 Mardi Gras. But things were disorganized, and we played without rehearsals or soundchecks and took some disappointing reviews. The album sold about a quarter-million copies and stalled at No. 142. The RCO All-Stars were never able to develop the momentum we needed to continue as any kind of permanent organization, but it was fun while it lasted. (Rick Danko's solo LP got to No. 119 at around the same time.)

I did a lot of press interviews, trying to keep up interest in the new band. But what the reporters wanted to know about was . . . The Band. The official line was that we had a movie and a triple album coming out, and that we were gonna get together and record. A little more than a year after *The Last Waltz,* I was quoted in *Rolling Stone* regarding The Band:

" 'We never played no fruit rock, no punk rock. We never wore dresses onstage or put no paint on our faces. We never blew up any bombs onstage. We didn't suck off any snakes onstage. We didn't wear tight pants or them big turquoise rings. We didn't take a piss onstage or throw any TVs out the window that I can remember. But today the music business has gotten so it's like Vietnam: a few guys making a lot of money, some guys getting cut up, and in five years ain't much of it even gonna be *worth* a pinch of shit.'

"Given The Band's unerring taste and integrity," the article continued, "its honest failures and its respected place in American musical culture, Helm's growling carries a certain weight."

And that's how I felt about the music business at the time, and in some ways still do.

Warner Bros. released *The Last Waltz* as a film and three-LP album in April 1978. As far as I was concerned, the movie was a disaster.

I'd had almost no contact with Robbie Robertson during the eighteen-month postproduction period on *The Last Waltz.* I'd heard on The

Band grapevine that Robbie's wife had thrown him out and that he'd moved into Marty Scorsese's house on Mulholland Drive, where they lived the wild life of true Hollywood bachelors and blow buddies. Marty had the windows of the house blacked out and an air-filtration system installed so there was no need to see the sun or open the windows to breathe. Marty was editing *The Last Waltz* while Robbie worked on the soundtrack. They edited the movie to please themselves.

John Simon: "I'm pretty sure that Levon is the only honest, live element in *The Last Waltz,* with the exception of Muddy Waters's vocal. Everything else was overdubbed and redone. Levon was basically gone, because he was disgusted with certain of the business practices. Robbie asked him to do his part over again, but Levon had nothing to do with it. He told me that he just didn't think any of it was fair.

"Robbie was right in that there were some good reasons for overdubbing the whole thing. Richard wasn't singing well, Rick's bass was out of tune, and Robbie wanted to improve his guitar solos. Also, the horns were recorded completely out of balance and had to be redone in New York with arrangements Henry Glover and I put together. The great thing was that Levon didn't need to do it over. He got it right the first time, and those were the drum tracks used in the final mix. I don't think Levon even knew that any overdubbing was taking place."

There were problems with the film as well. They had almost no footage of the actual event: the Thanksgiving feast, the orchestra, people dancing, the clowning around backstage. Bill Graham had refused to be interviewed—he was said to be angry that Robertson hadn't properly thanked him for producing the lavish, labor-intensive show— and so was only barely credited in the film. Scorsese had watched the dress rehearsal with his thumb up his ass and neglected to shoot, the dummy. That was unfortunate, because some of the rehearsal was better than the concert. Neil Young had delivered a good version of "Helpless," but performed with a good-size rock of cocaine stuck in his nostril. Neil's manager saw this and said *no way* is Neil gonna be in the film like this. They had to go to special-effects people, who developed what they called a "traveling booger matte" that sanitized Neil's nostril and put "Helpless" into the movie.

I took Ronnie Hawkins with me to a screening of *The Last Waltz* just before its official release. All The Band was there, plus family, friends, people who'd worked on the project. For two hours we watched as the camera focused almost exclusively on Robbie Robertson, long and loving close-ups of his heavily made-up face and expensive haircut. The film was edited so it looked like Robbie was conducting the band with expansive waves of his guitar neck. The muscles on his neck stood out like cords when he sang so powerfully into his switched-off microphone. Hawk kept nudging me and laughing at this. Halfway through he whispered, "Was Richard still in the group when we did this?"

Because there were almost no shots of Richard in the movie. And very little of Garth. Rick and I were better represented because we sang a lot. But where was Richard? In the interviews he was depicted prone on a sofa at Shangri-La, his hair wild and eyes shining like wet moons, looking like Che Guevara after the Bolivians got through with him. Garth looked like he wanted to be somewhere else. I was all but spitting in Scorsese's face. Rick was a brooding presence under a leather hat, playing a track from his solo album instead of being interviewed.

It was left to Robertson, the film's producer, to tell its story, in which a band of brothers who'd been on the road for sixteen years—sometimes stealing food to survive a hellacious circuit of one-night stands in bucket-of-blood roadhouses owned by Jack Ruby—finally decided that "the road" was too dangerous an address to occupy any longer. "Sixteen years on the road, and the numbers start to scare you," Robertson earnestly told Scorsese, his hooded eyes rimmed with kohl. "I couldn't live with twenty years on the road. I couldn't even discuss it."

The world-weary angst with which these and other lines were delivered was making Ronnie laugh. Hell, he'd been on the road twenty years and it hadn't killed him. I'd nudge Ronnie to make him stop, and then Robertson would come out with something like, "Yeah, the road has taken many of the great ones: Hank Williams, Otis, Jimi, Janis, Elvis. It's a goddamn impossible way of life." The Hawk howled at that one. Fade to black and roll credits over "The Last Waltz Suite" as The Band shrinks to these little figures that eventually diminish to nothing on the screen.

Silence in the screening room. I was in shock over how bad the movie was. Nine cameras on the floor, and there wasn't even a shot of Richard Manuel singing the finale, "I Shall Be Released," his trademark song. It turned out that of the nine cameras, only two were used in the movie. No film of Muddy Waters kissing me on the head, right onstage. Nothing showing how Garth Hudson led the band and inspired us all. It was mostly Robertson, showing off and acting like he was the king.

The lights came up. I lit a cigarette and looked at Hawk, who pounded me on the back and loudly exclaimed, so everyone could hear: "Hey, son, don't look so glum. The goddamn movie'd be awright *if it only had a few more shots of Robbie.* Haw haw haw haw haw!!!"

So that's the story of *The Last Waltz.* Predictably, the reviews were excellent for the movie, if not the album, which was judged to be more of the same from us. Critics called the movie the best and most sumptuous film ever made about a rock concert, and I suppose that's true. But Warner Bros. charged the movie and record against advances we'd been paid, and to this day, despite a worldwide video release, we've never seen any money from the project. The Band never delivered any records to Warners, either, and eventually Shangri-La was shut down.

Richard was still in his bungalow down by the beach when it came time to move out. I think they wanted to rent it out to defray some of the operating expenses of the place. But Richard liked it down there and didn't want to leave. So they turned off his phone, then the gas. I went down to visit him and found him cooking minute steaks on an upside-down electric clothes iron. The thing was set on "cotton." Richard would drop a pat of butter on the hot iron, slap on a steak, flip it over, drop another butter pat, and eat it right off the grill, so to speak. When they finally got him out of there it took them a couple of days to clean out the two thousand Grand Marnier bottles they found.

Today people tell me all the time how much they loved *The Last Waltz.* I try to thank them politely and usually refrain from mentioning that for me it was a real scandal. Over the years we've heard people say that drugs affected the quality of the music and the film, and it would probably be hard to argue with that line of reasoning from any rational point of view. In hindsight, it was probably one of the reasons I was against the whole idea in the first place. If I was going to blame someone, I'd start with Robertson and Scorsese. I've certainly read interviews where they blamed themselves. They admitted that they got pretty far out there. You just can't let things blow up in your head that big. None of us is as important as he wishes he was. *New York, New York* bombed when it was released, and Scorsese himself ended up in the hospital that September. His doctors told him to change his life or die.

As for Robbie, he eventually got back with his family and pursued the movie career that he'd wanted badly enough to put The Band behind him. I want to be careful here not to deny Robbie's contribution to all our careers. He was certainly a catalyst for what happened to The Band and deserves his place of honor in the history of our music. But to this day I don't fully understand why he had to let go of it the way he did. Some of us were going through bad times, and it was a sin not to reach out and help them if you were able. Music is a special category to my way of looking. It's sinful, the things that haven't been done for certain artists over the years. To me it was unforgivable.

I had a good reason for not inviting my new girlfriend, Sandra Dodd, to The Last Waltz. She was a part of my life I wanted to keep separate from the conflict and turmoil of that event. She was the one I turned to when the going got rough, and eventually . . .

Let's ask Sandy to remember those times for us:

"I was raised and went to school in Virginia, where my dad had a construction company. I graduated from high school in '67 and went to college in Florida. When the first Band records came out I really loved them, but never managed to see the group until they came to Washington with Bob Dylan in 1974. It was the first time I saw Levon. I heard his voice before I saw him, because I'd never seen a singing drummer and didn't understand who was singing until I noticed the drummer kind of hidden behind his drums and a big Tiffany lamp they had onstage. I loved the way he kind of sang *sideways,* and he was also putting out more energy than anyone else onstage. The other guys seemed a little bored.

"Then I moved to Lake Tahoe with some friends, and they knew Rusty Kershaw, who was making a record in L.A. with Neil Young called *On the Beach.* We all went down to L.A., and that's where Levon and I met. Actually, I didn't think he even noticed me that much. The next day I'm doing laps in the pool at the Sunset Marquis, and I get to the end of the lane and see this *gorgeous* pair of palomino cowboy boots.

"It was Levon, smiling and looking down at me in the pool. He said he'd come to take me to get some sushi. I'd never eaten raw fish before. I guess I fell in love with him right then.

"But I also got scared. I asked myself, *Why does he want to go out with this little bumpkin from Virginia?* So I didn't let him pursue me. I went back up to Tahoe with my boyfriend, but couldn't get Levon out of my mind. I'd write letters and bake cookies, and sent them to an address on the Pacific Coast Highway in Malibu: Shangri-La. And I didn't really hear from him, except for a postcard with his phone number at the Miramar Hotel.

"Next time I was in L.A. I called the number. Rick Danko answered. 'Oh, yeah, Levon told me all about you. He's not here right now, but come on over anyway because he'll be right back.' I asked where Levon was, and Rick said, 'Ah, he's out getting the children.'

"I thought, *Oh no. He didn't say anything about having kids.*

"So I summoned all my courage and went over to the hotel. I went up to Levon's apartment, but now Rick was gone. Instead there was this huge bearded man in cowboy boots splayed out all over the bed, and some kids running around. The man was Ronnie Hawkins, and the kids were Amy and Ezra. I was shy, so I sat in the chair closest to the door to wait and see if Levon would be back. So I'm sitting there, and Amy was figuring things out even though she was only five. She came up and whispered, 'There's a big, hairy monster right behind this curtain, and he's going to get you if you don't leave.'

"Then Levon came back. He sat down next to me, took my hand, and I've been his woman ever since. I asked him if he was married, and he shook his head. 'Hell, *no!*' was all he said, and I was so relieved, because I was really falling for him. I mean, it hit me *hard.* Any woman's who's really fallen for a man will understand what I mean. I had to stay, so I checked into the Miramar, and my parents sent me a little money to live on. I was this twenty-six-year-old kid, but I felt something very powerful, and Levon was so sweet to me. He's a gentleman of the old southern school who believes a woman shouldn't want for anything if a man can help it.

"But then his business was over in California, and he went back to Woodstock to work on the studio he was building in his barn. I went back to Virginia, but now we stayed in touch. This is winter of '75–'76. He invited me to Woodstock, and I went to visit.

"I went back to Virginia after that and was in a pretty bad car wreck. Levon came down to see me, and I think I knew then that I'd found the right man for me.

"After The Last Waltz I came out to California and moved into the Miramar, where Levon was living while they were doing the interviews for the movie and getting the many business deals worked out. Libby found out about me, realized that Levon had a girlfriend, and immediately served support papers on him. He would get up in the morning, stuff wads of contracts and legal paper into a briefcase, and head downtown in his BMW to see the lawyers. At night we'd go up to Shangri-La, where the movie interviews were being filmed, and I think they were finishing an album as well.

"Levon and I stayed together through this long, confusing time. Eventually many issues regarding the children couldn't be worked out, there was a custody battle, and we all had to go to court and lay out our lives for the judge. Levon had always been very honest about not wanting to get married, of not wanting a wife to worry about, but now things changed. Both our mothers wanted to see us married to each other, and we wanted to affirm our bond to Amy so we wouldn't be just 'living together.' So we got married on September 7, 1981, and here we still are today."

Chapter Ten

THE NEXT WALTZ

Allow me to rewind a bit.

In November 1978 a thirty-three-year-old progressive congressman named Bill Clinton was elected governor of Arkansas. I think he was one of the youngest people ever to be governor. He'd worked for our senator William Fulbright, and had taught at the university's law school. Before he got married he'd roomed with our old friend Paul Berry, who had embarked on his own career in banking.

When it came time to choose a band to play Bill Clinton's gubernatorial inaugural ball in January 1979, Paul suggested us. It turned out the governor was a Band fan, so it didn't take a hell of a lot of prodding. That month, the Cate Brothers and I put a group together and played the "Diamonds & Denim Gala" in Little Rock. We met Bill and Hillary Clinton and helped our fellow Arkansawyers bring our new governor in with style. Bill Clinton was our governor for the next fourteen years, until it was time for him to move on in his career. But that's when we first shook hands and said how ya doin'?

Cut to February 1979, and I'm speeding out of Nashville in the back of a station wagon with actor Tommy Lee Jones and a fifth of Wild Turkey. We're on our way to the location in Kentucky where director Michael Apted is about to begin production on *Coal Miner's Daughter*, a biopic based on Loretta Lynn's best-selling autobiography. Sissy Spacek is playing Loretta, Tommy Lee is her husband, Doolittle Lynn, and—I can still barely believe it—the part of Loretta's father, Ted Webb, the coal miner of the title, is being played by me.

The reason Tommy Lee and I are driving down together is because he's supposed to teach me how to act during the ride. Believe it or not, that is the deal.

After *The Last Waltz* was released the year before, The Band scattered. I was the only one still living in Woodstock. Rick and Elizabeth Danko stayed in Malibu, more or less keeping an eye on Richard Manuel. Garth lost his house in a Malibu brushfire that also claimed the homes of Neil Young and other friends. Garth lost some of his instruments in the fire, as well as most of Richard's possessions, which had been stored in Garth's basement. Garth and his wife, Maud, then moved to Agoura, on the other side of the mountains. Robertson was fending off film offers in the wake of his chiseled performance in our movie, and there were rumors he was going to produce and star in a movie about carnival life, something he'd always been interested in.

I decided to remain in Woodstock. I loved the town and the people and the way of life too much to sell my house and relocate. Sandy and I would go down to Arkansas for a few months every year and rent a place, just to get away. ABC Records took the RCO All-Stars to Japan for a few weeks, and we sold out every hall we played. I knew I was going to love Japan when I noticed they had rice on their currency instead of emperors and statesmen. Farmers were almost revered. This was clearly a people who had their priorities straight.

At airport customs this young officer walked me right into a booth and performed a major search of my luggage. After scrutinizing my passport like a jeweler, he said, "You may go." I said, "Nice doin' business with ya," and left. I'm walking toward the exit, and a little girl in a khaki uniform comes and says, "Excuse me, Mr. Helm, may I search your boots?" I said "Yes, ma'am, of course," and she found my pocketknife. But that was no problem, and after we passed through two more rings of security, including .50-caliber machine guns mounted on army jeeps, it was hard to even find a policeman in Japan. I was already in love with the food, but the landscape and the people made a huge impression as well. The audience in Osaka wouldn't let us go until we'd played some Band songs, which sent them into rapture and made me sad we'd never gone over there to play before. But Japan in those days was terra incognita for rock and roll bands. Coming back through Hawaii three weeks later, the U.S. customs officer said, "Mr. Helm, you're not foolish enough to have any drugs on you, woudja?" And I said, "Buddy, after two weeks in Japan, you *know* I don't have any drugs." Because the country was dry as a bone.

Also in 1978 I went down to Muscle Shoals Sound studios in Sheffield, Alabama, to cut my second album for ABC, produced by Duck Dunn. We used that famous Roger Hawkins–Barry Beckett rhythm section they had there, plus Steve Cropper on guitar and the Cate Brothers on vocals. This album, *Levon Helm,* was released late in 1978 but didn't make the charts without a tour to back it up. I was wondering what the hell I was gonna do.

That's when I got the call that Michael Apted wanted me to read for *Coal Miner's Daughter.*

I think it happened because my friend Brad Dourif brought Tommy Lee Jones to a Band concert when they were working on a movie called *The Eyes of Laura Mars.* Tommy Lee was a Texas boy who had been to Harvard and knew acting cold, and he and I got along real well from the start. So when Michael Apted was in Nashville working on preproduction for the Loretta Lynn movie, Tommy Lee kind of threw my name in the hat when they started having trouble casting the part of Ted Webb. Apparently they couldn't find anybody in Hollywood that was "country" enough for the role. So I was proposed, and I think Conway Twitty might've put in a word to Loretta for me. Apted screened *The Last Waltz* and then had one of his people call me up. I figured that acting and singing were part of the same ball game and actually had the temerity to show up.

So I went to Nashville, and we sat in Apted's office with the script. I immediately felt like a total fool. I'm reading Ted Webb's part, and Michael's reading Loretta's part and calling me Daddy, and I'm calling him Loretta. I'm thinking, *Why don't they give this part to Brad? He's the all-pro actor.* My only acting experience had been in high school more than twenty years before, and I thought my reading sounded awkward and amateurish. In the end I just threw up my hands and had to laugh. Hell, I'd failed, but it was probably just a damn cameo anyway. Apted said thanks a lot, and I went back to Arkansas and told Sandy that I'd blown my "screen test."

Three days later they called and said I had the part. I put down the phone, and Sandy said, "Lee, who was it?"

I said, "Honey, I feel like I've just rolled a pair of sevens!"

I was flattered as hell. If I'd had to sing or dance, I don't know if I could've done it, but the part was such an honorable one. This man had labored in the mines for his family, and growing up in the cotton fields, I knew what it was like to bend over and sweat when you work. I felt that I knew what it was to work for the company store. I was also so scared of blowing it that I got real ambitious and researched the part until I felt I could *be* Ted Webb. I went up to Kentucky and met Loretta and her family. I talked to "Moonie," Loretta's husband, about Ted, studied photographs, and spent time with his son Herman Webb, Loretta's brother, and tried to pick up on Herman's ways a little. My main concern was getting it so that it didn't irritate the family, that it would seem realistic to them. They were my most important audience. In the end it wasn't a big transition because I've been around people like the Webbs all my life. Loretta's parents were a little like mine. I knew that families like ours made up in love for one another what they might have lacked in material things. That was the feeling I wanted to create. Add the basic formality to people that makes life in the South a bit more pleasant, and that was the character.

That, plus the mines. Michael Apted arranged for me to spend a few days in a coal mine to see what it was like. They got out the obsolete brass dodgers and other old tools. I talked to the miners and their families to see what their lives were like. And I was real impressed. To be down there day after day takes a certain kind of nerve that I don't have. We shot the mine parts of the film in a real mine, no props, and I was a little spooked by the claustrophobic conditions. Hang out in a coal mine for a couple of days, and you realize how strong these people have to be to survive.

So we're driving to the location, and Tommy Lee is giving me the Jones crash course in acting.

"Levon, the most important thing you got to remember is, *never* look at the camera. It doesn't exist. *Forget* about it. You know your lines [the cast had already sat down in Nashville and read through the script a couple of times], and Michael is gonna walk you through your scenes until you're comfortable.

284

"Next, don't move too quickly. There's a rhythm, and you find it and plug into it. Don't talk too fast either. You have to exaggerate your emotions to get your point across, but not too much. Let the director be the coach, and then do it your own way, and you're gonna be great, man. Cause everyone's excited about working with you. We're all tickled you got that part."

As the level on the Wild Turkey fell, Tommy continued to educate me about how to be on a movie set, how to deal with the assistant directors, the property masters, who to listen to, and who to watch out for. When we stopped at a little grocery in Kentucky, Tommy Lee started getting into it with the teamster who was driving us. I noticed the other customers were miners whose blue-gray eyes peered out of faces covered in coal dust. They were looking kinda funny at Tommy Lee, and I whispered, "Let's get outta here now."

Tommy thanked me the next day for saving him from himself. And by the time we pulled into the Suburban Motel in Whitesburg, Kentucky, Tommy Lee had managed to turn me into the beginnings of a movie actor.

They took me out to the location, and it was like going back in time. The film crew had rebuilt Butcher Hollow, Loretta's hometown, completely, down to the number of corncribs behind the houses. Ted Webb's house was re-created from old photos, but without the back porch and wall so the camera could come in. When the girls—Loretta and her sister—came in, they looked around and said, "No . . . no . . . out . . . that goes . . ." because the set designer had started out a little too fancy. Ted Webb didn't own no brass bed. But eventually they got it accurate, down to the old newspapers lining the walls to keep out the cold.

We started work late in February and filmed for about six weeks, until old Ted Webb passes away. You had someone combing your hair, getting you dressed, telling you what you had to do, so it wasn't any real problem. They had a terrific team of actors, and all of them helped pull me through. I even helped choreograph a scene where Tommy picks Sissy up and sashays her through the screen door after I give them my blessing to marry. It was a pretty nice dance move they did. Michael Apted was terrific. There was a difficult scene where I had to beat Sissy with a switch for staying out too late with Tommy Lee, a scene that seemed beyond my abilities at that time. I had to grab her and bring that switch down hard on her dress, and Sissy was so adorable that all the crew were scowling at me while I tried to play this right.

"*Cut!* OK, we'll do it again." And Michael would come over and say, in his veddy British voice, "It looks good, but if only you'd try it a little slower and mean it more. D'yew know what I mean?"

He actually made it fun for me to try to pull it off. He let us actors change words around a little to suit the way we spoke, and gave us enough slack to make something up. On the last take I brought that switch down like a whip and then broke it over my knee. I stomped through the door, like the scene called for, and the whole crew was making faces at me and whispering, "Booooo!" "Bully!" "Brute!" But it was a take.

I was sad when my character died and my part of the movie was over. I didn't really want to get into the coffin for the big wake scene, but I also didn't want to be thought of as superstitious or "difficult." So I told Michael Apted he'd have to get in first to show me how to look. So he kind of warmed the thing up for me, good sport that he is. As the "mourners" gathered around to sing "Amazing Grace," I had to sit bolt upright. It was like coming back to life.

"*Cut!*"

"It's my funeral," I told them, "and if you're gonna sing 'Amazing Grace,' it's gotta be the old-fashioned, traditional way." And I taught 'em in my dead man's makeup how to do it shape-note style like they would've back in the holler in those days. Some of the ladies they'd hired as extras turned out to be church choir singers, so once we got it off the ground it didn't sound too bad. We rehearsed it a few times, then I got back in the coffin, and we shot the scene.

They wanted me to cut a version of Bill Monroe's "Blue Moon of Kentucky" for the movie sound track, and I had to swallow hard on that one and ask the producer how he'd like to follow the Blue Grass Boys and Elvis Presley. But I went into Bradley's Barn Studios in Nashville with the Cate Brothers and Fred Carter, Jr., and after we did "Blue Moon" we figured why not put a little hay in the barn, so we cut twenty more tracks. Around the time *Coal Miner's Daughter* came out in 1980, MCA (which had gobbled up ABC) released ten of these under the title *American Son.*

Coal Miner's Daughter was a hit movie, and I got surprisingly good reviews. There was buzz of a possible Best Supporting Actor nomination by the Academy, but of course none was forthcoming. But I did manage to throw a scare into a few people all the same. I was and remain terminally modest about my acting abilities, but after that quite a few movie offers started to come my way, and for the next decade I took as many as seemed interesting. If there was a part for a country-type hick, I had a good shot at it. (And *Playboy* went and wrote that Levon Helm and Dolly Parton were the three best things to hit Hollywood that year.)

Five years after *The Last Waltz* I began to really miss The Band. I needed to be out playing music, so I teamed up with the Cate Brothers and went on the road, starting in Canada and then heading down to the States, where we played in theaters. The Cates, with my nephew Terry Cagle on drums, would open with a few of their own hits—"In One Eye and out the Other," the ballad "Let It Slide"—and Ernie's great vocals and Earl's sizzling guitar would get everyone warmed up. I'd show up halfway through and get that double-drum attack going on things like "Milk Cow Boogie," "Summertime Blues," "Willie and the Hand Jive," and "Bring It On Home." At first we relied on Band material, but eventually we were doing only "The Weight," which the customers basically demanded to hear, and "Evangeline," familiar to our fans from the movie (and I got to play mandolin). I was more comfortable doing the American blues numbers I'd grown up with— Sonny Boy, Muddy—and the old rock and roll songs like "Short Fat Fannie."

In 1982 I made an album for Capitol at Muscle Shoals and went on the road that spring playing clubs with the Muscle Shoals All-Stars. We'd get that jungle thing happening with "Willie and the Hand Jive," and people would just dance. Rick Danko was restless too and went out as a duo with Paul Butterfield.

A few months later Rick came back to Woodstock to sell his house. We ran into each other outside Judge Forno's Colonial Pharmacy on Mill Hill Road, and suddenly we realized we had to play music to-gether. Rick is one of these people who is just so musical that he makes anyone who plays with him look good and feel better. Then Rick looked around and realized that Woodstock had shed its posthippie aura and had settled back into the quiet Catskill artists' colony it had been for the sixty-nine years prior to the Woodstock Festival. He called Elizabeth in California and told her to pack up the kids and come on home. In early 1983 Rick and I did a club and college tour as an acoustic duo, playing a few Band songs (on the theory that sometimes less is more) and "Caledonia," with Rick on guitar and me on harp and everyone in the house clapping along as the rhythm section. We sold out the Ritz in New York City and got booked into the Lone Star Café, one of our favorite places to play.

At five o'clock on a February evening Rick and I were doing our soundcheck when Bob Dylan strolled in wearing a cashmere coat and a big fur hat. He was between tours and said he was just hanging out in the Village when he heard we were playing. He said, "Whatcha playin' tonight?" and I told him we liked to open with "Don't Ya Tell Henry," one of his songs. He borrowed one of Rick's guitars, I picked up the mandolin, and we played some old tunes together. He stayed until about nine o'clock, then disappeared.

Two hours later Rick and I were into "Short Fat Fannie," the ninth song of our set, when we got word that Bob was hanging around the bar. Rick called him up to the stage, he took off his hat, and was handed a guitar. And amid the pandemonium of the packed house we played a rather liquid "Your Cheatin' Heart" before launching into a funny medley of "Hand Jive" and "Ain't No More Cane."

We had a few laughs and a beer in the dressing room after the show, and then Bob was out the door, into the night. It would be a few years until we saw him again.

Muddy Waters died that year.

My film career was active enough in those days. I worked on the CBS series *Seven Brides for Seven Brothers* and played the part of Major Jack Ridley, General Chuck Yeager's sidekick in *The Right Stuff*. One night at the film's desert location, I winked at Sam Shepard, who was playing General Yeager, and the two of us kind of drifted off into the shadows, where I lit a joint one of the crew had laid on me. Out of nowhere General Yeager himself walked over and said, "What are you boys doing, smokin' pot?"

"Well, General," I said, eager to change the subject, "I know you like to fish, but did you ever do any catfish doggin' down in Arkansas?" Chuck Yeager just laughed at us and shook his head.

I'd usually try to see Richard when I was in California. He had stopped drinking in 1978, entered a detox program, and had been dry for several years. He seemed to be recovering from the behavior that had hurt him, and always would say something about getting The Band back together. "I thought we were just gonna take a *vacation*," he said. "I never wanted to put The Band into some kind of time capsule. Let's get back out on the road."

Well, that was always my intention, especially since I'd seen how much the Japanese loved our music. I figured we still had some frontiers to conquer. Garth was busy working with a new band, the Call, and became an iconic presence on the new cable channel MTV, when the Call video "The Walls Came Down," featuring Garth's blistering synthesizer solo, went into heavy rotation. Robbie Robertson was working in Hollywood as musical director on Martin Scorsese pictures like *The King of Comedy*. When we re-formed The Band that summer, I said, "Let's not invite him," but I think Rick did call Robbie, and he passed. He told Rick he was afraid when we did *The Last Waltz* that people would think it was one of those phony show-biz retirements and that we'd be back with the Big Comeback someday, and he just didn't want to do that.

But Richard told us he was gonna go nuts if we didn't do something, and Rick and I . . . well, we never had it any different. Being on the road was our way of life, and we thought we should embrace it instead of running from it. As usual, Garth was the key. If he wasn't willing, it wouldn't happen. He was the one who made the rest of us sound a little more schooled, a little more polished. Yes, he grumbled about touring, but it was in his blood too, and eventually he said yes.

The question had always been who would replace Robertson if The Band got back together. My vote went to Earl Cate, whose skills and good taste with the Fender Telecaster were unmatched in my opinion. But the Cate Brothers Band was a family affair in more ways than one, and it came down to not wanting to break them up. There was also a brilliant young guitarist in Woodstock, Jimmy Weider, whom we'd known for years and all wanted to play with. So we hired Jimmy.

We called Harold Kudlets up in Hamilton, Ontario, and told him to

289

book a tour of Canada for us. Then, so I wouldn't have to actually rehearse, we hired three of the Cate Brothers Band and put The Band on the road as an eight-piece group.

"Jeezus, Levon!" the Colonel exclaimed over the phone when I told him about this. "You're telling me that you're replacing Robbie with a *quartet?*"

We debuted in Toronto in early July, selling out all six thousand seats. Then we swung around Canada, with the Cates opening by themselves before being joined by the four of us: Me, Garth, Rick, and Richard, who was older, a bit wiser, and in pretty damn good form. His falsetto singing on "I Shall Be Released" was incredibly moving, and "You Don't Know Me," performed as a tribute to Ray Charles, usually brought down the house. We did "Cripple Creek" and "Mystery Train," and we could see that feelings ran high out in the audience. People sang along with these songs like they were old friends, and I think it was Richard who said to me after one show, "Levon, do you realize we have *become* these songs?"

I knew what he meant, even if I didn't feel that comfortable with the idea.

People would always ask about Robertson, and Rick or I would explain that all of us were here because we *wanted* to be. If it doesn't come from your heart, music just doesn't work. Robertson was the only one who ever came out and said he wanted to hang it up. The most important thing was that the four of us were proud of the show. It was fresh. Garth was finding new sounds and playing the best of his life.

On July 21, 1983, in San Jose, we made our first U.S. appearance as The Band since *The Last Waltz*. We always felt good about playing the Bay Area, where we had been reborn as The Band, and did a couple of more shows and played the New York Folk Festival before taking the thing to Japan at the end of the month.

We sold out four shows in Tokyo, two in Osaka, and other towns like Nagoya and Sapporo. And I mean the Japanese kids poured enthusiasm all over us like we were part of their folklore. I thought things were going pretty good, and we were so impressed by how together the Japanese seemed to be. One night Richard told me, "Levon, these people have so much respect for each other it makes me ashamed to be Western." There was actually a lot of tension because the Russians had just shot down the Korean airliner in the Sea of Japan, and people were pretty spooked.

We played theaters and clubs during the fall of 1983, and did a gig with the Grateful Dead at the Carrier Dome in Syracuse on October 22 before thirty-three thousand fans. We were pretty relieved that the press continued to be on our side. "The Band has context," one of the local papers said after the show. "Their music sounded as deep as the Old Testament. If one of the great, noble stone faces at Mount Rushmore grew a heart, opened its eyes, and began to sing, the voice would have to be that of Levon Helm." After a couple of sell-out shows at the Beacon Theater on upper Broadway in Manhattan, *Rolling Stone* wrote, "Perhaps most thrilling was the performance of the enigmatic, heartbreak-voiced Richard Manuel. Dark, handsome, and healthy-looking, Manuel romped through 'The Shape I'm In' and delivered the concert's high point, a tender rendition of 'You Don't Know Me.'"

Film roles kept coming my way. If Hollywood needed a sheriff or father figure, sometimes I got the call. In 1984 I played opposite Jane Fonda in an ABC movie called *The Dollmaker*. We filmed a dope smuggler movie called *The Best Revenge* in southern Spain for a Canadian outfit; another project called *Smooth Talk,* with Laura Dern and Treat Williams; and I played a southern sheriff in a chase picture, *The Man Outside,* which was shot in Arkansas and had other members of The Band in cameos. Things were going pretty good. Then in the spring of 1984 the agent called and said they wanted me to play a U.S. marshal in a western based on Willie Nelson's *Red Headed Stranger.* The script called for a couple of gun duels, so I went out back of my barn practicing quick-draw techniques with a .22 reproduction of a Colt .45 in a western-style holster.

Well, it ain't easy to come out and say I shot myself in the ass with it, but that's pretty much what happened. The gun went off in the holster, and I felt a searing pain as the bullet burrowed right behind my kneecap. First thing I thought was: *That's the leg you hit the bass drum with!* Second thing: *Levon, you've really done it this time.*

Sandy was in the house, and this friend of mine was there. I told him, "We have to *go*. I have *done it*. I've really done it. Damn thing's in there deep." We loaded up pretty quick, I laid the bad news on Sandy, and she went white, although not as white as I was.

First stop was the pharmacy. Richard Young was there, and so was Jane, his wife. She put a piece of gauze over the back of this gaping hole in the back of my leg. Joe Forno, Jr., who was looking after Richard Manuel's affairs, took over and got me to the hospital in Kingston. That started about ten real rough-ass hours. The first doctor who saw me shook his head and told us they *might* be able to save my leg. They took X rays and called the state police because it was a gunshot wound. Then they shipped me up to the big hospital in Albany. I spent the night with a slug in my leg, and in the morning the surgeon looked at me and said, "Mr. Helm, I'm gonna try to save your leg." And I begged him to do just that. The nurse said they could give me a local or put me all the way out, and I told 'em, "All the way out, because what you all don't understand is, this thing is on fire. It is on *fire!*"

I'd severed the tibial nerve, the main nerve running down the leg. They put it back together and repaired it, and said don't play the drums for a couple of years—if you can play at all.

So I took some time off. That summer I played guitar in a septet we called The Woodstock All-Stars, with a wonderful local girl named Cindy Cashdollar playing dobro. "Singing the blues," reported *The New York Times* of our Lone Star date, "the quality Mr. Helm expresses is a mixture of patience, true grit, and spiritual fire." Stan Szelest was the real star of that band.

On Labor Day The Band played a memorial for our late friend Dayton Stratton on the tenth anniversary of his death after the '74 Dylan tour. His wife, Lois, and eldest son, Randy, were carrying on the family business, and this was our first appearance in northwest Arkansas since the Hawks last played there in 1963.

The following year I sat down at the drums for the first time and realized I was going to be OK when I could play the "King Harvest" lick without too much pain. During the summer of 1985 we went on tour opening for Crosby, Stills, and Nash, but halfway through the tour we realized it just wasn't paying with eight people in the group. The Cates went home, we kept Jimmy Weider, and continued as a five-piece through the rest of the tour. For me it was heartbreaking to see the boys go, but there was nothing I could do.

We were doing most of this stuff without any real manager. "There *are* no more real managers," Richard Manuel would growl, and by that he meant the old-school types like Albert Grossman, who had a lot of power and looked after his clients. Albert and Richard were still connected, and there had always been talk of Richard writing and recording his own music. Joe Forno, Jr., was handling The Band's business and tour affairs. Various people came and went in this era who called themselves our manager, but they never did much for us.

In October 1985 The Band was booked at a big outdoor show in Portugal. When we arrived at the soccer stadium where the Avante Festival was to be held, we noticed a lot of pretty red flags and bunting flying everywhere. It was a stirring sight. We learned later we had played for the annual youth picnic of the Portuguese Communist Party.

In November Richard went to his hometown of Stratford, Ontario, because his old band the Rockin' Revols was reuniting after twenty-five years for a special show at the famous Festival Theater. Richard was nervous and excited. He'd rehearsed with his old mates the night before the show, and they realized they couldn't even remember what they used to play. "Levon," he told me later, "the people were just *there*. I could feel it, man. All the old crowd showed up, and there was this incredible teenage middle-age magic going on. People were yelling, 'Richard! Richard!' It was really something."

Everyone wanted to see the Beak, as Richard was universally known in those parts. He performed beautifully for his people, and they welcomed him home with a huge, warm ovation. I know it meant an awful lot to Richard that he was able to return home in absolute triumph that night.

Then Albert Grossman had a heart attack on a February night eight miles over the Atlantic. When the plane touched down at London, Albert was pronounced dead. He was sixty-one years old.

They had a memorial service in Woodstock. Richard sang "I Shall Be Released," and it tore everybody up. Robbie Robertson delivered a eulogy and said, "Every once in a while you meet a great teacher in life, and Albert's been my teacher."

Sitting in the back of the hall, John Simon wondered, *What could Albert ever have taught Robbie except how to be a son of a bitch in business?*

Albert was buried in a little grove behind the Bearsville Theater. In the summertime, young actors and actresses rehearse their lines in the clearing near his grave.

Albert's death really got to Richard. It may have even seemed like an abandonment, because Albert was looking after Richard's affairs, and I don't think that Richard knew who to turn to anymore when things got bad.

The following month we headed down to Florida to play some shows. The guy who was booking us had scheduled it so we were traveling hundreds of miles between relatively small clubs. It was a lot of traveling and not much dignity. Everyone had a cold, and the crew started referring jokingly to this trip as the "Death Tour."

We tried to laugh about it. We'd get to a club and set up, and someone would say, "Hey, Richard, how's the piano?" Richard would pantomime hanging himself. The quality of the shows came down to Richard's ability to perform. Could he sing the high notes to "Tears of Rage"? If he could, the shows were great. If not, no one liked them. He had started drinking since Albert's death, and, to tell the truth, all of us backslid from time to time. Rick and Elizabeth Danko were trying to use their considerable influence with Richard to get him to slow down, and Rick said something to him like, "We're disappointed in you."

But Richard just growled, "Don't nigger me, Rick!" He just wasn't gonna be told what to do at that stage of his life.

On March 3 we arrived at an upscale fern bar called the Cheek to Cheek Lounge in Winter Park, outside Orlando, Florida. We set up and checked in at the local Quality Inn Motel. Rick and Richard both had their wives along; Garth and I were traveling alone. That night we played two sets for capacity houses of people who'd paid eighteen dollars apiece to get in. They went nuts over "Rag Mama Rag," "Cripple Creek," "Dixie," and "The Weight." Richard did "You Don't Know Me," and it made me want to cry.

After the show, Richard went up to Garth, who was busy packing his keyboards, and thanked him profusely for twenty-five years of good music and appreciation. Garth acknowledged this, but he was preoccupied with getting his fragile synthesizers in their hard cases so they could be shipped to the next gig. Back at the motel, Richard said good night to his wife, Arlie, and then came to my room, where we talked until maybe two or two-thirty. He wasn't angry or too depressed, although he complained about the piano over at the lounge, and we did commiserate together on the hard touring conditions and the lack of respect it implied. He told me, "Levon, nothing hurts like self-doubt. When you put that whammy on yourself, it can be real bothersome. And playing these little joints after playing in Japan, you just feel you're slipping."

"I know what you mean," I told him. "You could get the feeling that you've slipped. But look: I like to think at the same time that every chance to play is a good time to test ourselves, then retest, and prove once again that *it doesn't matter*. All we have to do is set down, give it some concentration, and do a dozen tunes, whatever it takes, until you get that same enjoyment that the kid gets when he falls into the end zone with the ball in his arms.

"We're just musicians," I told Richard. "We're just working for the crowd. It's the best we can do."

Then we were just talking about songs and old movies on TV and people that we knew in common. Nothing seemed out of the ordinary. Around two-thirty Richard said he was going to his room for a few minutes and would come back to finish the movie we were watching.

Richard had left his room key in the room and woke his wife to get in. She said later he was annoyed and worked up about something, but I don't what. He lay down on the bed, and she went back to sleep.

When she woke up later that morning, she was alone. Arlie said that she thought Richard had gone out to sleep on the tour bus, so she went across the street to get some breakfast and returned with a bag of coffee and pastries. She went into the bathroom and found Richard hanging from the shower rod. That was when she started to scream.

I was dead to the world. There was pounding on my door. It took maybe five minutes just to rouse me. When I opened the door I heard Arlie screaming, "He's dead!!!"

I rushed into Richard's bathroom and basically went into shock. Rick was holding back tears, and Elizabeth gave me a horrified look I'll never forget. Richard had buckled his belt around his neck and looped the other end around the curtain rod, near the wall mounting where it would support his weight. Then he just sat down so hard that the screws had popped out of the mounting. But it had held, and Richard looked ghastly. I grabbed Richard and lifted him up while Rick got the belt loose. Then we carried him to the bed and got him down. I hit him in the chest, and I think Elizabeth tried cardiac massage, but hell, we knew he was gone. Paramedics arrived, and my hand shook violently as I lit a cigarette. Richard would have been forty-three in a few weeks. It was so sad and terrible to see this sweet, sad friend end like this. The tragedy was just overwhelming.

Soon the place was crawling with cops. They found an empty brandy bottle and an empty cocaine vial, and concluded that Richard had gotten drunk and committed suicide. Then the press got hold of it, and it was headlines all over the world the day after that.

When asked for a comment, Rick and I told reporters that we had *no idea* why Richard would end it all when we were selling out our shows, had just finished a movie, and were about to go into the studio to record.

But that wasn't it at all. I knew what Richard had done. He wasn't afraid of anything. I think he finally just got mad enough at the way things were that he sacrificed himself to shake things up, to make things change, to liberate himself from the earthly pain he lived with and expressed in his music. Richard had had a bellyful, and so he went right ahead and done it.

Because Richard was a true Christian man, you know? He knew that everything we're doing down here is just the blink of an eye, or however it's versed in the good book there. That's the way Richard looked at it.

Richard had flirted, maybe halfheartedly, with the Reaper a few times before, and every time God threw him back to us. This time He decided to keep Richard Manuel for Himself. Wherever he is now, you can bet that Richard's got a hell of a good band.

After the funeral in Canada, we actually went back on the road to keep some promises we'd made to club owners in Boston and New England. This was an insane thing to do, in retrospect, but Blondie Chaplin joined The Band and got us through until we could carry on no longer. We all attended a memorial for Richard in Woodstock, where his friends remembered Richard's sensitivity, humor, concern for others, and his utter and total commitment to music. Our friend Happy Traum spoke sadly of the demons that had pursued Richard throughout his life, and people could only nod sadly in agreement.

And so we put that chapter of our communal history to rest.

Now there were only three of us left: Garth Hudson, Rick Danko, and me. I think we decided to let things drift for a few years until the right opportunities presented themselves. I hunkered down in Woodstock with Sandy, enjoying life and occasionally taking to the road with the Cate Brothers. After Richard's death we had various augmented versions of The Band whenever called for. Fred Carter, Jr., played guitar on a tour we did in 1987 with Roy Buchanan opening some shows. I played some shows with drummer Max Weinberg of the E Street Band in 1987. Garth did a Band gig in Spain with the Cate Brothers one time because I didn't feel like going. (We always figured it was still The Band if Garth showed up. Garth also played in Marianne Faithfull's touring band around that time.) And after years of working on film scores, Robbie Robertson released a solo album featuring a song for Richard called "Fallen Angel."

Paul Butterfield died that year. Then Roy Buchanan in 1988. All around us, we could see that a certain way of life was taking its toll.

I did a few more film roles and was lucky to get enough voice-over and commercial work as an actor to keep the cash flow interesting. When I wasn't working I holed up with Sandy, and we usually had a couple of Arkansas boys living in the basement with standing orders to evict the stream of well-meaning but uninvited guests in constant search of Big Pink, The Band, and directions to the Woodstock Festival.

In 1988 our old and dear friend Ringo Starr checked into an Arizona clinic to dry out. When he came out, he got together with David Fishof, a New York agent, and they assembled a touring company called Ringo Starr's All-Starr Review. Ringo was going to do his old Beatles songs and needed some friends who had enjoyed a few hits of their own. So Ringo and David put their heads together and hired what I considered a dream band: Billy Preston and Dr. John on keyboards, Rick Danko on bass, Clarence Clemons on sax, Joe Walsh on guitar, and Jim Keltner and me on drums. With Ringo, we had three drum kits set up onstage. We took this out on the road in the summer of 1989, and some reviewers said it was one of the best shows they'd ever seen. The old Beatles fans were very emotional toward Ringo, and when Rick and I would do a few Band songs, the amphitheaters and sheds that we'd sold out would simply explode.

But my elation of our success was tempered by the death of my mother that year. People who are close to me say that I've never gotten over it. Does one ever?

Ringo's tour was rejuvenating. Rick and I felt excited about connecting so solidly with our fans. Some executives at CBS Records (which would soon be bought by Sony) thought the same way we did, and suddenly in 1990 The Band was offered a record deal. It felt like a real good second chance to get the people back on our side again, so we jumped at the contract and went to work at a studio near Woodstock with various writers, testing and recording songs.

I went home to Phillips County in May 1990 because I'd been invited to participate with Governor Bill Clinton in an unusual event.

The delta in May is green and beautiful, and it felt wonderful to be home. I went over to Turkey Scratch and saw our old family friend Sam Tillman, an eighty-year-old black retired farmer who reminded me that he'd had to put me over his knee once or twice.

So much in the delta had changed. Agribusiness had taken over the land, which was depopulated. The people now crowded into Helena and the other towns. All the farming is mechanized; the tractors have cold boxes so you can ride in comfort. You got Garth Brooks on the stereo. So much change, and yet still very much the delta of my roots.

Home is where they know you, and I had been asked to attend a ceremony at what was now called Historic Helena Depot. The Missouri Pacific railroad hadn't run through old Helena in a long time, and a great organization called Arkansas Heritage was restoring the 1912 depot as the home of the Delta Cultural Center. On May 12 they brought an old caboose down the line and hoisted it with a crane so it would sit behind the depot as part of the exhibits. At ten-thirty that morning, Governor Clinton said to me, "So, Levon, which of us is gonna go first?"

I looked at the governor, a big man with a wide smile and knowing eyes. The guy was a good five years younger than me. He was wearing a dark suit, 'cause this was official business. I'd just given him a couple of Band tie-dye shirts for his daughter, Chelsea.

I said, "What do you mean?"

"We have to say a few words. Why don't *you* go first?" This was the first I'd heard about giving a speech. But they pushed me out there in front of several hundred people gathered around the depot. I looked around and saw so many people I grew up with and knew. I flashed back to the day Thurlow Brown's big snake arrived in a broken crate at this old depot and they called Thurlow down to get it. I looked down Cherry Street, where Robert Johnson and Sonny Boy Williamson had walked. (Mr. Gist had just donated the building Sonny Boy used to rent for a Sonny Boy Museum.) Meanwhile, this red caboose was hanging in midair from a crane: totally surreal.

I just told the folks how my daddy had worked on that levee over there, and how his daddy probably had too. I told them how my parents had raised me and how the old levee camp music and swamp boogie that we liked to play down here had taken me all over the world, from Europe to Japan, but that the greatest honor I'd ever had was to be invited back to Helena that day to help dedicate a monument to the heritage we all shared in common. To me, that was the greatest.

When I finished, they were polite enough to applaud. I felt someone patting me on the back and turned. It was Bill Clinton.

By the end of 1990 we had gotten The Band the way we wanted it. As a peculiar facet of The Band's penchant for teamwork, Richard had been both drummer and piano player, so it took two musicians to take his place. Randy Ciarlante was one of the best drummers I knew, and he was good enough to come on board to anchor us while I played my harp or the mandolin. For piano we tapped the great Stan Szelest, our former colleague in the Hawks and one of the best rock and roll piano players anywhere. Stan had some good songs he was working on, and he and Garth liked to play their accordions together. My father, J.D., was living with me that fall. We used to take him to Band shows, and sometimes he'd sing along on some old song like "In the Pines." Those were good days, and I was full of hope that we were on our way into a whole new era.

Then we had a whole series of calamities.

In January 1991 Stan began to feel chest pains while rehearsing at my barn. Joe Forno was driving him over to the hospital when Stan suffered a heart attack and just died in the car. He was only forty-eight years old. We tried to comfort his wife, Caroline, as best we could, and she was a comfort to us as well, but it was a devastating

299

blow. Then in April, a cruel month, Henry Glover died at age sixty-five. He'd been my mentor for more than thirty years, and it was a terrible loss for everyone who knew him. Only a few weeks later our barn burned to the ground. Faulty stove wiring was the verdict. The damn fire took near everything we had, although a concrete storage vault containing my archives and other important material survived intact. If Caroline Szelest hadn't smelled smoke and woken us all up . . .

So J.D. returned to Arkansas to live with my sister Modena, and Sandy and I rented a house near Bearsville and tried to regroup. We had an album to do and gigs to play, so we invited Billy Preston into The Band. We'd known and loved this master musician—one of only two to play with both the Beatles and the Stones—for many years, and Rick and I had really dug his work on Ringo's tour. Billy is a dancer, a showman who flashes lightning up onstage. His energy was just what we badly needed at that point, but then he had some legal trouble over in Malibu, where he has a ranch, and a California judge wouldn't let him come to Woodstock.

That summer of 1991 Sony changed its mind. The executives who had believed in us thought they'd spotted a dismal trend in the lack of success of Robbie Robertson's second solo album, as well as those of some other over-forty rockers who shall remain nameless. They bought out our record deal, and we didn't have anything to say about it.

I tried not to let this stuff annoy me too much. We rebuilt the barn better than ever, this time out of good Catskill stone that isn't gonna burn, God willin'. My daughter, Amy, is as beautiful as her mother and is beginning her own career as a singer. She's got a great blues style and even got her picture in *Rolling Stone* with her old college band, Big Blue Squid. Meanwhile, Garth and I try to accommodate as many people as want to make the pilgrimage to Bearsville to record with us, and I'm in the fortunate position of turning down film roles and commercials that don't seem quite right to me.

But anytime Ben & Jerry's calls, I'm there.

We filled The Band's piano chair with Rick Bell, another old friend from Canada. He was one of the Hawks that Albert Grossman had lured away to Janis Joplin's great band many years before, so Rick is like family to us.

300

John Simon was recording a solo album in Woodstock early in 1992 for Pioneer in Japan, and some of us in The Band were helping him out when we realized that we had to work together again. Nobody, we understood, knew us like John. An independent record company in Tennessee called Pyramid Records picked up our option, so to speak, and that's where that part of the story stands for now. John Simon is currently producing our next album.

Later in 1992 we got a call to appear at the big show in New York marking Bob Dylan's thirty years of recording for CBS. We showed up at Madison Square Garden as a sextet: mandolin, two guitars, two accordions, and a trap drum. Backstage was like a reunion of our entire career, including John Hammond, Jr., Neil Young, Eric Clapton, Ron Wood, Johnny Cash and family, Tom Petty, Roger McGuinn, and many more than I can remember. We met a new generation of stars, like Shawn Colvin, Mary Chapin Carpenter, and the guys in Pearl Jam. The stage band was Booker T. and the MGs, including Duck Dunn and Steve Cropper.

When it was our turn, Eric Clapton did us the honor of introducing us. He came onstage before we went on and said, "In 1968 an album came out called *Music From Big Pink*. It changed my life, and it changed the course of American music. Ladies and gentlemen, The Band."

We walked out amid cheering. It had been many years since we'd faced down a crowd that big. We were all extremely proud to be there, because we all knew the debt we owed Bob Dylan could never be repaid. We were a bar band when he found us. We'd grown up and practiced our craft in honky-tonks and dance halls. We learned every-thing—songwriting, recording, stage shows—from watching him. It meant a lot for us to pay tribute to him that magical night.

There were six of us: Garth, Rick, Jimmy Weider, Rick Bell, Randy Ciarlante, and me. We did "When I Paint My Masterpiece" in a two-accordion arrangement. Afterward Danko and I barged in on Bob to thank him for inviting us. It had been ten years since I'd seen him. "Glad you could make it," he said, shaking hands. "I'm gonna be seeing you again soon." I was going to ask what he meant when they called him up onstage to do his songs.

*　*　*

301

And so that's my story. I'm fifty-three years old as of this writing and still going strong. The Band works as much as it can, and when we come to your town to promote our new record, we're expecting to see you there.

As for the other characters in our ongoing drama, let me see if I can summarize . . .

My daddy, Jasper Diamond, passed away in late 1992 at the age of eighty-two. My two sisters and brother, Mary Cavette and her sisters, Anna Lee Williams, Fireball Carter, and Mutt Cagle are all alive and well, thank God. But Harold Jenkins—Conway Twitty—passed on in 1993.

Ronnie Hawkins still lives up in "Mortgage Manor North" outside Toronto and still plays the bars up there. His son Robin and beautiful daughter Leah are in the band, and when the Hawk gets goin' on "Who Do You Love," that old rockabilly spirit comes alive. Hawk may be pushing sixty, but some things never change. Not long ago Rick and Elizabeth Danko were at the airport in Oslo, Norway, waiting for a plane to New York. At the other end of the lounge they heard a familiar voice going, "Yeah, these young girls only impress me when they bring their own apparatus!" Rick turned to Elizabeth and said, "Do you know who that sounds like?" Sure enough, it was Ronnie coming through town on one of his own Scandinavian tours.

Colonel Harold Kudlets is retired in Hamilton, Ontario. Morris Levy died in 1990 with jail time hanging over his head. The old Hit Man of Roulette Records never served a day, no matter what they said about him.

Woodstock is Woodstock again. As a friend of mine said the other day, "Woodstock is still great. The only reason that Butterfield and them aren't hanging out here anymore is that they're dead."

Libby Titus, mother of my daughter, lives in Bob Dylan's old house above Woodstock, and in New York, where she's involved in the music business. Albert Grossman's widow, Sally, still runs Albert's Bearsville empire. Jane Manuel works for the organization.

Rick Danko works as a solo artist when The Band is inactive. He had to endure the loss of his son, who died of a breathing ailment while at college. He has since collaborated with folk singer Eric Andersen and Norwegian singer Jonas Fjeld, and remains my brother in arms. Garth Hudson keeps busy as a sound consultant to synthesizer manufacturers, and he's working on computer software relating to the history of R&B and jump-band music. He and his wife, Maud, recently moved back to their house near Woodstock after years in California.

Robbie still lives in Southern California. His wife is a successful therapist specializing in drug and alcohol recovery. Robbie is in the music business, releasing albums and working on other projects, most recently one involving the late Roy Orbison's last recordings. Every year he helps to induct great musicians into the nonexistent Rock and Roll Hall of Fame that will supposedly be built in Cleveland some day.

It ought to be in Memphis, or—even better—Helena, Arkansas.

Not long after Bob Dylan's thirtieth-anniversary concert, Bill Clinton of Arkansas was elected President of the United States. And as true sons of Arkansas, The Band had the honor of providing the musical entertainment for the "Blue Jean Bash," an unofficial inauguration barbecue for twenty-five hundred Arkansawyers and Bill Clinton's campaign staff, held in the National Building Museum in Washington, DC, three days before Bill took office.

We had a soundcheck in the hall—the largest indoor columned building in North America—on the night before the show. Artist Peter Max was hanging his giant posters, and the champion barbecue chefs who'd come up from Little Rock were preparing giant ice sculptures of razorback hogs. The Cate Brothers were on the bill, along with Dr. John, Clarence Clemons, Vassar Clements, Steve Stills, and other old friends. The Secret Service were all over the place, and it looked like the Blue Jean Bash was gonna have some *visitors*.

Around midnight I was playing drums with Randy Ciarlante and Porky, who plays with the Cates, when a figure crouched down at my left elbow. He had on a baseball cap and a pair of dark glasses. A hooded sweatshirt lettered "New York Americans" was pulled over his hat. It seemed that he was talking to me.

I looked again. It was Bob Dylan.

I knew he'd come. His manager had called Joe Forno a few days before to say that Bob wanted to be there with us when Arkansas took over the country.

And now Bob was saying, "So, uh, Levon, howya doin'? What's up?"

I said, "Bob, anything you wanna do is fine with us, 'cause we really appreciate you coming by."

Communication between us was more instinctive than anything else.

303

I said, "We're just playing some blues, but, you know, if you call a tune we'll be there."

He thought for moment, and said, "How's about 'To Be Alone With You'?"

Bob showed up the next night and came on after the Hawk had finished "Who Do You Love." The crowd screamed in delight when Bob walked out at the end of the show in his cowboy hat and went into "To Be Alone With You." U.S. senators were dancing next to the stage! The finale was "I Shall Be Released," and it seemed like everyone knew the words. Being the mischievous type, Bob Dylan didn't sing along.

Yeah! That's all she wrote. I've come a long way from Turkey Scratch, but in my heart I'm still Lavon, the hambone kid in the 4-H show. In fact, the main thing that still gets my juices flowing is to get over to the venue on the night of the job, wherever it might be, anywhere in the world. The man that's running the joint knows we're coming, and he invites me in and helps me set up my stuff. We play some music, and then he pays us. That's the only way I ever wanted it.

As for The Band, we never sold millions of records or got attacked by groupies, but we're still here. We never thought our "career" was more important than the music. That's our whole story right there.

"They were grown men," wrote *The Philadelphia Inquirer*, "who had climbed the mountain together, spoken to the gods, and returned to the valley, where they once again became mortal."

Hell, all I know is that I haven't had to cultivate cotton since I was seventeen.

ACKNOWLEDGMENTS AND SOURCES

The authors wish to extend special thanks to Rick Danko and Garth Hudson.

Also to the late J. D. Helm, Modena Cagle, Mary Cavette, Paul and Mary Berry, Edward Carter, C. W. Gatlin, Sam Tillman, Ben Story, and Jim Howe of KFFA, Helena, Arkansas.

Also to Bill Avis and Ronnie Hawkins.

Also to Jane Manuel, John Simon, and the family of the late Stan Szelest.

Also to Richard Bell, Randy Ciarlante, and Jim Weider.

Also to Joe Forno, Jr., without whom . . .

Also to the memory of Ralph Shultis, and to his grandson, Paul Shultis, Jr., who has continued the finest tradition of building homes in the Catskills.

Also to Elliott Landy.

This book was researched in Phillips County, Arkansas, and Ulster County, New York, between 1990 and 1993. David Fishof and David Vigliano helped fire it up. Jim Landis thought it was a good thing. Judy Moore and Henry Pinkham gave it shelter from Catskill summer thunderstorms. Chris Davis maintained editorial standards. The David Bieber Archive of Boston, Massachusetts, provided rare documents and recordings, as did James Isaacs and Andy Robinson. James Henke made available *Rolling Stone* magazine's extensive file on The Band.

Special thanks to Paul Bresnick, Ben Ratliff, Philip Bashe, and all our friends at William Morrow and Company for helping our story make the harrowing transition from manuscript to print.

Love to Sandy Helm and Judith Arons.

Special mention: for friendship above and beyond—Don Tyson, Duck and June Dunn, Ace Kutsuna, Hayden McIlroy, Jake and Arlene Christofora, Judge and Mrs. Joseph Forno, Sr., and Leon "Butch" Dener. Mojo navigation: Joel Zoss.

Also to Tommy Lee Jones, Brad Dourif, and Jane Fonda for opportunities I could only dream about as a kid.

The authors of the following texts, from which quotations not already cited in the text are taken.

Alfred G. Aronowitz, "Friends and Neighbors Just Call Us The Band," *Rolling Stone* (August 24, 1968).

Joshua Baer, "The Robbie Robertson Interview," *Musician* (May 1982).

Rob Bowman, "Life Is a Carnival," *Goldmine* (July 26, 1991).

Dix Bruce, "Levon Helm," *Mandolin World News* (Summer 1983).

Jay Cocks, "Down to Old Dixie and Back," *Time* (January 12, 1970).

Sara Davidson, "The Band in Suits and Ties," *The Boston Sunday Globe*, June 1969.

Bill Flanagan, "The Return of Robbie Robertson," *Musician* (October 1987).

Robyn Flans, "Levon Helm," *Modern Drummer* (August 1984).

Howard Gladstone, "Robbie Robertson," *Rolling Stone* (December 27, 1969).

Ralph J. Gleason, "The Band at Winterland," *San Francisco Chronicle*, May 17, 1969.

Tony Glover, "Music From Big Pink," *Eye* (October 1968).

Michael Goldberg, "The Second Coming of Robbie Robertson," *Rolling Stone* (November 19, 1987).

Bill Graham and Robert Greenfield, *Bill Graham Presents* (Doubleday, 1992).

Ronnie Hawkins with Peter Goddard, *Last of the Good Ol' Boys* (Stoddard, 1989), the Hawk's autobiography.

Robert Palmer, "A Portrait of The Band," *Rolling Stone* (June 10, 1978) and "Robbie Robertson," *Rolling Stone* (November 14, 1991).

John Poppy, "The Band: Music From Home," *Look* (August 25, 1970).

Tony Scherman, "The Wild Youth of Robbie Robertson," *Musician* (December 1991).

Robert Shelton, *No Direction Home: The Life and Music of Bob Dylan* (Beech Tree Books, 1986).

Ruth Spencer, four-part interview with The Band, *The Woodstock Times*, March 21–April 11, 1985.

Max Weinberg with Robert Santelli, *The Big Beat* (Contemporary Books, 1984).

INDEX

307

Index